The Politics of the New South Africa

Pearson Education

We work with leading authors to develop the
strongest educational materials in politics,
bringing cutting-edge thinking and best learning
practice to a global market.

Under a range of well-known imprints, including
Longman, we craft high-quality print and
electronic publications which help readers to
understand and apply their content, whether
studying or at work.

To find out about the complete range of our
publishing please visit us on the World Wide Web at:
www.pearsoneduc.com

The Politics of the New South Africa
Apartheid and After

Heather Deegan

Longman

An imprint of Pearson Education

Harlow, England • London • New York • Reading, Massachusetts • San Francisco • Toronto • Don Mills, Ontario • Sydney •
Tokyo • Singapore • Hong Kong • Seoul • Taipei • Cape Town • Madrid • Mexico City • Amsterdam • Munich • Paris • Milan

Pearson Education Ltd
Edinburgh Gate
Harlow
Essex CM20 2JE
England

and Associated Companies throughout the world

Visit us on the World Wide Web at:
http://www.pearsoneduc.com

First published 2001

ISBN 0 582 38227 0

British Library Cataloguing-in-Publication Data
A catalogue record for this book can be obtained from the British Library

Library of Congress Cataloguing-in-Publication Data
Deegan, Heather.
    The politics of the new South Africa : apartheid and after / Heather Deegan.
        p. cm
    Includes bibliographical references and index.
    ISBN 0-582-38227-0
        1. Apartheid--South Africa. 2. Anti-apartheid movements--South Africa. 3. South Africa--Politics and government--1961-1978. 4. South Africa--Politics and government--1978-1989. 5. South Africa--Politics and government--1989-1994. 6. South Africa--Politics and government--1994- 7. South Africa. Truth and Reconciliation Commission. I. Title.

    DT1757 .D44 2001
    968.06--dc21

                                                    00-063205

10 9 8 7 6 5 4 3 2 1
05 04 03 02

Typeset by Photoprint, Torquay, Devon
Printed in Malaysia,

Contents

Contents

List of abbreviations and acronyms

ANC	African National Congress
AZAPO	Azanian People's Organisation
AZASO	Azanian Students' Organisation
CODESA	Convention for a Democratic South Africa
COMSA	Commonwealth Observer Mission to South Africa
COSAS	Congress of South African Students
COSATU	Congress of South African Trade Unions
CP	Conservative Party
FOSATU	Federation of South African Trade Unions
GNU	Government of National Unity
IBA	Independent Broadcasting Authority
IEC	Independent Electoral Commission
IDASA	Institute for Democracy in South Africa
IFP	Inkatha Freedom Party
IMC	Independent Media Commission
MPNP	Multi-Party Negotiating Process
MK	Umkhonto we Sizwe (military wing of ANC)
NGO	non-governmental organisation
NP	National Party
NPA	National Peace Accord
OAU	Organisation of African Unity
PAC	Pan Africanist Congress
RDP	Reconstruction and Development Programme
SACP	South African Communist Party
SADF	South African Defence Force
SANNC	South African Native National Congress
SANNGO	South African National NGO Coalition
SAP	South African Police (apartheid era)
SAPS	South African Police Service (post-apartheid era)
SARDC	Southern African Research and Documentation Centre
TEC	Transitional Executive Council
TRC	Truth and Reconciliation Commission
UDF	United Democratic Front
UNISA	University of South Africa

Preface

South Africa has had such a dreadful history and suffered devastating evil. Yet now the nightmare of apartheid is over the country has shown a great capacity for good (Archbishop Desmond Tutu 1999).

The ending of the 'nightmare' of apartheid and the election of Nelson Mandela in 1994 have been positive and heartwarming events that captured the attention of international audiences. Yet as the country sought to rehabilitate and affirm the human rights of all people, some feared that the nation would lapse into violence and bloodshed. Such were the great divisions and animosities between racial groups, the argument went, that only retribution and revenge would emerge. South Africa did not follow that path but moved forward and away from its 'dreadful history' with dignity and hope. Yet, the issues confronting President Mbeki are, in part, related to the apartheid period. The country's asymmetrical development has produced a first/third world society: an industrialised, urban, technological society running in parallel with an impoverished rural hinterland. In understanding the challenges that confront a changed South Africa, therefore, we need to look back at the country's past. In fact, the Truth and Reconciliation Commission, instituted in 1996, has done just that in its attempt to help the nation to come to terms with its history and to forge a sense of understanding and reconciliation. Through a process of public hearings, at which people spoke of their painful experiences, the commission cast new light on the former activities of government agencies, liberation movements and the wider population.

This study provides an appraisal of critical moments in South Africa's history: segregation and racial supremacy, black opposition, politics under apartheid, and violence and terror. But it also covers more recent events: the transfer of power in 1994, enfranchisement and political realignment, the post-electoral period of adjustment and socio-economic transition, the findings of the Truth and Reconciliation Commission, and the 1999 elections. The important issues that still confront the young democracy – governance, the economy and crime levels – are considered in a final chapter. While the apartheid period provides a historical framework, the text places an emphasis on the contemporary pace of change, which has radically altered the trajectory of the country. The work also contains qualitative and quantitative data, so providing the reader with detailed information and combining the accessibility of a textbook with first-hand empirical research.

The writer has researched in South Africa since 1995, in part funded by the Nuffield Foundation. She is a Fellow of the Africa Institute of South Africa, Pretoria, and was a visiting lecturer in the Politics Department of the University of Witwatersrand in 1998. During the 1999 elections she conducted a range of interviews with public opinion organisations, institutions and agencies of civil society, international observers, and the secretariat of the Independent Electoral Commission.

Many individuals participated in interviews and meetings and the writer would like to particularly thank the following: Marius Steyn of the Independent Electoral Commission, Robert Jones of the Electoral Institute of South Africa, Professor Tom Lodge and Professor

Noam Pines of the University of Witwatersrand, Dr Denis Venter, Professor Jack Spence, members of the African Studies Association of South Africa, the Southern African Study Group of the Royal Institute of International Affairs, and all those who assisted in the accessing and collection of research information. The writer alone, however, is responsible for views and opinions expressed in the work.

Acknowledgements

The publishers are grateful to the following for permission to reproduce copyright material:

Map 1.2 from *The Voortrekkers* published by Cassell & Co. (Meintjes, J. 1972); Tables 2.1, 6.3 from 'The Surplus People Project' in *Race Relations News* published by the South African Institute of Race Relations (SAIRR), May/June 1983 and 1996; Maps 2.1, 5.1, 5.2 from *South Africa in the 20th Century* published by Blackwell Publishers Ltd. (Barber, J. 1999); Tables 2.5, 2.6, 2.7 from *Capitalism and Apartheid* published by Gower Publishing (Lipton, M. 1985); Tables 3.2, 4.2, 4.3 from *South Africa: Time Runs Out* published by the Ford Foundation (Schrire, R. 1991); Tables 3.4, 8.8, 8.9, 8.10, 8.11, 8.12, 8.13, 8.14, 9.11 from *South Africa: The Challenge of Reform* published by Owen Burgess Publishers for the Human Sciences Research Council (HSRC), South Africa (van Vuuren, D.J. (ed.) 1988); Table 3.5 and Box 5 from *Launching Democracy in South Africa* published by Yale University Press (Johnson, R. and Schlemmer, L. 1996); Table 4.1 from *Annual Surveys 1985–89* published by SAIRR; Map 4.1 from *Changing Fortunes: Diplomacy and Economics in South Africa* published by the Ford Foundation (Jaster, R., Mbeki, M., Nkosi, M., Clough, M. 1992); Tables 5.6, 5.9, 5.10, 5.11, 5.12 from *The Election Book* published by Institute of Democracy in South Africa (IDASA) (Mattes, R. 1995); Tables 6.1, 6.2 from *Country Profile: South Africa* published by The Economist Intelligence Unit, 1996/97; Table 6.9 from *Gender on the Agenda* published by the Centre of Policy Studies, South Africa (White, C. 1995); Tables 6.13, 6.14 adapted from *Public Opinion survey No. 8* published by IDASA, May 1996; Table 7.1 from *Opinion Poll* conducted by HSRC 1996; Figures 7.1 'Butcher Boys', 7.2 'Self Defence and Stability Unit' from Sculpture and Photomontage Exhibition, Grahamstown, 1995 (Jane Alexander, Sculptress, 1985/86); Tables 7.3, 7.4 from *From Truth to Transformation* published by Catholic Institute for Race Relations (CIIR); Tables 8.1, 8.10 compiled from Independent Electoral Commission (IEC) *Progress Reports,* Pretoria, 1998/99; Figures 8.1, 8.2, 8.3, 8.5(a), 8.5(b) from *Nazo Elections 1999* and Tables 8.5, 8.6, 8.7, 8.21 published by IEC, 1999; Table 8.4 from *Election Update 99* No. 13 published by Electoral Institute of South Africa (EISA) May 1999; Figure 8.4 from 'Make Yourself Heard' programme by EISA; Tables 8.15, 8.16, 8.17, 8.18, 8.19, 8.20, 9.1 from *Opinion 99* published by IDASA, Figures 9.1(a), 9.1(b), 9.2 published by *The Star Newspaper*, Johannesburg/ Independent News and Media Group; Tables 9.2, 9.3, 9.4 from Bureau of Market Research, University of South Africa, published by the *Sunday Times of South Africa* 1998.

Text extracts:

Extracts from 'Consequences of Gross Human Rights Violations on People's Lives' in *Truth and Reconciliation Commission Report* Vols 2, 5, courtesy of CIIR; Appendix 2: Extracts from State President F. W. de Klerk's *Opening Address to Parliament*, 2 February 1990, Appendix 4: *Bill of Rights* 1996, reproduced under South African Government Printers Copyright Authorities Nos. 10872 dated 18 August 2000 ; Appendix 3: Extracts from speech by Nelson Mandela given in Capetown, published by *The Star Newspaper*, Johannesburg/Independent News and Media Group, 11 February 1990.

Every effort has been made to trace the copyright material. However, in the event that any have been overlooked, the Publishers will make the necessary amendment at the earliest opportunity.

Part I

Historical forces

Chapter 1

Union and segregation

In 1910, a new constitution combined the areas of the Transvaal, the Free State, Natal and the Cape into a union and effectively established the boundaries of a single country (see Figure 1.1). Although central government was instituted under the Union, regional variations continued to exist. The Cape, for example, retained the right to have a non-racial franchise based on property rights, whereas in the other regions black political rights were not upheld. Cape Town became, as it remains, the legislative capital, while Pretoria and Bloemfontein were the administrative and judicial locations, respectively. The Union consolidated the interests of the white population over the black community, a situation that was further demonstrated in the Natives Land Act of 1913. This Act was intended to prevent Africans buying land in areas designated as white, and to stop black tenants living on farms unless they provided an annual minimum of ninety days labour to the landowner.[1] The Act also forbade the purchase or lease of land by Africans outside certain areas referred to as reserves and by doing so 'established the principle of land segregation'.[2] These areas, which were adapted in 1936, became the 'basis of the "homelands" of the apartheid era'.[3] By 1910, South Africa was 'a powerful settler state', yet only around 20 per cent of the population of the newly formed territory could be classified as white or European.[4] The country had attracted European settlers, but the effect could not be compared with the colonisation of North and South America or Australasia.

The origins of segregation

A major preoccupation among historians of South Africa has been the need to explain and account for the establishment of segregation. Whose interests did it serve? Why did it become so entrenched? How did it affect the economy? Did it mark the beginning of the ideology that was later to manifest itself in the policy of apartheid? Segregation has been defined as the territorial and residential

---

[1] Beinart 1994: 54; for an excellent account of South Africa's political history, see Barber 1999.

[2] Worden 1995: 49.

[3] *Ibid.*: 50.

[4] Denoon and Nyeko 1984: 138.

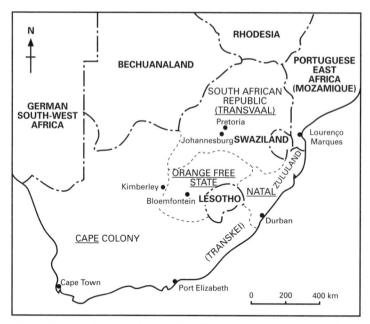

Figure 1.1 The Union of South Africa, 1910. Province names are underlined (source: Shillington 1987)

Box 1.1 The peoples of southern Africa

The San (Bushmen) communities occupied most of the southern African region. They were short in stature and lived a hunter-gatherer lifestyle. The San were displaced by the Khoikhoi (Hottentots) communities, who were nomadic pastoralists. The Khoikhoi had developed a pastoral culture by the time of European contact. In the Iron Age and until the fifteenth century AD, Bantu-speaking peoples migrated southwards, developing more complex community structures. In 1652, Jan van Riebeeck established a colony at the Cape of Good Hope to serve as a shipping port for the Dutch East India Company. The colonists were initially known as Boers and latterly as Afrikaners. Interbreeding occurred between the San, Khoikhoi and Afrikaners, which led to the formation of a new ethnic group known as the Cape coloureds. Indians were brought to the country as indentured workers. The racial categories Black African, coloured, Indian and white are still used today as a way of distinguishing different groups.

separation of peoples based on the idea that black and white communities 'have different wants and requirements in the fields of social, cultural and political policy'.[5] The debate about the origins or formative years of segregation go back into

---

[5] M. Legassick, cited in Beinart and Dubow 1995: 44.

the nineteenth century and the policies of the British colonial administration. African reserves were established by the British, while African chieftancy survived in Natal under British rule. When the British were in control, local authority was devolved to African chiefs, who were instrumental in maintaining order. According to Shula Marks, this divide and rule approach was part of British colonial policy and reflected racial perceptions.[6] Certainly, notions of racial superiority formed part of the general pattern of colonial rule into the twentieth century. Martin Legassick pinpoints the origins of segregation to the period after the South African War of 1899–1902 between the British and the Afrikaners. The purpose of the war had not been to establish complete British authority throughout the region but to assist the forces of colonialism to gain ascendancy over the Afrikaners.[7] Nevertheless, through its victory Britain was able to institute a general colonial strategy and begin to define 'native policy'.

The conquest of the Transvaal and the Orange Free State in 1900 began six years of British supremacy in South Africa before moves towards Afrikaner political independence eventually culminated in the Act of Union in 1910. These were critical years, argues Legassick, who points to the attitude of Sir Alfred Milner, the High Commissioner of South Africa between 1899 and 1902. He was a leading exponent of the need to 'reconstruct' South Africa in order to serve specific interests:

> The ultimate end [of colonial policy] is a self-governing white community supported by well-treated and justly governed black labour from Cape Town to the Zambesi (Sir Alfred Milner, cited in Legassick 1995: 46).

The notion of 'native' policy was a paternalistic vision of a subordinated society in which social welfare and social control would be introduced for those people designated as 'natives'. The South African Native Affairs Commission in 1905 outlined general attitudes towards 'natives'. As Legassick recorded: 'The rational policy is to facilitate the development of aboriginals on lines which do not merge too closely into European life, lest it lead to enmity and stem the tide of healthy progress.' With regard to education, the commission asserted: 'The character and extent of aboriginal teaching should be such as to afford opportunities for the natives to acquire that amount of elementary knowledge for which in their present state they are fitted.'[8] Yet for all the colonial assumptions of native inferiority and primitivism, the mining industry needed black labour. Inevitably, therefore, white and black communities could not be subjected to total separation. A question preoccupied administrators: how could the level of segregation be maximised without affecting the supply of black workers? A form of segregation was advocated in which the white and black races would each develop separately within their own given territories. As far as political arrangements were concerned, both white and black would fashion their own forms of representation. On

---

[6] *cf.* Welsh 1971; Marks 1970.
[7] Denoon and Nyeko 1984: 123.
[8] Legassick, cited in Beinart and Dubow 1995: 49.

the eve of 1910, then, a climate of opinion supportive of segregation existed in government circles.

> Complete segregation of the two races is manifestly impossible, for geography and economics forbids it. But some degree of segregation is desirable, especially in the tenure of land, for the gulf between the outlook and civilisation of the two colours (black and white) is so wide that too intimate an association is bad for both. For many years to come the two races must develop to a large extent on the lines of their own. (Philip Kerr, secretary of the Rhodes Trust, cited in Legassick 1995: 58).

Cheap black labour and industrial development

The discovery of diamonds in 1868 and gold in 1886 led to an economic boom in the late nineteenth century, and a pattern of reliance on migrant black labour began to emerge. Indigenous Africans, dispossessed from the land, became available as cheap labour. Workers were also imported from the Indian subcontinent and became yet another separate ethnic group. The nature of the relationship between racial segregation and the needs of the economy has been explored by a variety of historians. Christopher Saunders outlines the different perspectives, which he identifies as liberal or Marxist in analysis.[9] In the 1920s, William Macmillan was the first liberal writer to stress the importance of economics in the development of South Africa. He argued that the demands of industry and the quest for economic growth ran counter to policies designed to keep people apart. In effect, economic growth promoted further integration rather than increased segregation.[10] The growth of diamond mining under De Beers Consolidated Mines required the long-term provision of a regular supply of migrant workers. For the first few years of mining, it was not difficult to mobilise Africans to work in the mines, but there were fears that the flow of migrant labour might disappear. While white wage-earners in the diamond industry were employed in jobs requiring skills, black workers were in unskilled jobs. African workers began to be recruited on contracts for periods of several months at a time. During their contract period they lived in the compounds of the mine, thus ensuring that their employers had control over their labour and minimising any risks of strikes or demands for higher wages. White workers could not be treated in this way as their skills were much in demand elsewhere in other countries and they could always threaten to leave.

The early development of the Transvaal gold-mining industry was influenced by the example of diamond mining in Kimberley. A 'contract' labour force organised, disciplined and domiciled within the mining compound was accepted as both efficient and effective. According to Denoon and Nyeko, the gold-mining labour force included around 100,000 black workers from the rural areas and 10,000 white workers.[11] It was much cheaper for mine managers to employ

---

[9] For a full discussion of history and apartheid, see Lonsdale 1988.
[10] Macmillan 1930.
[11] Denoon and Nyeko 1984: 99.

migrant labourers, who were separated from their families and paid as single workers, than to allow African families to settle around Johannesburg, where employers would have been under pressure to pay higher wages. By 1900, the gold mines were producing over £15 million worth of gold each year and the Transvaal was the largest single source of gold on the world market.

The end of the nineteenth century marked a formative period of capitalist endeavour and expansion. In the years that followed the introduction of segregationist measures there was accompanying industrial growth, but the measures also led to clashes between employers and workers and between white and black workers. The interaction between economic development and racial segregation has been analysed by a variety of academics. One school of thought maintain that capitalists, e.g. mine-owners, found themselves operating within a racially determined environment and were obliged to adapt to it.[12] The Mines and Works Act passed in 1911 reinforced racial divisions in industry. Certain jobs could only be performed by those holding 'certificates of competency', which essentially meant that skilled positions were held by whites, while blacks undertook unskilled work. Primarily, the interests of the mine-owners were profit maximisation and the maintenance of low costs. Ideally, they wanted to pay white workers low wages and attempts were made to do just that, resulting in strike action. In respect of black workers, contract labour was the best option, but as African workers became more skilled in work such as rock drilling, an area that had been the preserve of white workers, mine-owners had an incentive to extend their black labour at the expense of white workers. By claiming tasks to be 'non-skilled' they could employ cheaper black labour. White workers fought to maintain their positions *vis-à-vis* low-wage black workers by organising a general strike of white employees in the railway and mining industries against the increased use of black employees.

Although white workers were pitched against black workers in this racially divided society, Merle Lipton points out that the Chamber of Mines, the mine-owners' organisation, opposed the legalisation of the so-called 'job colour bar' contained in the 1911 Mines and Works Act. In fact, she argues, 'rising costs and a falling gold price soon led to pressures from mine-owners to relax the job colour bar, thereby increasing the ratio of cheap African to expensive white workers'. In 1920, the Chamber of Mines recommended total abolition of the racially prejudiced job colour bar, but white miners' unions strongly supported the policy. Lipton explains:

> Mine-owners and white workers were prepared to precipitate a virtual civil war over the job bar because its effects were substantial for both parties. The factor in contention was the increasing cost of white labour, that is, the wages of whites comprising around 10–11% of the workforce, accounted for 25% of total working costs; African wages amount to 12%. The mine-owners' objectives of cheap labour and high profits were held in check by the resistance of white workers. The Transvaal Chamber of Mines Annual Report for 1918 stated that mining companies were

---

[12] For early studies of the issue, *cf.* Blumer 1967; van der Horst 1941; Frankel 1938.

reluctant to yield to a policy that not only raised costs but also artificially inhibited the advancement of the coloured population.[13]

However, it had to accept that 'public opinion is not prepared to see the substitution of coloured and native workers for white skilled and semi-skilled workers'.[14] In any case, more restrictive legislation was passed in 1923 with the Natives (Urban Areas) Act. This law enabled local authorities to enforce residential segregation between blacks and whites and forbade the granting of freehold property rights to Africans. Pass laws, administered by local authorities, were compulsory for black men in all towns in the Union. Africans without work could be 'endorsed out' of urban areas, and by 1930 entry into towns was restricted.[15] A network of legislation limited the freedom of African men, and the 1927 Riotous Assemblies Act allowed for the strict control of any disturbances.

Liberal historians believe that racial segregation may have worked to the advantage of industry in the early period, particularly with regard to maintaining a regimented black workforce, but as the economy grew an incompatibility between industrial growth and racial policies would develop. Ultimately, it was argued, economic growth would destroy racial segregation.[16] The period between 1915 and 1917 was marked by black worker activism against living conditions in the compounds and high prices in the mine stores. Other workers, for example those employed in sanitary works, demanded higher wages but also protested against pass law regulations and inadequate housing. As Worden asserts: 'The division of interest between black and white mine workers was now deeply entrenched. Any concession to one group threatened the position of the other'.[17]

Other analysts viewed capitalists as instrumental in maintaining segregation. Frederick Johnstone outlined a different understanding of the relationship between capitalism and segregation by arguing that both were 'collaborative'.[18] Industrial growth had occurred not in spite of white racism; rather, invested capital had appropriated the state's racial policies for its own ends. Industrial development in South Africa had taken on a particular form. Deep-level gold mining required a large labour force in the production of goods whose prices were fixed on the international market. Therefore, low-cost labour was essential to maintain profit margins. This situation was not only a problem of racial division and white dominance but also of class. Harold Wolpe believes that the repressive apparatus of the state, in the form of the police, army, prisons, courts, etc., was used to coerce all workers, black and white, in support of the employers.[19] The neo-Marxist approach saw the South African state 'as an instrument of class rule in a specific

---

[13] Lipton 1986: 112–13.
[14] cited in Smith 1976(b): 10.
[15] *Ibid.*: 9; Worden 1995: 43.
[16] *cf.* de Kiewiet 1941; van der Horst 1941.
[17] Worden 1995: 52.
[18] Johnstone 1976.
[19] Wolpe in Beinart and Dubow 1995: 65.

form of capitalist society'. Racial segregation and laws that upheld and reinforced such divisions actually 'served to mask the capitalist nature of the society and to dilute any form of opposition to the system'. The definition of racial groups was a construct of the social and political environment and embedded in legal, ideological and economic institutions. As Wolfe states:

> The colonial structure guaranteed the superior position and dominance of the white bloc as a whole and with it the specific interests of the different classes within that bloc. Correspondingly, it reproduced the subordinate position of the black groups and the different classes within it.[20]

These arguments are returned to in the following chapter, in which the relationship between class structures and the state is explored.

Racial supremacy

Racial separation is imperative, not only in the interests of a native culture, and to prevent the native traditions and institutions from being swamped by the more powerful organisation of the Whites, but also for other important purposes, such as public health, racial purity and public good order. The mixing up of two such alien elements as white and black leads to unhappy social results – racial miscegenation, moral deterioration of both, racial antipathy and clashes, and to many other forms of social evil ... It is, however, evident that the proper place of the educated minority of the natives is with the rest of their people, of whom they are the natural leaders, and from where they should not in any way be dissociated (J.C. Smuts (prime minister 1919–24), cited in van den Berghe 1967: 114).

Tradition, culture and character have all been invoked to explain the nature of Afrikaner attitudes towards race. Although the British also adopted racially prejudiced policies, one view has identified segregation with the early attitudes and personal dispositions of Afrikaners in the early nineteenth-century Cape frontier. It was there, the argument goes, that the 'trekboers' confirmed themselves as a strong racial group grappling with the 'black enemy'.[21] To 'trek' meant to migrate or move on, and a 'Voortrekker' was a person who took the lead in the migration. The 'Great Trek' involved Afrikaner families rejecting British control in the Cape and leaving to travel northwards in search of land. The trek was extremely difficult in terms of both terrain and conflict, but many Afrikaners saw it as 'God's will': between 1836 and 1846, around 13,000 people trekked out of the Cape Colony (see Figure 1.2).[22] The distribution of these Voortrekkers by the end of the 1840s foreshadowed the dimensions of South Africa today. According to Anthony Lemon, two consequences of the Great Trek are absolutely fundamental to an understanding of the country's subsequent development. First, the frontier between white farmers and Africans was extended from 320 to more than 1600

---

[20] Wolpe 1988: 31.
[21] Saunders 1988: 16.
[22] Meintjes 1973.

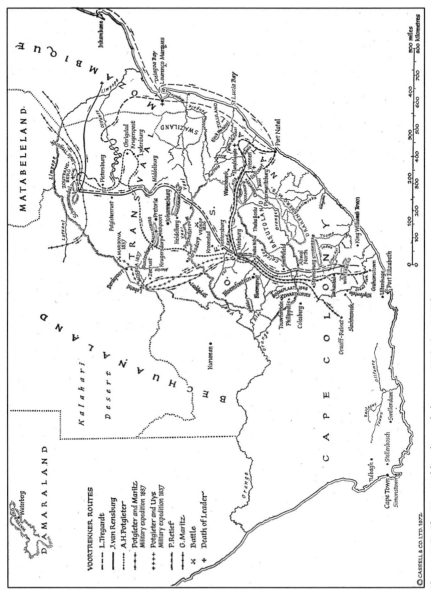

Figure 1.2 The Voortrekkers' march (source: Meintjes 1973)

kilometres. From the middle of the nineteenth century, black tribes were progressively confined to the arid west of the high veld or the malarial north. Second, the successful occupation of the high veld was critical as the region proved to be 'the richest parcel of real estate in the world and became the economic and political core of South Africa' when gold was discovered decades later.[23]

However, the trek was also to have a powerful effect on Afrikaner nationalism. The tenacity, endurance and self-respect that were such key components in facing isolation, fear and harsh conditions could, it is argued, fuel a contempt for those regarded as inferior. Certainly, descriptions of their lifestyle as 'a joyless existence' have been recorded, with trekkers finding justification for their way of life in the Old Testament of the Bible.[24] In the context of racism, Walker claims that it was on the frontier that the trekboers came to identify themselves as white and superior to a black enemy. The strong sense of racial identity and prejudice was forged into the interior by the Voortrekkers and subsequently became enshrined in the Union of South Africa.[25] In short, it was these 'frontier' ideas that were seen to underpin the segregationist policies inherent in white supremacy. Herman Giliomee believes that discrimination and prejudice are seldom justified as ends in themselves but rather as the consequence of upholding ethnic rights and interests. Political leaders identified the Afrikaners' uniqueness in the development of the country, and General Hertzog, prime minister in 1924, claimed the Afrikaners as pioneers of South African civilisation and as such, their special role was not to be assimilated.[26] Hertzog saw differences in blacks and whites in terms of 'civilisation' and believed it was the duty of whites to protect civilisation. However, relations between Afrikaners and the English were uneasy, with domination and conflict very much part of the scene, while Cape coloureds were regarded as not 'socially part of the white nation'.[27] Afrikaners, then, had a specific ethnic identification, beyond skin colour, which they wished to preserve apart from English, African or coloured influences.

Racial identity has also been explained in terms of ethnos theory, which assumes that human beings have distinct natural social entities, or 'ethnies'. These structures cannot be organised artificially, because they are culturally determined. Racial differentiation takes place only after these associations are established. Within this interpretation, the differentiation into biological types was a consequence of ethnic differentiation, therefore notions of 'race' could be replaced by ideas of 'culture'. If racial segregation was to be dignified by a non-white supremacist rationale, then cultural ethnicity could be introduced as a way of understanding and justifying differences between peoples.[28] Saul Dubow, in analysing the development of a segregationist ideology, explores the related

---

[23] Lemon 1976: 25.
[24] Meintjes 1973: 10.
[25] *cf.* Walker 1930; Meintjes 1973.
[26] Giliomee 1989: 34.
[27] *Ibid.*
[28] Kuper 1988: 44–6.

issues of social Darwinism and cultural relativity. Social Darwinism applied the evolutionist principle to races of people, whereby a 'natural' hierarchy existed between different races, but racial 'advancement' could be achieved over time. These views were sometimes linked with the notion of eugenics, which reinforced fears of moral degeneracy and physical degradation if races intermingled.[29] In the context of South Africa, Dubow sees social Darwinism expressed in three distinct areas: first, the debate about the relative intelligence of blacks *vis-à-vis* whites, with blacks being generally regarded as 'backward'; second, the abiding fear and horror of 'miscegenation', the mixing of blacks and whites, which would produce 'race fusion' and threaten to eliminate white civilisation. Given the population ratios in South Africa, with Africans far outnumbering whites, these views were particularly powerful. Political concessions for blacks were often seen as the first step towards 'social equality', which would ultimately lead to the 'swamping' of the white minority. The third issue was that of urbanisation and anxieties about the development of a black proletariat in the cities. As Dubow points out, in the opinion of many, 'Africans were "naturally" party of the land. Cities were portrayed as an "alien environment" for which they were not ready.'[30]

The notion of 'culture' became popular in the 1920s and 1930s as the term could be interchanged with 'civilisation'. By stressing the role of culture, white and black communities could retain their identities. 'The duty of the native', as Dubow records, was 'not to become a black European, but to become a better native, with ideals and a culture of his own.'[31] The concept of 'cultural adaptation' allowed different racial groups to fit into their own environments and was employed as a rationale for segregation. The alternative to adaptation was assimilation, which was seen as both undesirable and potentially dangerous. These views were prevalent in Europe and underlined Britain's colonial policy, not only in Africa but also in the mandated territories in the Middle East. The British Colonial Office had long espoused paternalistic sentiments with regard to its imperial policy by declaring that it was 'only concerned for its wards' in its various territories.[32]

However, any assumption that blacks would be relatively unaffected by European influences and particularly by the development of industry was misplaced. The Native Affairs Department was aware of 'an awakening of racial consciousness'.[33] A host of strikes and riots against pay and conditions clearly revealed 'a growing inclination among Native workers to adopt European methods for the redress of grievances'. Although the principle of segregation became generally accepted, there were nuances in its precise definition. The Hertzog view was gen-

---

[29] Beinart and Dubow 1995: 154.

[30] *Ibid.*: 155.

[31] Dubow, quoting Werner Eiselen in *ibid*: 162.

[32] Thames Papers Box 1, File 5, Middle East Centre, St Antony's Oxford, cited in Deegan (1984).

[33] Beinart and Dubow 1995: 165.

erally racist, strident and emphasised the 'economic and political exclusion of Africans from a common society', while Smuts's position was more paternalistic and favoured 'a moderate segregationist solution'. Yet as Dubow asserts: 'Common to both strands of segregationist ideology was an unashamed paternalism towards Africans and an unquestioning commitment to the maintenance of white supremacy.'[34]

Politics

The first government following the Union of South Africa was led by Louis Botha and the South African Party (SAP). It was a coalition of all the Afrikaner parties from the separate colonies. The electoral arrangement was as follows: members of the lower house were elected by the adult male, white population, except initially in the Cape, where a minority of electors were coloured or African. The constitution allowed for a marginal advantage to be given to rural voters. The opposition to the government was led by the Unionist Party, which was a coalition of non-Afrikaner politicians led by leaders of the mining industry, and the small Labour Party. Segregation as a formal political policy had been put forward in the Union by the Labour Party in its manifesto in 1914.[35] At that time, the party consisted almost entirely of skilled British mine-workers, who were anxious to protect their privileged earnings. The white workers' trade union organisation was backed by the Labour Party. Interestingly, no Afrikaners sat on the opposition benches, and there were only a few English-speaking representatives on the government side. Yet, there was a general fluidity of political affiliation and diversity within the SAP. According to Denoon and Nyeko, there were liberal Cape politicians within the SAP who had close personal relations with some African political leaders and felt distinctly uncomfortable with the 'explicit racism of the northern Afrikaners'.[36] The South African Party, initially under the leadership of Louis Botha until his death in 1919 and then under General Jan Smuts, ruled the country until 1924. However, in the election of 1920 the party only managed to cling on to power through an alliance with the Unionist Party (see Table 1.1) and in 1924 it was heavily defeated at the polls.

J.B.M. Hertzog became prime minister of a National Party–Labour Party coalition that formed a pact government (see Table 1.2). Herzog's main objectives were to win complete emancipation from British control and to provide greater protection for Afrikaners. In fact, the National Party gained support because it took up strong Afrikaner causes and the issue of white poverty. The combined factors of agrarian change, indebtedness, the war and cattle disease contributed to a higher incidence of white poverty. Beinart maintains that the boundaries between white and coloured people were particularly uneven in the Cape, where poor Afrikaner

---

[34] *Ibid.*: 168.
[35] Smith 1976(b): 10.
[36] Denoon and Nyeko 1984: 164.

Table 1.1 1920 South African election

Party	Seats in parliament
Nationalist Party	44
South African Party	41
Unionist Party	25
Labour Party	21

Table 1.2 Governments and prime ministers 1910–1999

1910–1919	South African Party: Louis Botha
1919–1924	South African Party: J.C. Smuts
1924–1933	Nationalist–Labour Pact: J. Hertzog
1933–1939	United Party: J. Hertzog
1939–1948	United Party: J.C. Smuts
1948–1954	National Party: D.F. Malan
1954–1958	National Party: J.G. Strijdom
1958–1966	National Party: H.F. Verwoerd
1966–1978	National Party: B.J. Vorster
1978–1989	National Party: P.W. Botha
1989–1994	National Party: F.W. de Klerk
1994–1999	African National Congress: Nelson Mandela
1999–	African National Congress: Thabo Mbeki

whites began to lose their identity and cohabit with English speakers and Africans.[37] The fact that whites were entitled to vote, unlike poor blacks, and therefore were a political constituency, had a direct impact on politicians. In a sense, they had to take notice of this section of the electorate, either in terms of wooing them as potential supporters or stemming their political activism. From the inception of the Union, Denoon and Nyeko argue, 'the ministers of the cabinet worked in two main directions: seeking ways to satisfy the demands of major white political interests and developing means of coercing the rest of the population'.[38] A tranche of legislation was passed that boosted white supremacy, including the 1927 Immorality Act, which forbade extramarital sexual relations between blacks and whites. In 1933, Hertzog and General Smuts formed a coalition government, and their parties merged the following year to form the United South African National Party. However, a small group of disaffected Afrikaners split off to form the Purified Nationalist Party under the leadership of D.F. Malan. Two pieces of legislation in 1936 further reinforced the subordinate role of Africans in

---

[37] Beinart 1994: 77.
[38] Denoon and Nyeko 1984: 165.

both society and politics. Because Africans were regarded as essentially rural dwellers who migrated to work in cities but actually belonged on the land, the Native Trust and Land Act enlarged the amount of territory deemed appropriate for African occupation to 13 per cent of the country. In fact, these tracts of land were to form the basis of the 'homelands' some years later.[39] The Representation of Natives Act removed Cape Africans from the electoral register and provided for their separate representation in both houses of parliament, while a Native Representative Council was set up to advise the government on African matters.[40] Denoon and Nyeko provide a stark picture of black African life in the city: 'Industrial relations had been clarified by the solidification of the industrial colour bar and arbitration procedures which ignored African unions; the lives of urban Africans were determined by pass laws and residential segregation.'[41]

The segregationist legislation of Louis Botha's government acted as a catalyst for organised black political unity. Delegates from throughout South Africa met in 1912 in Bloemfontein to form the South African Native National Congress (SANNC), which was renamed the African National Congress (ANC) in 1923 (see Box 1.2). Its aims were to unite tribes and races in defence of their rights, but as Tom Lodge points out, it was far from being a mass movement. Although the congress included some chiefs and rural leaders, its members were still primarily middle-class men who feared 'being thrust back into the ranks of the urban and rural poor'.[42] Some congress leaders disagreed with militant actions such as strikes and protests and favoured achieving the organisation's aims through persuasion, for example by appealing to Britain. However, the appeals of delegations to Britain in 1914 urging protest against the Land Act and again in 1919, pleading for British recognition of African rights, were ignored. The SANNC had hoped to exert influence by petitions, delegations and journalism, but the ineffectiveness of such approaches had become clear by the end of the decade. In 1927, J.T. Gumede was elected president of the ANC and he tried to revitalise the organisation to

---

Box 1.2 The objectives of the South African Native National Congress, 1912

First Constitution: This organisation aims to encourage mutual understanding and to bring together into common action as one political people, all tribes and clans of various tribes or races and by means of combined effort and united political organi-sation, to defend their freedom, rights and privileges.

Source: Worden 1995.

---

[39] The 'homelands' are dealt with in Chapter 2.

[40] Beinart 1994: 170.

[41] Denoon and Nyeko 1984: 169.

[42] Lodge 1983: 2.

fight against the discriminatory legislation being passed by the government (see Figure 1.3). However, in 1930 he was voted out of office, and the organisation was weakened.

The ANC described itself during the 1930s as a 'careful organisation' that was in decline. According to Nigel Worden, the ANC lost influence during that decade because its 'cautious and conservative orientation towards the reserve chiefs and the aspiring African commercial and middle classes provided little link with the majority of the population facing rural impoverishment and urban proletarianisation'.[43] The ANC later admitted that it had become inactive during the 1930s under its conservative leadership.[44] Certainly, ANC leaders found it difficult to 'steer a path between liberalism, rural traditionalism and urban radicalism'.[45] Given the size and diversity of South Africa, regional organisations tended to follow local concerns. During the 1920s, the ANC was largely supplanted by the Industrial and Commercial Workers' Union of South Africa (ICU), which was a general union formed in 1919. It was an active and popular organisation in rural and urban areas during this period and was believed to have a membership of around 100,000 by the late 1920s.[46] Individual ANC members were involved in

Figure 1.3 ANC cartoon (source: *Mzabalazo*, 1994)

---

[43] Worden 1995: 83.
[44] *Mzabalazo*, 5.
[45] Beinart 1994: 99.
[46] *Ibid.*: 101.

the ICU and supported it, although organisationally the ANC was a separate entity. However, the ICU was also subject to factionalism and fragmentation into regional groupings. By the late 1920s, it too had diminished in force and effectiveness. For many involved in trade unionism, the ICU experience suggested that although African workers could be easily mobilised, the state was too strong and ruthless to be overthrown, or even redirected. Once all vestiges of black political suffrage had been legislated away, it was unlikely that any negotiated arrangement could be made with the government, and the ANC was forced to recognise that at some stage a different strategy would have to be adopted.

The Inkatha liberation movement grew from a cultural organisation of the same name founded in the 1920s by the Zulu monarch King Solomon. The objectives of that organisation were 'to preserve the unity of the Zulu nation', particularly as people's rights were being undermined and their land removed.[47] King Solomon sought to inculcate traditional values at a time when 'crushing indignities' were being heaped on black people. Shula Marks believes that the origins and development of Inkatha owed much to the 'deliberate resuscitation of traditional views' by the Zulu royal family.[48] King Solomon provided a focal point and central figure, and the founding of Inkatha was a deliberate attempt to reduce tensions that had arisen within Zulu society as a result of the growth of internal social stratification. Divisions occurred in Natal between black workers and black farmers who owned land and employed labour. These socio-economic differences gave rise to uneven responses to the ICU. The organisation was regarded positively in industrial centres, where working conditions were severe and the margin of profit was high. But in rural areas, and especially on black farms, profit margins were insufficient to pay high wages.[49] It would, however, be misleading to overestimate the number of black farmers, who were, according to Marks, 'the privileged few' in the 1920s. With the extension of white farming activities into cotton and sugar in the Natal region, there had been massive evictions of blacks from the land, particularly following the introduction of the 1913 Land Act.

The Second World War

Tensions between Hertzog and Smuts within the government grew during the build-up to the Second World War over their respective attitudes to the impending war. Hertzog wanted South Africa to adopt a neutral position, while Smuts felt that the country should support Britain. These views were debated in parliament, and Smuts won a narrow vote of 80:67. The coalition government split and Hertzog left, taking some of his old supporters with him. Some Afrikaners adopted pro-Nazi positions and created a variety of paramilitary groups. One organisation, the Ossewa

---

[47] Inkatha Freedom Party 1987: 30.
[48] Marks 1970: 106.
[49] *Ibid.*: 108.

Brandwag (OB), had formed in 1938 and drew considerable Afrikaner support: 130,000 in the Transvaal and 60,000 on the Rand.[50] Forged either out of a dislike of imperial Britain or a real identification with fascist sentiments, OB organised terror groups and attempted to sabotage the country's war effort. Nevertheless, 150,000 whites joined up to fight in the war, and around two-thirds of these were Afrikaners. In the 1943 general election, although Smuts's coalition won a majority with sixty-seven seats, Malan's National Party won all forty-three opposition seats. Malan had emphasised Afrikaner ethnic identity during the electoral campaign. Ironically, Beinart believes, had it not been for the impact of the Second World War on South African society, which actually broke down segregationist policies and fuelled Afrikaner racial fears, there may have been a softening of government policies. However, as pro-Nazi groups attracted support in the late 1930s, there were strong indicators that society had become more polarised and potentially extremist even before the weakening of segregation during the war years.

The important strategic role played by South Africa in the Second World War made inroads into the policies of movement control and job reservation. More Africans crowded into the urban areas, especially the shanty towns on the fringes of the cities. For a short period, from 1943 to 1946, the pass laws and 'job colour bar' laws were relaxed, largely because in the absence of white labour, industry needed black workers. As Merle Lipton explains: 'The job colour bar, pass laws and migrant labour were all criticised as unjust and inefficient, deterring ambition and competition.'[51] Running in tandem with these changes were policies on the extension of training facilities for blacks in order to expand the supply of skilled workers. A combination of occupational advance and government policy led to increases in black wages. The 1945 National Education Finance Act freed black education from its dependence on African taxes, and blacks became eligible for old age pensions. In 1942, the Department of Native Affairs recommended the abolition of the pass laws and in 1947 African trade unions were recognised. Table 1.3 displays the increases in the total number of black children in school between 1940 and 1950, although even at its highest it is only one-fifth of the number of white children attending school. But, as Lipton points out: 'the reforms of this period were limited to socioeconomic policy, politically there was little progress.'[52]

In terms of black and coloured political activity, the 1940s reflected a renewed awareness. The ANC believes that it had 'new life and energy' during that decade and acted against the rise of 'extreme Afrikaner nationalism.'[53] In 1944, the ANC Youth League was formed. Its young leaders included Nelson Mandela, Walter Sisulu and Oliver Tambo, who argued that Africans would be freed only by their own efforts. In part, their activities stemmed from the fact that more people had moved to the cities in the 1940s to work in new factories and industries. They

---

[50] Beinart 1994: 131.
[51] Lipton 1986: 21.
[52] *Ibid.*
[53] *Mzabalazo*, 6.

Table 1.3 South African educational statistics by race 1910–1950

	Year	Population (in thousands)	Total No. in school (in thousands)	% getting post-primary education	Total state expenditure (in £ millions)
Whites	1910	1256	165	10.8	1.6
	1920	1500	314	13.4	6.3
	1930	1798	371	16.0	8.4
	1940	2153	416	21.2	10.7
	1950	2620	507	22.0	25.4
Black Africans	1910	3953	186	–	0.1
	1920	4630	185	1.5	0.3
	1930	5858	287	1.5	0.6
	1940	7116	471	2.6	1.0
	1950	8347	767	4.2	5.8
Coloured and Asian	1920	707	56	–	–
	1930	880	100	1.4	0.5
	1940	1069	175	3.0	1.0
	1950	1353	266	3.6	4.7

Source: van den Berghe 1965: 298.

began to form their own community organisations, such as the Squatters Movement. The Natal Indian Congress used passive resistance against laws that restricted Indians from buying land, and their campaign was supported by the ANC. In 1946, 75,000 African mine-workers came out on strike for higher wages, and troops were called in to drive the men back to the mines at bayonet point. The Second World War's fight against fascism had heightened political awareness and union activity, but when the wartime shortage of workers ended, blacks found themselves under increasing pressure. The 1946 mine-workers' strike 'turned out to be the end of the phase of militant unionism, rather than the beginning'.[54] Whites began to feel uneasy about the flow of Africans to the towns, and many believed that the government had become too lenient towards blacks.

The 1948 general election

The leader of the National Party, D.F. Malan, had upheld Afrikaner ethnicity during the 1943 election, but in 1945 the party spoke out strongly in favour of a 'firm native policy'.[55] Again, 'cultural' factors were invoked to rationalise the party's recommendations that controls over African urban settlement should be

---

[54] Beinart 1994: 127.
[55] Worden 1995: 92.

strengthened and the reserves further consolidated. Segregation would be extended and racial inequality would continue. The National Party adopted an explicitly 'Afrikaners first' programme and fielded no English candidates. In fact, the Transvaal National Party excluded Jews.[56] The party wanted Afrikaner domination and all the symbolism that accompanied it, e.g. pre-eminence for the Afrikaans language, a republic, and rejection of the Commonwealth. The United Party entered the election campaign divided between its liberal and conservative wings although seemingly committed to the view that the segregationist policy of migrant labour was socially and economically undesirable.

The results of the 1948 elections were affected by the favourable loading of rural votes in the allocation of parliamentary seats. The United Party gained more votes, particularly in major urban areas (see Table 1.4), yet because of the weighting, the National Party gained more seats. The election confirmed the rural base of the National Party, and although it made some inroads in Johannesburg and Pretoria among Afrikaner miners, railwaymen and steelworkers, its largest gains were in the Cape and Transvaal. Almost half the National MPs were farmers or connected with agriculture, and although the United Party was primarily an urban party, 20 per cent of its MPs were farmers. For the first time since 1910 the party in power was exclusively Afrikaner.

> Today South Africa belongs to us once more. For the first time since Union, South Africa is our own, and may God grant that it will always remain our own (victory speech by Prime Minister Malan after the 1948 General Election).

Table 1.4 South African elections 1948

Party	Number of votes
United Party	524,230
National Party	401,834
Labour Party	27,360
Afrikaner Party	41,885

Source: van den Berghe 1965: 295.

The National Party's policy of explicit racism appealed to white workers, who felt threatened by black urbanisation during the Second World War, but its central core of support came from large-scale farmers. Nelson Mandela recalls the shock of learning of the National Party's victory: 'I was stunned and dismayed. We knew that our land would henceforth be a place of tension and strife.'[57] Although the National Party only entered government because of the intricacies of South Africa's electoral system, it was to consolidate its support and remain in power for the next forty-six years.

---

[56] Lipton 1986: 276.
[57] Mandela 1994: 128.

Part II

The rise and fall of apartheid

Chapter 2

Apartheid and the state

Forced segregation

In 1948, the Nationalist government inherited a system of segregation that was showing signs of collapse. Industrial development had so accelerated the urban movement of Africans that many 'white' areas were in fact largely black. A government commission set up by the former administration, under Justice Fagan, concluded that total segregation was impracticable and advocated the acceptance of a permanent 'native' population in urban areas. The Nationalists rejected this recommendation and set about entrenching segregation by rooting it in the ideology of apartheid. The country would be divided into racial zones. Like the old segregationist policies of the 1920s, geographical segregation was to be the key to white domination, since it removed blacks from the field of white competition and contained them permanently in their own areas. One of the first speeches made at the opening of parliament in 1949 stressed the government's intention 'to take the necessary steps to give effect to their policy of segregation'.[1] The flow of native labour to farms and cities would be 'channelled more effectively' and the natives would be 'encouraged to equip themselves for increased participation in and responsibility for their own services ... within their own territory and their own community'.[2] As James Barber makes clear, the National Party did not wish to halt industrialisation and economic growth but rather 'to control its social implications by imposing strict segregation based on racial hierarchy'.[3]

The Group Areas Act, one of the Nationalist government's first pieces of legislation (see Box 2.1), had far-reaching effects on racial segregation. It provided for the extension throughout South Africa of areas of land that were designated for the exclusive occupation by each racial group: 'white', 'coloured', 'Asiatic' (Indian) and 'Native' (later termed 'Bantu' or African). These classifications were categorised in the Population Registration Act of 1950. Land held by Indians and coloureds in city centres was expropriated by the government, and residents were resettled in housing estates on the peripheries of cities. The black population who lived in Sophiatown, one of the oldest black settlements in Johannesburg, had

---

[1] *Hansard*, January 1949, cited in W. de Klerk 1991.

[2] *Ibid.*

[3] Barber 1999: 124.

Box 2.1 Legislation of the National government

1949 **Immorality Act** – extended the existing ban on sexual relations between whites and Africans to prohibit all sexual contact between whites and coloureds and Indians

1950 **Suppression of Communism Act** – organisations that supported communism were banned.

1950 **Group Areas Act** – extended the principle of separate racial residential areas on a comprehensive and compulsory basis.

1951 **Bantu Authorities Act** – established government-approved chiefs in the reserves but no provision for African representation in the towns.

1952 **Abolition of Passes and Coordination of Documents Act** – all Africans had to carry a reference book to include an employer's signature renewed each month. This became a new form of pass law.

1953 **Reservation of Separate Amenities Act** – enforced social segregation in all public amenities, such as transport, cinemas, restaurants and sports facilities. Separation was later enforced in schools, colleges and universities.

1953 **Bantu Education Act** – all African schools brought under the control of the Department of Native Affairs; independent missionary schools for Africans were phased out. Imposition of a strict curriculum that stressed 'Bantu culture' and prepared students for manual labour.

1953 **Criminal Law Amendment Act** – prescribed heavy penalties for civil disobedience.

1954 **Natives Resettlement Act** – gave the state the power to remove Africans forcibly to separate townships.

1955 **Natives (Urban Areas) Amendment Act** – rights of Africans to live in a town were confined to those who had been in continuous residence for 10 years or had worked for fifteen years with a single employer. All others needed a permit to stay longer than three days.

---

their homes destroyed under the Group Areas Act and they were moved to Soweto. Sophiatown had been one of the few places where Africans had been able to buy housing plots before the 1923 Urban Areas Act. Despite its poverty and overcrowding, Sophiatown had a special character and symbolic cultural significance. Nelson Mandela remembers the ANC's efforts to prevent the removal of residents but, finally, Africans were forced out of the area by 2000 troops and eighty trucks.[4]

The creation of racial residential segregation at national and city levels required the relocation of large numbers of people. Table 2.1 outlines the various types of removal adopted and the numbers involved. Between 1955 and 1980, it is estimated that around 3.5 million people, predominantly black, Indian and coloured,

---

[4] *Mzabalazo*, 9; Mandela 1994: 173–82.

Table 2.1 Population affected by removal or relocation, 1955–1980

Type of removal	Numbers
Eviction of black tenants, squatters and surplus labour from 'white' farmland	1,129,000
Clearance of 'black spots' and 'homeland' consolidation	674,000
Urban relocation and removal from 'white' areas to 'homeland' townships	670,000
Removal from unauthorised (spontaneous) urban settlements	112,000
'Group area' removals arising from racial rezoning	834,400
Relocation due to development schemes and clearing sensitive areas	23,500
Political moves such as banishment and flight from oppression	50,000
Other miscellaneous moves	30,000
TOTAL	3,522,900

Source: the Surplus People Project, as reported in *Race Relations News* (SAIRR), May/June 1983.

were relocated. The term 'black spots' described parcels of land bought by Africans freehold before the 1913 Land Act. The elimination of those pieces of land was an important feature of the consolidation of the 'homelands'. The creation of the 'homelands' (or 'Bantustans') was an extension of the separated areas that had been demarcated as 'African reserves' in 1936. Black South Africans were to be restricted to the separate territories that they had been allocated as part of the segregationist policies of the interwar years, but under the Nationalist government, mobility would be strictly controlled. According to the 1955 amendment to the Natives (Urban) Areas Act, only so-called *'bona fide'* Africans were entitled to be in urban areas longer than 72 hours: that is, those Africans who could produce documentary proof that they had been in continuous residence in the area for ten years or with one employer for fifteen years and were without a criminal record. Africans who could not produce such documentation were removed to the homelands. The Population Registration Act of 1962 fixed the racial classification of coloured people legally in order that they could no longer pass as whites on physical appearance.

The new minister for native affairs, Dr H.F. Verwoerd, commissioned a comprehensive development plan that ultimately became the official blueprint of apartheid policy. The report of the Commission for the Socio-Economic Development of the Bantu Areas within the Union of South Africa, known as the Tomlinson Commission, was published in 1954. This document defined apartheid as a combination of science and culture. The balance of the report was concerned with the implementation of segregation, that is the consolidation and development of the 'Bantu areas' or black homelands. Interestingly, the report contained no suggestion that race was a crucial factor in policy. In fact, it looked to the traditional segregation of South African society in terms of religion, civilisation, social arrangement and economic status. It recognised that historically there had been conflict between communities and that a clear demographic imbalance between different peoples existed. For Adam Kuper, the Tomlinson Report attempted 'to found a policy of discrimination on a basis other than simple racialism', and he points to the cultural and ethnic factors that infused Afrikaner discussions of the 'Native question' in the 1920s.[5] While Beinart and Dubow accept that the rhetoric of apartheid bore 'considerable similarities to white supremacist statements of the segregation era', its distinctive and appealing quality was the prospect of 'Afrikaner ethnic exclusivity'.[6] In any case, the political context was different: British colonialism was ending and power rested in the hands of the Afrikaner Nationalist Party. Merle Lipton explains the government's 'Afrikaner first' policies, whereby Afrikaners were given preference in jobs and entrepreneurial opportunities. The state sector was expanded and 'Afrikaner hegemony was extended over senior posts in the civil service, armed forces and judiciary'. Effectively, 'the state sector became an Afrikaner preserve'.[7]

Yet it would be erroneous to believe that a government that represented the interests of Afrikaners, who comprised only 12 per cent of the entire population, did not gain support from other white communities. The English-speaking communities were economically dominant in the mining and commercial spheres, and clear divisions existed between 'liberal-minded' groups, who were uncomfortable with apartheid, and those 'conservatives' who generally supported it. The United Party seemed unable to mount a vigorous campaign against the government, and its ambiguity led some coloured leaders to suggest that the party was hypocritical and equivocal in its stand against apartheid. Certainly, Afrikaners were caustic in their response to English speakers with jokes in their newspapers claiming that 'the English joined the Progressive Party, voted for the United Party and thanked God for the National Party'.[8] Although some English-speaking South Africans left the country to organise campaigns against apartheid overseas, those who stayed benefited economically from the government's policies. English-speaking manufacturers and industrialists were able to increase output, and gold production alone expanded markedly. Foreign investment, attracted by cheap labour, further enhanced white prosperity. The increased votes gained by the National Party in general elections during the 1950s (see Tables 2.2 and 2.3) indicate that support came from English-speaking voters.

---

[5] Kuper 1988.
[6] Beinart and Dubow 1995: 12.
[7] Lipton 1986: 282.
[8] *Ibid.*: 305.

Table 2.2 South African general election results, 1953 and 1958

Total votes polled by:	Year of Election	
	1953	1958
National Party	598,718	642,069
United Party	576,474	503,639
Labour Party	34,730	2,670
Liberal Party	–	2,934

Source: van den Berghe 1967: 295.

Table 2.3 South African general election results: seats gained in parliament 1948–1958

Year of Election	1948	1953	1958
National Party	70	94	103
United Party	63	57	53
Afrikaner Party	9	–	–
Labour Party	6	5	

Source: van den Berghe 1967: 286–7.

Black opposition

The ANC Youth League's Programme of Action, which called for strikes, boycotts and defiance, was formally adopted by the ANC in 1949, one year after the National Party came to power. The programme led to the creation of a defence campaign against the government's oppressive legislation. In defiance of the government's strict policies of racial separation, in which every social area was designated for 'Europeans only'/'Whites only' or 'Non-Europeans', black Africans went to shop counters that were for 'Whites only', and Indian, coloured and some white 'volunteers' entered African townships without permission. Teachers and pupils called for a boycott of state schools in protest against the Bantu Education Act. The defence campaign called for 'national freedom' and political independence from white domination. All forms of segregation were rejected. The government, in response, tried to stop the campaign by banning its leaders and passing new laws to prevent acts of public disobedience. But the campaign made considerable strides and forged closer cooperation between the ANC and the South African Indian Congress. Initially, this cooperation was not easy as many within the ANC felt that the interests of the Indian and coloured communities were different from those of Africans. As Nelson Mandela remembers: 'I doubted whether or not they could truly embrace our cause.'[9] Nevertheless, obstacles were overcome and new

[9] Mandela 1994: 129.

organisations were formed: the South African Coloured People's Organisation (SACPO) and the Congress of Democrats, an organisation of white democrats.

These groups, together with the South African Congress of Trade Unions (SACTU) formed the Congress Alliance. The alliance canvassed people's opinions and presented what came to be known as the 'Freedom Charter' (see Box 2.2), a document that was written after a year-long campaign in which activists collected popular demands. It called for equal access to health, education and legal rights and demanded that all apartheid laws and practices be set aside. According to Nigel Worden, the vision of a 'strongly democratic and multiracial' South Africa informed the ANC's thinking and provided an ideological benchmark of opposition to apartheid right into the 1990s.[10] Certainly, some of the clauses contained in the Freedom Charter were later to be included in South Africa's democratic constitution in 1996, and the ANC still sees the Freedom Charter as an important expression of its policy of non-racialism. In fact, contained in the membership section of the ANC's 1994 constitution is the declaration that new members must pledge to abide by the 'aims and objectives of the ANC as set out in the Constitution and the Freedom Charter'.[11] In 1996, forty years after the adoption of the charter, the national executive committee of the ANC announced a celebration of the event. The Freedom Charter is seen as the 'first systematic statement in the country of the political and constitutional vision of a free, democratic and non-racial South Africa'.[12] As its clauses demonstrate, the document was a powerful statement of resistance to apartheid, and although the South African Communist Party helped to draft some sections it raised political principles that continue to be relevant. For Tom Lodge, the charter 'emphasised the ANC's commitment to a populist notion of people's sovereignty'.[13] But it would be misleading to regard its economic clauses as guiding principles to the ANC governments of either Nelson Mandela or Thabo Mbeki.

Nevertheless, during the 1950s, not everyone in the ANC agreed with the policy: 'A small minority of members who called themselves Africanists, opposed the Charter. They objected to the ANC's growing cooperation with whites and Indians, whom they described as foreigners.'[14] The differences between Africanists and those in the ANC who supported non-racialism could not be overcome, and in 1959 the Africanists broke away to form the Pan Africanist Congress (PAC). The structure of the ANC, until the late 1950s, was largely federal in character, with 'each province constituting a fairly autonomous organisational unit, an arrangement which helped to sustain ideological diversity'. Essentially, the ANC represented 'a broad church accommodating socially conservative and radical nationalists, democratic socialists, liberal constitutionalists and Marxists of various persuasions'.[15] Yet political dis-

---

[10] Worden 1995: 105–6.
[11] ANC 1994a: 5.
[12] Robertson 1991: 221.
[13] Lodge 1996: 191.
[14] *Mzabalazo*, 1994: 14.
[15] Lodge 1996: 190–1.

Box 2.2 The ANC's Freedom Charter, 1956

South Africa belongs to all who live in it, black and white, and no government can justly claim authority unless it is based on the will of the people:

- Every man and woman shall have the right to vote for and stand as a candidate.
- The rights of the people shall be the same regardless of race, colour or sex.
- All people shall have equal rights to use their own language and to develop their own culture and customs.
- All apartheid laws and practices shall be put aside.
- The mineral wealth beneath the soil, the banks and monopoly industry shall be transferred to the ownership of the people as a whole.
- Restriction of land ownership on a racial basis shall be ended.
- Freedom of movement shall be guaranteed to all who work on the land.
- All shall have the right to occupy land wherever they choose.
- No one shall be imprisoned, deported or restricted without fair trial.
- The courts shall be representative of all the people.
- All laws which discriminate on grounds of race, colour or belief shall be repealed.
- The preaching and practice of national, race or colour discrimination and contempt shall be a punishable crime.
- The law shall guarantee to all their right to speak, to organise, to meet together, to publish, to preach, to worship and to educate their children.
- All shall be free to travel without restriction from countryside to town, from province to province, and from South Africa abroad.
- Pass laws, permits and all other laws restricting these freedoms shall be abolished.
- The state shall recognise the right and duty of all to work and to draw full unemployment benefits.
- The aim of education shall be to teach the youth to love their people and their culture, to honour human brotherhood, liberty and peace.
- Education shall be free, compulsory, universal and equal for all children.
- The colour bar in cultural life, in sport and in education shall be abolished.
- A preventive health scheme shall be run by the state.
- All people shall have the right to live where they choose, to be decently housed and to bring up their families in comfort and security.
- Peace and friendship amongst all our people shall be secured by upholding the equal rights, opportunities and status of all.
- Let all who love their people and their country now say:

  These freedoms we will fight for, side by side, throughout our lives until we have won our liberty.

agreements within and between groups in black politics in the 1950s did not generally lead to violence, because of the 'strong moral commitment to peaceful conduct by a Protestant missionary-trained leadership'. Equally, black organisations were relatively weak and too small to compete with each other.[16]

The presence of communists in the ANC leadership inevitably attracted criticism from liberal quarters. The mainly white South African Communist Party (SACP) was seen to have an agenda that played directly to the Soviet Union. Therefore, the party would not be averse to manipulating resistance movements in South Africa. Also, the activities of the SACP accentuated the government's claims of communist agitation. Stephen Ellis believes that it was more or less 'an open secret that leading ANC members, such as J.B. Marks, Govan Mbeki [father of President Thabo Mbeki] and Moses Kotane, were Communist Party members'.[17] Nelson Mandela and Oliver Tambo were not communists and at one stage were highly ambivalent about associating with such an organisation.[18] The ANC was by far the leading force in the Congress Alliance, but clandestine communist activity did take place within the wider 'umbrella' organisation.

Those who supported the Freedom Charter were accused of treason, and 156 ANC and Congress Alliance leaders were charged. The government claimed that the charter was a communist document, and since such activities had been banned since 1950, its publication was a criminal offence. The government also tried to prove that the ANC and its allies proposed to violently overthrow the state. Ninety-one people were finally committed for a trial that lasted three years, eventually ending in 1961. Ultimately, the judges found that although the ANC and Congress Alliance had worked together in order to replace the existing state with a radically different one, it could not be proved that such a state would result from violent revolution or be a communist one. 'It was impossible,' argued the judge, 'for the court to come to the conclusion that the ANC's policy was to overthrow the state by violence', and those accused were finally acquitted.[19]

The Federation of South African Women, founded in 1954, coordinated incidents of pass burning and mounted a campaign against government legislation that forced women to carry passes. The highpoint of the women's campaign was their 20,000-strong march on the government's Union Buildings in Pretoria. There were many other community struggles in the 1950s, including bus boycotts against raised fares, demonstrations against bans on political meetings and a large revolt by the people of Pondoland, who demanded representation in parliament, lower taxes and an end to Bantu education. Thirty people were sentenced to death for their part in the rebellion. However, for all the passive resistance of the 1950s, the state seemed too strong for opposition to have much impact. In fact, to some analysts the state was already losing its democratic features and acquiring 'many

---

[16] *Ibid.*
[17] Ellis 1992: 149.
[18] Mandela 1994.
[19] South African Institute of Race Relations 1962: 62.

of the characteristics of a police state'.[20] Merle Lipton believes that these changes were facilitated by three mechanisms of the state: direct coercion, indirect coercion and psychological/ideological controls. Direct coercion by the state took the form of political intimidation of and physical violence against those who engaged in non-violent passive resistance. Black activists and whites who supported them or who promoted interracial cooperation were regularly subjected to house arrest, whippings, heavy fines, beatings, police surveillance, harassment and torture. Fear of physical violence inevitably had an impact on radical opposition. Indirect coercion manifested itself in the bureaucratic controls and the legalistic restrictions on the lives of Africans, especially the pass laws, which governed the mobility of the black population. Through the expansion of laws the state could now intrude into the lives of everyone, and officials were given a range of formal powers to grant or withhold passes, permits and official approval for jobs, housing, education, family residence, and so on. The government's insistence on maintaining racially designated areas had to be monitored continuously. There was even a policy on so-called 'racial borderline cases', that is, those people who were deemed to be on the border of white/coloured or coloured/African categories. By 1961, 57,981 cases had been presented to race appeal boards, which designated the 'racial' group into which a person would be placed.[21] As Lipton observes, the personal denigration of racial categorisation was never 'petty or marginal'.[22] Psychological and ideological controls were effected by the state through the astute use of propaganda and the censorship of opposing views. The actual process of institutionalised social separation made it difficult for communities to interact with each other. With the government losing respect for constitutional rights and political dissent, passive opposition was ineffective. This raised the question of violent protest, but many critics of the government were unprepared for such a strategy. That is, until the events of Sharpeville took place.

Sharpeville, state control and separate development

On 21 March 1960, the Pan Africanist Congress asked people to leave their passes at home and gather at police stations in order to be arrested for contravening the pass laws. People gathered in large numbers at Sharpeville in the Transvaal and at Nyanga and Langa near Cape Town. The crowds were unarmed and engaged in passive opposition. The police opened fire on these people, killing sixty-nine, many of whom were shot in the back; 186 were wounded. These actions provoked widespread unrest and strikes in the country and a storm of protest internationally. The United Nations passed resolutions of condemnation. A state of emergency was declared and supporters of the ANC and PAC arrested and detained. Under the emergency regulations, it was later announced that ninety-eight

---

[20] Lipton 1986: 297.
[21] South African Institute of Race Relations 1962: 85.
[22] Lipton 1986: 297.

whites, thirty-six coloured persons, ninety Asians and 11,279 Africans had been detained. Both the ANC and the PAC were ultimately banned. To many observers, the policy of non-violent resistance against the state had failed. The ANC outlined the limitations of extra-parliamentary protest:

> The general strike was suppressed with the utmost vigour. Other protests were increasingly broken by police brutality and the use of orthodox mass demonstration as an effective weapon was demonstrably not feasible. Legal opposition was rendered ineffective by bannings, exile and the imprisonment of activists and leaders. All opposition by legal or peaceful means was rendered impossible.[23]

Without any legitimate electoral channels for the majority of the population to use, there seemed only one route for oppositionists to take: violent struggle. Umkhonto we Sizwe (Spear of the Nation) (MK) was founded in 1961 as an underground guerrilla army 'to hit back by all the means within our power in defence of our people, our future and our freedom'.[24]

Looking back from the perspective of the 1990s, the ANC believes that the formation of Umkhonto we Sizwe was one of its major strengths, or 'pillars of struggle', against apartheid.[25] Within eighteen months of its inception, the organisation had carried out 200 acts of sabotage against government property and buildings. All cadres were under strict orders that no person be harmed during these actions. However, Umkhonto we Sizwe included a large number of communists in its ranks and leadership. For many years, its chief military strategist and chief of staff was Joe Slovo, who was later to become general secretary of the South African Communist Party. The government responded to the activities of MK with even harsher methods of repression. Laws were passed that upheld the death penalty for sabotage and allowed police to detain people for ninety days without trial. In 1963, police raided the secret headquarters of MK and arrested its leaders. These arrests led to the Rivonia trial, where the leaders of the MK were charged with attempting to cause a violent revolution. The Rivonia defendants included Nelson Mandela, Walter Sisulu, Govan Mbeki, Raymond Mhlaba, Elias Motsoaledi, Andrew Mlangeni, Ahmed Kathrada and Dennis Goldberg. All were found guilty and sentenced to life imprisonment.[26] The ANC admits that after the Rivonia trial, the underground structure of the organisation was all but destroyed and the South African state became far more powerful.[27] In the space of a few years, the government's defence spending increased and army manpower rose from 8000 to almost 44,000 (see Table 2.4). For some analysts, the events at Sharpeville marked a high point of resistance that could not be sustained, while others saw the killings as a 'dramatic turning point' in the country's history.[28] Perhaps the

---

[23] ANC, 1994b.

[24] *Mzabalazo*, 1994: 17.

[25] ANC 1994b.

[26] See Chapter 9.

[27] *Mzabalazo*, 1994: 17.

[28] *cf.* Lipton 1986: 302 and Worden 1995: 107.

Table 2.4 Estimates of expenditure for defence and police (£ million)

	1960–61	1961–62	1962–63	1963–64
Defence	21.8	35.8	59.9	78.5
Police	18.1	19.2	20.4	25.4
Total	39.9	55.0	80.3	103.9

Source: van den Berghe 1067: 308.

final judgement on the brutality of gunning down unarmed people should be left to the findings of the judicial commissions of inquiry that investigated the events at Sharpeville and Langa. The reports found that the majority of people who demonstrated were anxious and frustrated at having no constitutional channels through which they could make their grievances known to the government. The crowds who amassed at Langa did so not to engage in violent insurrection but because they actually believed that a senior government official would be attending to listen to their views. The police were found to have acted in an undisciplined manner by using force without warning and resorting to unlawful shooting. Regarding the charges of incitement to violence at Sharpeville, the reports found that there was 'not sufficient justification for the very extensive firing' which killed so many people.[29]

International reaction

Following the events at Sharpeville, the United Nations General Assembly passed a resolution calling on all member states to consider taking separate and collective action, in accordance with the UN Charter, to 'bring about the abandonment by South Africa of policies based on racial discrimination'.[30] A few months earlier, the International Commission of Jurists had produced a detailed report of conditions in South Africa and sent copies to the United Nations and governments across the world. The report declared that South Africa's systematic policy of racial separation penetrated every aspect of life and was supported by a rigid and all-embracing network of legislation. This policy 'denied to a vast majority of the population those opportunities without which the legitimate aspirations and dignity of a human being could not be realised'.[31] The commission analysed the effects of the application of apartheid in various fields. The pass law system, it found, resulted in 'flagrant abuses of the law involving arbitrary arrest and detention', creating a situation that could only be described as 'legalised slavery'. An educational system for non-whites that was deliberately constructed to prepare blacks 'for their acceptance of an inferior social, economic and political status' was 'contrary to the

---

[29] South African Institute of Race Relations 1962: 54–5.

[30] *Ibid*.: 285.

[31] *Ibid*.: 293.

generally accepted concepts of justice and principles of human rights'. The report also condemned the fact that the 'very expression of opposition to or protest against the policy of apartheid constituted a criminal offence'.[32] It called on the international community to be aware of the 'full legal and moral implications' of apartheid and hoped that South Africa would face the future with justice and foresight.

The commission's report was a severe indictment of apartheid, and international attention focused on South Africa. A host of African states withdrew their diplomats, and many instituted a boycott of South African goods. Numerous resolutions were passed by African conferences condemning 'the vicious economic exploitation, brutal political oppression and savage social degradation of the oppressed majority of the people in South Africa'.[33] The Nobel Peace Prize was awarded to ex-Chief A.J. Luthuli, who had been president-general of the banned ANC. The Nobel committee stated that 'in spite of the unmerciful South African race laws, Luthuli had always urged that violence should not be used'. At the time of the award, he was banned from attending gatherings and was confined to a rural area in the district of Natal. He was granted a ten-day passport in order to receive the prize in Oslo but was refused permission to accept an invitation to visit the United States. The South African minister of the interior condemned the decision to grant Luthuli the Nobel Peace Prize, arguing that the former ANC leader had failed to promote peaceful community life within the country. The government, therefore, felt that it could not support the award and believed that the Nobel Peace Prize should no longer be held in high esteem.[34] Irrespective of the views of the international community, the Nationalist government continued to pride itself on standing firm against external threats.

Dr H.F. Verwoerd, the prime minister, blamed communist propaganda for creating a climate of dissent within the country and masquerading as defenders of freedom: 'The communist factor which is responsible for much of the frustration, incitement, hatred, attacks and slogans often shelters behind humanistic, liberal and moral propaganda.' The international criticism, which could only be appeased by the government instituting full political and electoral rights to all people, irrespective of racial group, was dismissed by Verwoerd as objectives destined to lead to deterioration, chaos and communist control. At stake here was national survival against the threat of world communism. The only alternative, according to Verwoerd, was national reconstruction based on racial differentiation. But it could be achieved neither by white domination over the whole population nor by black majority rule. In order to 'establish peace and tranquillity and harmonious relations, each racial unit must be guided to a form of self-government suited to it'.[35]

[32] *Ibid.*

[33] Resolution on South Africa adopted by the Third All-African People's Conference, Cairo, March 1961.

[34] South African Institute of Race Relations 1962: 29.

[35] Dr H.F. Verwoerd's speech to parliament, *Hansard*, January 1962, cited in F.W. de Klerk 1999: 8–9.

The government's policy, then, was to pursue a programme of 'separate development', which would not rest on 'suppression or discrimination based on race or colour'. White and black communities would have their own areas in which they would have dignity and autonomy, but no racial group would have rights outside their own territories. This policy became known as the 'Bantustan' programme. The Promotion of Black Self Government Act, passed in 1959, defined eight so-called ethnic 'nations'. The stage was set for a more formalised separation of the races.

The 'homelands'

It is the intention of the government to consult with the Bantu (Black) people on how to grant self-government as speedily as they themselves wish and are able to accept it. This will have to be done in such a way as to allow these communities to function on a healthy, efficient and truly democratic basis, so as to ensure the maintenance of friendship and co-operation with the Whites. Thus the position of the Whites will at the same time be safeguarded (Prime Minister Verwoerd's statement to parliament, Hansard, *19 January 1962).*

The very word 'homeland' has unpleasant connotations, and as Beinart points out it attempted to 'lend legitimacy to the state's policy of exclusion'.[36] The programme of separate development provided a façade behind which deeply racist policies were pursued. The rationale behind the policy assumed that migrant black workers were simply *'Gastarbeiters'* or 'guestworkers', in much the same way as, say, Turkish workers were in Germany. The government argued that as blacks had their own homelands why should they want social and political rights outside their territories.[37] Laws were passed curbing the number of blacks in urban areas, with the 1964 Bantu Labour Act prohibiting Africans 'seeking work in towns or employers from taking them on unless they were channelled through the state labour bureaux'.[38] These restrictions were part of the separate development policy, which was intended to discourage the drift of black people towards the towns. Another part of the government's plan was the encouragement of industries on the borders of the homelands so that black workers could travel to work on a daily basis. Tax incentives were introduced to persuade companies to relocate, but difficulties were experienced in the recruitment of white managers as well as in general running and transport costs.

Initially, eight 'Bantu homelands' were set up, although later there was a total of ten (see Figure 2.1). The 1963 Transkei Constitution Act set up a legislative assembly with sixty-four chiefs and forty-five elected members. Whites were not allowed to vote, but they continued to work in the Transkei as administrators.[39]

---

[36] Beinart 1994: 203.
[37] Denoon and Nyeko 1984: 199.
[38] Worden 1995: 109.
[39] Denoon and Nyeko 1984: 200.

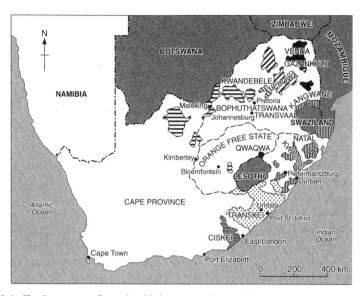

Figure 2.1 The Bantustans (homelands) (source: Barber 1999)

Economically, the homelands were dependent upon South Africa as the possibility of self-sufficiency was remote and, in the mind of the Nationalist government, undesirable. Some chiefs decided to appropriate power to themselves: for example, in KwaZulu, the head of Inkatha, Chief Gatsha Buthelezi, decentralised some policy making from central government. During the 1960s, the population of the homelands rose by 70 per cent, largely through forced removals of black people from designated 'white areas'. Although, by 1965, 38,500 houses for African occupation had been completed in homeland towns, many people were relocated to areas that were remote and barren. The Council of the Institute of Race Relations found that the overall result of the separate development policy was that the 'vast majority of Africans have no "right" to be anywhere where they can earn a living'. The Reserve Africans were nearly all dependent on outside employment.[40] Apart from the inconvenience of long-distance commuting to work, Africans had to travel to 'white' towns for most goods and services. The more blacks left the homelands to go to work in the large 'white' cities, the greater the deterioration of economic conditions in the reserves.

Essentially, the relationship between the homelands and the cities exemplified the fundamental contradiction of South African society, that of the integrated economy dependent upon black labour and the political expedient of enforcing separation to ensure white rule. As Gavin Maasdorp argues, the location of border industries in the white areas and the exclusion of important natural resources from the homelands perpetuated their 'labour reservoir' function.[41] In any case, for eth-

---

[40] South African Institute of Race Relations 1962: 130.
[41] Maasdorp 1976: 28.

nically homogeneous homelands to be legitimate, specific concepts of ethnic identity had to exist. As Worden points out, in some cases such as Zululand and the Transkei, 'the argument that the Bantustans were the rightful historic home of a particular ethnic group coincided with common perceptions'. But elsewhere this was not so.[42] Some homelands were scattered and fragmented pieces of land with no common domiciliary ethnic group, and many were undesirable for commercial agriculture. Even if ethnic identity was accepted as a legitimising rationale, if taken to its logical conclusion there was no reason why two Xhosa homelands, the Ciskei and the Transkei, should be separated. According to the government, the cultural, linguistic and historical differences between the homelands were so great as to preclude any form of unity, but when ethnic groups straddled two homelands this was manifestly not the case. By stressing territorial and ethnic fragmentation, the government could not only divide black opposition but also maintain white supremacy.

Although separate development and the institution of the homelands policy was a political expedient in that it was aimed at breaking African nationalism, it nevertheless created a brand of African leaders who upheld their tribal identities and became increasingly aware of their political roles. The emergence of these black political figures attracted accusations of collaboration with the government. It was certainly the policy of the government to co-opt local chiefs, and many acquired considerable wealth, power and patronage. Bureaucratic expansion and black entrepreneurial activity took place in the homelands, all of which stemmed from government loans and grants. A new form of political concept emerged, that of black federation. Chief Mantanzima of Transkei announced plans for a new African-controlled 'superstate' that would unite Ciskei, Transkei, East Griqualand and all white areas to the Indian Ocean. This proposed state would be called Xhosaland, and all races would have equal rights protected by a constitution. Xhosaland would then seek federation with other black homelands, most notably KwaZulu.

In November 1973, six homeland leaders met and issued what became known as the 'Umtata Declaration'. Black federation was perceived as both territorial association and demographic unity between people sharing common cause and similar aspirations. Chief Buthelezi stated: 'We can keep black unity before the eyes of our followers through the idea of working towards a federation of black states as a goal.'[43] Whether there would have been any real agreement among the chiefs about how federation would operate is open to debate but, certainly, different notions of federation were discussed in the existing political parties. The United Party supported a federal plan in which three levels of power and authority were proposed: a white parliament at the centre of South Africa, a multiracial federal assembly and fifteen racially defined and constituted legislative assemblies. The fifteen assemblies would consist of four white assemblies, two coloured, one

---

[42] Worden 1995: 112.
[43] Best 1976: 43.

Asian and eight African. The difficulties with any discussion of black federalism as an expression of black unity or opposition to the Nationalist government were twofold. First, the homelands were dependent on the government and were, in fact, a creation of its apartheid policies; and, second, all other formal black opposition had been banned, jailed or forced into exile. As Worden states, the homelands were forged only through 'systematic and ruthless state intervention'. While for J.B. Peires, ethnicity in the homelands was largely imposed by the South African government and reinforced with 'newly invented ceremonies and rituals'.[44] Yet the policy succeeded in creating great mistrust between Africans involved in the liberation struggle and those traditional homeland leaders who were seen as colluding puppets of a racist government.

Class and the state

The general economic processes of capitalist transformation, proletarianisation and class formation in South Africa were mediated by imperial control, or what Marxists call 'monopoly capital'. One of the main economic features of imperialism was the export of capital in search of profit. By 1914, the level of foreign, predominantly British, investment in South African mining was between 60 and 80 per cent. Karl Marx had viewed capitalism *per se* as a form of robbery in that workers were not paid the real value of their labour; their labour's surplus value instead went to the capitalist in the form of profit. The desire for more profit would provide an incentive for employers to drive down wages.[45] Thus an increasing polarisation of society into a small clique of capitalists and a great mass of miserable exploited workers would continue. Marx described the process: 'Along with the constantly diminishing number of magnates of capital, who monopolise all advantages … grows the mass of misery, oppression, slavery, degradation, exploitation of workers.'[46]

To obtain high monopoly profits in South Africa, then, the mine-owners combined two forms of labour, white skilled and black unskilled. Blacks were exploited through the use of 'feudal forms of exploitation'; that is, traditional precapitalist social structures were maintained through the incorporation of the reserve areas. Bernard Magubane believes that the black migrant labourer was 'super-exploited', because wages could be kept exceptionally low as it was assumed he would gain subsistence from the land.[47] This was the manner in which capitalism was expressed during colonial rule, and in the case of South Africa the white working class became a creation of imperialism. The nature of the white working class has been described by Simons and Simons:

---

[44] Peires 1995: 256.
[45] *cf.* Freedman 1971: xv; Magubane 1983.
[46] Karl Marx, cited in Freedman 1971.
[47] Magubane 1983.

White working men, set in authority over African peasants, despised them and also feared them as potential competitors. Employers, concerned mainly to maximise profits, exploited the weak bargaining position of the peasants and substituted them, when this was expedient, for the better paid whites.[48]

Marx recognised that at particular stages of industrial development there would be 'competition between workers themselves'. Equally, it should be remembered that employers wished to pay low wages to both black and white workers in order to maintain high profit margins but were prevented from doing so by the job colour bar. Certainly, white workers assumed a privileged position in the imperial economy of South Africa and one they wished to maintain, hence the strikes and revolt in 1922 against any changes to the job colour bar in favour of black workers.

The relationship between class and race in South Africa has been much disputed. The dominant ideology in a state, believes Nicos Poulantzas, is the power that rests with certain classes and is embodied in a series of institutions: churches, political parties, trade unions, schools, universities, media, press, publishing, culture, and so on. These institutions become part of a state's ideological apparatus that indoctrinates wider society. Political domination could not be maintained through the use of physical repression alone but demanded 'the direct and decisive intervention of ideology'.[49] In a Marxist definition, the state represented specific class and economic interests. In the context of South Africa, the apartheid state represented white capitalist interests, but it was also a particular kind of state, one in which, a form of 'internal colonialism' operated.[50] Wolpe argues that the notion of colonialism as a 'special type' explains the development of South Africa's political structures. He believes that the Freedom Charter gave voice to the idea of internal colonialism, which delineated a 'colonial relationship between black and white people and a developed capitalist economy all within the confines of a single national state'.[51] In fact, the ANC defined internal colonialism as such:

> On one level, that of 'white South Africa', there were all the features of an advanced capitalist state in its final stage of industrial monopolies and the merging of industrial and finance capital ... But on another level, that of 'non-white South Africa' there are all the features of a colony. The indigenous population was subjected to extreme national oppression, poverty, exploitation and lacked all democratic and political rights. Non-white South Africa was the colony of white South Africa itself.[52]

The existence of an internal colonial state raised questions regarding the nature of the class structure. As Wolpe asserts, the situation of the black classes was 'vastly inferior' to that of the corresponding white classes, whatever the criteria of measurement, e.g. the amount of capital invested, the level of wages, the rate

---

[48] Simons and Simons 1969: 32.
[49] Poulantzas 1970: 302.
[50] Wolpe 1988: 28–9.
[51] *Ibid.*
[52] ANC 1994b.

of income, the supply of skills.[53] Joe Slovo, general secretary of the SACP between 1986 and 1991, pointed out that in the case of the black middle strata, class mobility could not proceed beyond a certain point, and this point was defined in racial rather than economic terms.[54] The colonial structure in the country there-fore guaranteed the superior position and dominance of the white bloc as a whole and with it the specific interests of different classes within that bloc. On the one hand, the imperatives of race cut through class boundaries to the extent that racial identity predominated over class position. Yet on the other hand, groups such as homeland chiefs were identified as following different *petit bourgeois* class interests from their fellow proletarianised Africans working in the mines.[55] Table 2.5 out-lines the racial occupational structures that existed in South Africa between 1960 and 1980. Although there were movements in some occupations, the numbers of blacks, Indians and coloured people in administrative and managerial positions remained low and actually dropped in the case of Africans. However, there was a considerable proletarianisation of black workers in production and labouring employment.

Table 2.5 Racial occupational structure (thousands) 1960–1980

Occupation	Year	Whites	Coloured	Indians	Africans	Total
Professional/technical	1960	138	14	5	48	206
	1980	371	51	23	205	650
Administrative/	1960	59	1	2	6	68
managerial	1980	126	3	4	5	138
Clerical worker	1960	276	9	8	19	313
	1980	505	70	53	211	839
Sales worker	1960	97	10	23	29	160
	1980	196	38	37	180	451
Service worker	1960	59	118	15	711	902
	1980	156	153	17	1174	1499
Agricultural worker	1960	117	128	12	1475	1731
	1980	89	155	6	1734	1992
Production worker	1960	376	214	43	1316	1949
and labourer	1980	434	387	104	2304	3230
Unclassified	1960	28	9	17	286	391
and unemployed	1980	28	71	12	702	813
Total economically	1960	1150	554	126	3890	5720
active	1980	1905	928	226	6524	9613

Source: Lipton 1986: 404.

[53] Wolpe 1988: 31.
[54] Slovo 1976: 126.
[55] *cf.* Worden 1995, Wolpe 1988.

During the 1960s, the South African economy underwent change as foreign investment increased and the local sector of the economy began to take off. It is important to recognise that although the National Party established its political pre-eminence after gaining office in 1948, in terms of capital ownership it did not control large sectors of the economy (see Table 2.6). As Merle Lipton asserts, the Afrikaners 'lacked the economic strength and financial know-how to prevail over metropolitan capital on their own'. A critical role was played by local English capital: 'without the financial strength and skill of this local English/Jewish capital' it is doubtful whether South Africa's national industrial growth could have been achieved. The proportion of mining dividends paid to overseas investors fell from the very high level of 82 per cent in 1918 to 46 per cent by 1945 and 29 per cent in 1964.[56] These trends indicate that the South African 'English' were more than capable of pursuing their own economic interests rather than those of the colonial power. It also suggests that whatever the political differences between the Afrikaners and the South African English, or their relative class rankings within the hierarchy, both communities could forge economic strategies that enhanced their positions.

Certainly, the South African state did not conform to the pattern of 'underdevelopment' that was to become so prevalent among newly independent ex-colonial states. Yet, as Merle Lipton points out, it had 'all the ingredients that should have made it an ideal exemplar' of that form of state. In terms of capitalist development, a dominant role had been played by foreign mining capital, which generated great profits for overseas investors. Black Africans were subjugated under British colonialism, and the mining industry was instrumental in the exploitation of black workers. At one point, the country's development might have been viewed as subordinate to the interests of imperial capitalism; that is, South Africa would remain a primary producing nation dependent upon the export of its raw materials to the developed world with little or no indigenous investment. However, capitalism was capable of bending to the demands of the proletariat,

Table 2.6 Afrikaner percentage share of ownership of private sector

	1938/39	1954/55	1975
Agriculture	87	84	82
Mining	1	1	18
Manufacturing and construction	3	6	15
Commerce	8	26	16
Transportation	n/a	14	15
Liquor and catering	n/a	30	35
Finance	5	10	25

Source: Lipton 1986: 411.

---

[56] Lipton 1986: 258.

especially when workers' organisations called for political concessions from the state. In fact, the success of the white working class in South Africa replicated the struggles of workers in other industrialised countries as they pushed for political and economic representation. According to Lipton, the Afrikaners' struggle against the imperial interests of the British made them 'successful nationalists'.[57] Yet their success was mirrored by the 'misery, oppression, degradation and exploitation' of black workers, and at once the debate returns to the issue of race.

Over a long period in the development of capitalism in South Africa, the structures of racial domination in the political sphere provided a legal framework for the institution of discriminatory practices in the workplace. This situation occurred during the country's colonial period and later under apartheid regulations. Race, then, was part of South Africa's historical economic development, but when the National Party came to power on a policy aimed at suppressing emergent black opposition it met the demands of a mixed class constituency, i.e. the interests of both white farmers and the white working class. According to Wolpe, the government, fearing the growing proletarianisation of blacks and their potential to undermine the state, instituted repressive measures as a means of controlling mass protest.[58] Although racial disparities of wealth were enormous, in contrast to the periods of labour resistance and protest of the postwar years, the 1960s were quiet. The ANC admits that there were few signs of resistance during that decade. The reasons were twofold: the apartheid state had grown stronger as it extended its control over all aspects of people's lives; and the1960s witnessed a period of considerable economic growth. After the economic dip following Sharpeville, gross national product increased by over 5 per cent per annum. As Table 2.5 indicates, employment for white and black workers increased, although differentially, in all sectors of the economy.

Table 2.7 Sectoral wage comparisons (in South African rands)

	Whites			Blacks		
	1952–53	1969–70	1975–76	1952–53	1969–70	1975–76
Manufacturing and construction	1348	3633	6119	266	609	1265
Gold mines	1736	4329	7929	113	208	947
White agriculture	–	1845	4008	72	135	491

Source: Lipton 1986: 410.

---

[57] *Ibid.*: 367.
[58] Wolpe 1988.

Chapter 3

Apartheid and the struggle

Economic pressures in the 1970s

If the 1960s witnessed a period when resistance against apartheid appeared to be undermined by the power of the state, the 1970s represented a time when people renewed their fight against the system. South Africa's economic expansion had been forged by a labour force comprised of white management and unskilled black labour (see Table 2.5). Inevitably, a time came when economic growth was restricted by the white community's inability to provide the skills and internal market needed to support a growing economy. Domestic economic weaknesses were compounded by changes in a world economy rocked by dramatic increases in the price of oil, leading to reduced demand for many of South Africa's primary commodities. This development created a reduction in earnings from exports, coupled with an increase in the price of imports resulting from the massive oil price hike. Between 1975 and 1985, South Africa's economic growth rate dropped to 1.9 per cent per annum.[1]

The migrant labour system was adapted to an economy that was based on mining and agricultural needs that required a small percentage of highly skilled individuals in supervisory roles and a large supply of unskilled labour. Despite the success of South Africa's economy during the 1960s, on closer inspection the migrant labour system resulted in low productivity. Output per worker in manufacturing industry increased by only 12 per cent between 1963 and 1970.[2] The migrant labour system and the restrictive nature of recruitment through labour bureaux began to have an impact on the economy. By the beginning of the 1970s, the mining industry was short of 2000 skilled workers, which effectively acted as a break on the expansion of the industry. Mine-owners began to foment opposition to the job colour bar. Harry Oppenheimer, the chairman of Anglo-American, and Tom Muller, chairman of the Afrikaner company General Mining, both wanted the government to change the job colour bar so that black workers could engage in more skilled work. Such moves would then allow white workers to take up more specialised employment. White trade unionists, however, were against such a policy at the time. During the period of recession between 1973 and 1976,

---

[1] Schrire 1991: 12.
[2] Lemon 1976: 43.

prices of goods began to rise sharply, making it even more difficult for black workers to survive on low wages. It was against this background that black protest was renewed and a series of strikes followed. Some activists claimed that the strikes were political actions of the African proletariat against minority rule and the system of apartheid, yet they were generally concerned with issues of higher wages and better working conditions.[3] The strikes involved more than 200,000 workers, with the first major action taking place in Durban. More strikes broke out in Cape Town, East London and the Rand, later extending to other parts of the country. The Durban strikes were spontaneous, as workers had no trade unions and very little organisation. However, they gained some success and a series of pay increases were introduced in 1973. Average wages for black miners rose by 78.8 per cent between 1973 and 1974 as mining companies shifted away from their former policy of recruiting cheap foreign black workers.[4]

Employers decided to raise wages chiefly to expand the domestic market. It had long been known that the lower-paid spent more of their income on necessary items, which were often locally produced goods such as furniture, blankets and clothes. As the wages of black workers rose, more and more businessmen became aware of the buying power of Africans. However, apartheid worked against the potential increase in demand in the African market. Social apartheid excluded blacks from restaurants, theatres and hotels, while curbs on black home ownership restricted the activities and potential profits of financial institutions.[5] Apartheid structures also created a situation in which Africans were playing an increasingly important role in various industries in South Africa yet were excluded from any industrial negotiations. As black purchasing power grew, the incentives to remove apartheid and improve services and facilities for Africans increased. Shops and department stores refused the demands of some whites to stem the influx of black shoppers into white towns. Equally, black workers could not continue to be treated as subjugated labour, especially as businesses began to realise that the policy was affecting their profit margins. In short, strict apartheid policies were starting to be bad for white businesses.[6]

The living conditions of workers had been an issue raised both in strike actions and in the mine riots of 1973–75 during which 135 men died and 500 were injured. The single-sex compounds in which 97 per cent of black workers were forced to live were appallingly squalid. The institutionalised policies of apartheid created a situation whereby men were separated from their families, who lived in the rural areas. The migrant labour system acted against any initiatives that would improve and upgrade workers' skills, because of the high turnover of workers and the lack of career opportunities. If workers were to have their skills raised, employers would need to contribute towards housing for workers' families in order to

---

[3] Magubane 1983: 48.
[4] Lemon 1976: 45.
[5] Lipton 1986: 164.
[6] *Ibid.*

stabilise their working conditions. It should be remembered that in 1977 around 50,000 workers broke their work contracts in the mines because they were unprepared to accept the conditions of work. The government legally recognised black trade unions in 1979, after which union membership grew rapidly, from 808,053 in 1979 to 1,406,302 in 1984.[7] Between 1979 and 1981, the number of strikes increased from 101 to 342 per year. The police intervened aggressively in nearly half the strikes and injected a bitter political dimension into industrial conflict. Lodge argues that in contrast to early communist initiatives, the trade unions of the 1970s emphasised 'tight factory-based organisation and highly trained shop-steward leadership'.[8] In 1979, FOSATU (Federation of South African Trade Unions) was formed. It stressed the importance of establishing workers' rights in employment and emphasised strong shop-floor organisation on a factory-by-factory basis.

Soweto, education and youth action

The activism of black workers energised other sectors of the black community. University students and local voluntary associations began to become active in work-related concerns and became known as 'community unions'. Community unions adopted a more political approach, such as encouraging the public to boycott products made in factories that were the target of strikes and recruiting members through mass meetings held in the townships. These groups were born out of a series of fiercely contested strikes in Cape Province in 1979, where they attempted to compensate for the vulnerability of unskilled workers in mass dismissals. Workplace interests were seen as inseparable from community interests, both of which demanded political activity.[9] In some centres, community unions such as the South African Allied Workers' Union in East London, represented in themselves an impressive political force, pioneering a combination of industrial and communal rebellion. Other developments were taking place in black schools and universities, particularly the emergence of the black consciousness movement. Although the 1953 Bantu Education Act was explicitly intended to instil compliance and passivity into black youth through its restricted form of elementary education, the outcome was very different. In the early 1970s, the number of black students in elementary schools rose to 2.75 million from 750,000 in 1953. By 1976, that figure had increased to 3.75 million students. The South African Students' Organisation was formed in 1969 in a spirit of black consciousness:

> We, the Black students of South Africa, having examined and assessed the role of Black students in the struggle for the emancipation of Black people in South Africa and the betterment of their social, political and economic lot and having unconditionally declared our lack of faith in the genuineness and capability of multi-racial

---

[7] Lodge and Nasson 1991a: 38.
[8] Lodge 1996: 192.
[9] Lodge and Nasson 1991a: 39.

organisations and individual whites in the country to effect rapid social changes ... do commit ourselves to the realisation of the worth of the Black man, the assertion of his human dignity and to promoting consciousness and self-reliance of the Black community (Constitution adopted by the South African Students' Organisation, 1970).

Black consciousness in a broad sense was concerned with upholding black pride and self-assertion and, in a way, was modelled on similar developments in the United States. But in the South African context, 'black consciousness' included coloured and Indian peoples and became a more radical concept than the notion of black ethnicity that prevailed in the homelands. The defining principle among some activists remained the exclusion of whites from organisations functioning in black communities. During the 1970s, the state harassed black consciousness leaders and arrested their leading activist, Steve Biko. Biko's death while in police custody led to an international outcry and public inquest. Biko, it was revealed, had been 'kept naked for the eighteen days he was in the police cells, was manacled to the floor of the interrogation room and was transported naked in a semi-comatose condition seven hundred miles'.[10] Yet the inquest cleared the police of any wrongdoing. The events surrounding the death of Steve Biko were not uncovered until 1996.[11]

The activities in Soweto were equally grim. What had started as a march through Soweto by 15,000 students protesting against the compulsory use of the Afrikaans language in schools ended in 'brutal suppression' when the police opened fire, killing several students, including a 13-year-old, Hector Peterson. Following these killings, workers went on strike in Johannesburg, Cape Town and the Eastern Cape, schools were burned, administrative buildings were attacked and there were general uprisings in townships. By the end of 1976, 575 were dead and 2389 had been wounded in the conflicts.[12] Nomavenda Mathiane, a journalist from Soweto, witnessed and recorded the events of June 1976:

> Soweto was engulfed in pain, blood and smoke. Children saw other children die. They saw their parents shot. On June 17, I watched as bodies were dragged out of what had been a shopping centre on the Old Portch Road. I saw figures running out of the shop, some carrying goods. They ran across the road like wild animals, dropping like bags as bullets hit them. I saw billows of smoke shoot up as white-owned vehicles burned. I thought the world had come to an end. I heard leaders inside and outside Soweto plead for reason and I saw people detained and killed (Mathiane 1989).

The impact of the Soweto killings was to last for years in the memory of the ANC. One of the first declarations made by the newly elected government in 1994 was the announcement of a public holiday, Youth Day, to commemorate the sacrifices that the young had made at Soweto. The harrowing image of the dead body of

---

[10] Dugard *et al.* 1992: 64–5.
[11] For further details of Steve Biko's death, see Chapter 7.
[12] Worden 1995: 119.

Hector Peterson being carried away from the scene marked the memorial pamphlet of that fateful day, 16 June 1976 (see Figure 3.1).

The 1977 opening address to parliament was made while the country was still in the grip of domestic unrest, but it was clear that the government had been shaken by events:

> It may justifiably be said that 1976 was a watershed year for the Republic of South Africa, a year characterised on the one hand by far-reaching developments on the international scene and on the other by the emergence within the Republic of elements who believe that the attainment of meaningful political rights for all our peoples is only possible by totally destroying, if need be through violence and bloodshed, the existing political, economic and social order (*Hansard*, 21 January 1977).

The Cillie Commission was appointed by the government to investigate the 1976 revolt and found that it was the work of 'outside agitators' with ANC involvement.[13] Certainly, the ANC had changed its tactics since a consultative conference held in Morogoro in Tanzania in 1969. This meeting had called for an all-round struggle. Both armed and political resistance had to be used to defeat the apartheid state, and a campaign of mass political education and agitation was adopted. The ANC opened up its membership to non-Africans, while its mission abroad coordinated an international political campaign. The object was to ensure political, military, economic and cultural isolation of the apartheid regime. It was also aimed at mobilising political, material and human resources for the national liberation movement.[14] During the 1970s, the ANC underground movement issued pamphlets calling on the community to support students by linking their struggles against education policy to the wider campaign for national liberation.[15] Inevitably, the relationship between the ANC and the South African Communist Party became much closer. Within the ANC alliance, by the mid-1970s many important positions were held by SACP members, who 'controlled access to education, funds and foreign travel'.[16] Also after 1976, ANC camps in Angola were controlled by Soviet and East German security personnel. The circumstances of exile and armed struggle contributed greatly to the influence of the SACP and also led to the ANC becoming 'heavily reliant on support from the Communist bloc'.[17] Another impetus for the campaign was provided by the success of anti-imperial forces in Mozambique and Angola and the collapse of their 500-year Portuguese rule, resulting in the fall of their colonial governments. Many young people left South Africa and 'flooded the ranks of Umkhonto we Sizwe (MK)', but the young who stayed continued to find themselves at the centre of political conflict. Black youth had been mobilised through struggles over the content and quality of education in schools and colleges, but their activities

---

[13] *Ibid.*

[14] ANC 1994b.

[15] *Mzabalazo*, 19.

[16] Ellis 1992: 153.

[17] Johnson and Schlemmer 1996: 2.

June 16

ANC

South African Youth Day

A tribute to the youth

Published by ANC Youth League
51 Plain Street, Johannesburg

Figure 3.1 The 1994 ANC pamphlet commemorating events in Soweto on 16 June 1976

became part of the wider fight against apartheid. As Nomavenda Mathiane recalls: 'Nine years after June 16 1976 violence was a blanket worn in the townships. There were locations entirely without teenagers. Many had fled to avoid the police, others had gone to look for schools elsewhere and many had escaped into exile'.[18]

The principles of the Bantu education system had been condemned as 'unsound in principle and harmful in practice' as far back as 1961.[19] In a prescient report, the South African Institute for Race Relations asserted that although Africans had no alternative but to accept the operation of the Bantu Education Act, they would never agree to its aims or its practice. Ironically, the object of black resentment against educational policy in the early 1960s was the policy of 'vernacular instruction' in schools. This meant that Africans were taught in their own languages, rather than in English or Afrikaans. At that time, it was argued, the Bantu languages, although acceptable in everyday usage, were deficient in scientific and abstract terms. Consequently, fluency in an 'official' language was necessary in order for blacks to participate in commercial and industrial life.[20] Fifteen years later, it was the matter of the Afrikaans language being made the compulsory medium of instruction in part of the school curriculum that triggered the Soweto demonstration. Yet this time problems in schools had been simmering for a long period. A range of disturbances had occurred in African schools across the country in 1961, and various protests had taken place at the black University College of Fort Hare. Children were expelled from schools, students were sent home from college, university lectures were suspended, classes were boycotted, police patrols were introduced, knives were confiscated, and so on. Verwoerd's policy of maintaining white power and privilege by limiting black education to a bare minimum had always been provocative and potentially dangerous. But for Verwoerd the apartheid system was 'like a brick wall' and every brick was important. If one was discarded the whole wall would collapse.[21]

Verwoerd was assassinated in 1966 by a white oppositionist, and John Vorster succeeded him as prime minister. Vorster's background was hard-line nationalist: he was an ex-Greyshirt who had been interned as a Nazi sympathiser during the Second World War and, later, as minister of justice, had introduced detention without trial.[22] Vorster's response to events was to improvise only when the situation demanded action. He strived to maintain unity within the National Party but was willing to resort to authoritarian measures if necessary. While under Verwoerd, expenditure on African education was minimal and fixed, Vorster reversed Verwoerd's strategy and bowed to the economic necessity of creating a larger pool of skilled and semi-skilled black workers. Vorster's demise came in 1977 when he was involved in a financial scandal, but the new prime minister,

---

[18] Mathiane 1989: 31.
[19] South African Institute of Race Relations 1962: 236.
[20] *Ibid*.
[21] Johnson and Schlemmer 1996.
[22] Lipton 1986: 314.

Table 3.1 High school graduates in South Africa by racial group, 1978–1988

	1978		1988	
	No. of graduates	Percentage of all graduates	No. of graduates	Percentage of all graduates
African	7,767	13	98,050	51
Coloured	3,668	6	14,235	7
Asian	2,758	5	12,577	7
White	45,888	76	66,309	35
Total	60,081	100	191,171	100

Source: Race Relations Survey 1978/79.

Table 3.2 University enrolment in South Africa, 1979–1989

	1979		1989	
	Number	Per cent	Number	Per cent
White	118,000	78	156,000	52
African	16,000	10	105,000	36
Coloured	7,000	5	18,000	6
Indian	10.000	7	18,000	6
Total	151,000	100	300,000	100

Source: Schrire 1991.

P.W. Botha, accelerated Vorster's policies. Black education was gradually given more resources, and the Botha government moved to reduce differences in government spending on education. Table 3.1 indicates the number of high school graduates between 1978 and 1988, while Table 3.2 displays university enrolment between 1979 and 1989. *Per capita* expenditure on African education increased from 68.84 rand in 1978 to 237 rand by 1985. The question that must be asked is 'Why did the government introduce these reforms?'

Attempts to make apartheid work

In the first phase of Botha's leadership, pressures built up in the business community as two government-commissioned reports proposed changes that would promote economic growth. The Wiehahn Report recommended that African rights to trade union membership and registration be recognised, while the Reikert Commission favoured the dismantling of white job reservation, although black mobility would continue to be curbed. Apartheid was not to be dismantled; rather, the system was to be modified in order that it could work better. Botha recognised that South Africa was 'moving in a changing world' and that the country had to 'adapt or die'.[23] He adopted a dual approach. On the one hand, he used tough rhetoric on internal affairs and a belligerent posture in foreign policy to reassure whites that blacks would be excluded from national politics and would exercise their political rights in the homelands. There was no question of 'one person, one vote' in his time, he asserted. On the other hand, Botha took every available opportunity to educate the white electorate that socio-economic reform had to take place. The need for semi-skilled black labour was not in doubt, and it was this business requirement that led to the educational changes for blacks. Although Botha recognised that 'the moment you start oppressing people ... they fight back', he was no white liberal and without business pressures it is unlikely that apartheid would have been 'modified' out of any sense of injustice. He believed economic changes could be introduced that did not undermine the basic objective of apartheid, that is, the maintenance of white supremacy. Botha declined to tamper with legislation on public facilities and sports segregation and retained the Separate Amenities Act. However, some small incidences of social integration took place when special permits were granted that allowed Africans to eat in white restaurants.

The National Party's homelands policy continued to be crucial to the preservation of Afrikaner political power. One of Hendrik Verwoerd's original notions about the utility of the homelands scheme was that at some stage the flow of Africans from these areas into 'white' South Africa would halt and be reversed. However, given the parlous conditions in the homelands this had not happened, and blacks were still moving into white areas. Botha's initial response was to try to make the policy work through 'dynamic leadership, good organisation, territorial consolidation, additional land and greater economic development'. If more homelands became independent, went the argument, 7.8 million blacks would be independent citizens of the homelands. This situation would leave only 6.25 million blacks within South Africa, and that number would be less than the total of 7.8 million whites, coloureds and Asians living in the country. In such a numerical position, far from being a dominant majority, blacks would actually become a minority in South Africa. This would put an immediate stop to international criticism of apartheid, Botha believed: 'When so many black people are independent, it will be useless for South Africa's enemies to continue pleading for one man, one vote.'[24] However, events were to turn out differently.

The homelands strategy had always been predicated on the assumption that industry would relocate to adjacent areas and so provide employment for Africans, but it met with little success. There had, in any case, been considerable criticism of industrial decentralisation, the main argument being that it created 'artificial and unsustainable' growth in peripheral areas.[25] The engine of the economy

---

[23] cited in *ibid.*: 50.
[24] Schrire 1991: 52.
[25] Todes 1998.

remained in the established industrial areas of Johannesburg, the Western Cape, Durban and Port Elizabeth, and as these areas continued to expand, a steady flow of rural Africans sought work. Botha sought to tackle this problem by providing new economic regions and a new development bank to help to finance regional development. But the problems remained and were exacerbated by corruption and inefficiency in homeland bureaucracies, growing unemployment, and rapid population growth. Ultimately, Botha came to realise that neither 'determination nor better management' would make the homelands more successful economically. Large numbers of Africans would seek work where they could find it, making black urbanisation inevitable. Blacks would continue to be permanent residents in 'white' areas irrespective of the rigours of apartheid. Demographic, economic and social forces had produced a growing urban African population that had few personal ties or interests in the homelands. In a National Party policy document, it was accepted that Dr Verwoerd's vision of 'grand apartheid' had failed and that the homelands were neither economically viable nor politically legitimate.

If regenerating the homelands had been a failure, then Botha hoped that improving the conditions of townships might act as a means of stabilising society. Business joined the National Party government in this endeavour by funding the Urban Foundation, an organisation that supported programmes to improve housing and facilities in townships. Although urban blacks would not be granted any political rights in parliament, they were allowed to participate in community councils. This was a system of African-run local government structures that had administrative responsibilities and budgets resourced by local rates and taxes. Again, this was a policy that failed, for a number of reasons: first, it was inadequately resourced, consequently requiring increases in rents that caused great hardship and a fierce political backlash; second, it lacked legitimacy, and Africans saw the measures as an attempted palliative to their demands for real political representation; and, third, it eventually collapsed during the 1980s under the weight of the radical policy of 'ungovernability' that was introduced as part of the resistance struggle.

The pass laws, or 'influx control', designed to limit black movement into the cities, had been part of the earliest policies of racial discrimination to be introduced in South Africa. Between 1916 and 1986, an estimated 20 million Africans were prosecuted for 'pass law' offences. Under pressure from business, in 1985 the government began to admit publicly the need to abolish the pass laws. The policy had always been oppressive, as blacks were forced to carry a passbook at all times under penalty of arbitrary arrest. In 1986, the pass laws were abolished, but there were still important restrictions. The repeal was accompanied by a policy of 'orderly urbanisation', which essentially implied a tightening of the anti-squatting, vagrancy and slum clearance laws. Equally, while all races were issued similar identity cards, each individual was coded according to race.

The tricameral parliament

Botha's most elaborate scheme to rearrange apartheid was the introduction of a constitutional referendum. On 2 November 1983, whites voted on the constitutional proposals (see Box 3.1). Robert Schrire points out, during the referendum

---

Box 3.1 Constitutional proposals presented to the white electorate in the 1983 referendum

• The setting up of a tricameral parliament with a House of Assembly for whites, a House of Representatives for coloureds and a House of Delegates for Indians.
• An executive president, chosen by an electoral college consisting of fifty members elected from the white chamber, twenty-five from the coloured chamber and thirteen from the Indian chamber.
• The president's term of office was linked to that of parliament.
• The president appointed the national cabinet.
• The president could dismiss ministers.
• A president's council made up of sixty members: twenty from the white chamber, ten from the coloured, five from the Indian, fifteen appointed by the president and ten selected by the opposition parties in all three chambers.

Source: Schrire 1991: 59.

---

campaign the government received 'considerable support from the business community'.[26] In a 70 per cent turnout, two-thirds of voters supported the proposals and gave the government a resounding victory. Interestingly, the 'yes' vote included both Afrikaners and English speakers, but it would be misleading to regard the two communities as unanimous about the process of reform. In an opinion poll taken after the introduction of the tricameral constitution there were distinct differences in the responses of the interviewees, especially at the extremities of the questions, e.g. was reform too fast or too slow (see Table 3.3). The polarisation of responses has been attributed to changing class relationships among Afrikaners. As Afrikaners developed business interests and moved more decisively into the middle classes, their attitudes towards reform changed. Policies such as

Table 3.3 White attitudes towards political reform in South Africa, 1986

	Per cent	
	English	Afrikaans
Too fast	8	35
Just right	34	40
Too slow	48	15
Uncertain	5	6

Source: van Vuuren 1988: 256.

---

[26] Schrire 1991: 60.

the 'job colour bar' were not in the interests of expanding businesses although still of advantage to many working-class Afrikaners, who immediately felt threatened by economic reforms.[27] Without job reservation for whites, skilled black labour could push white workers out of industries. Consequently, the Afrikaner working class became more conservative and resistant to change.

The emergence of this class division highlights Harold Wolpe's interpretation of race masking class differentiation. Class interests were both functional and contradictory and could advance the interests of certain classes yet at the same time undermine the interests of others. In the racist state of South Africa a perverse situation emerged: while the business classes favoured racial reform because of their concern for higher profits, the white working class continued to support the subjugation of black workers.[28] The policy of reserving certain skilled and semiskilled jobs for whites was partially ended in 1979, the year after Botha took office. In 1983, the remaining categories were abolished with the exception of the mining industry, where Africans continued to be denied skill certificates, although many of them were actually doing the work. This last discriminatory barrier in the workplace was removed in 1987. Robert Schrire maintains that the basic philosophy behind the government's reforms was laid out in a statement by the business-backed Urban Foundation:

> Only by having the most responsible section of the urban black population on our side can the whites of South Africa be assured of containing on a long-term basis the irresponsible economic and political ambitions of those blacks who are influenced against their own interests from within and without our borders.[29]

While pragmatic reforms were being introduced in the labour market, largely at the behest of the business sector, the government decided to court the coloured and Indian communities by offering them political concessions. In this way, white power would not be compromised and non-African groups would be granted political rights. A new constitution would establish the process by which coloured and Indian representatives could be brought into central government. The African majority, however, was to be excluded.

The tricameral constitution was presented as a means of sharing power between the coloured, Indian and white communites, and each assembly had control over its own concerns, e.g. education, health and community administration. Central government dealt with all other matters (see Figure 3.2). The National Party claimed that the constitution was intended to join the coloured and Indian communities with whites to form a bloc of 2.5 million people and thus prevent a 'black-power onslaught'.[30] The party split as a result of this policy, and a conservative faction broke away. The government forged much closer links with business during the referendum campaign, and some business leaders were brought into

---

[27] cf. ibid.: 26; Lipton 1986: 66.
[28] Wolpe 1988: 76.
[29] Schrire 1991: 71.
[30] Johnson and Schlemmer 1996: 114.

ELECTORAL COLLEGE	STATE PRESIDENT	PRESIDENT'S COUNCIL
	• chosen by electoral college • five-year term • not member of any house	
• chooses the state president • has 88 members: 50 from House of Assembly 25 from House of Representatives 13 from House of Delegates		• advises state president on matters of public interest • rules in event of deadlock between houses • has 60 members: 20 from House of Assembly 10 from House of Representatives 5 from House of Delegates 25 appointed by state president (10 of whom are nominated by opposition parties in three houses)
	CABINET • executive authority for general affairs • appointed by state president	
	PARLIAMENT	
House of Assembly (White) • own affairs • 178 members • 5-year term	House of Representatives (Coloured) • own affairs • 85 members • 5-year term	House of Delegates (Indian) • own affairs • 45 members • 5-year term
	JOINT STANDING COMMITTEES • general affairs • consist of member of three houses	

Figure 3.2 The 1984 South African constitution

government commissions and management committees. Through organisations such as the Federated Chamber of Industries, the Afrikaanse Handelsinstituut and the Urban Foundation, businesses could influence government to introduce reforms that were beneficial to their respective industries. Consequently, taxes were lowered, currency regulations were changed and the controls on the movement of blacks from rural areas into the cities and towns were abolished.

The 1983 referendum did not permit the coloured and Indian communities to express their views on whether or not they wanted such a parliament. The government rejected the idea of holding a referendum in which coloureds and Indians could vote on the proposed constitution. Instead, the government decided that direct elections to the new parliament would be held in August 1984. In the elections, the actual numbers who turned out to vote were variable (see Table 3.4).

Table 3.4 Coloured turnout in the 1984 parliamentary elections

	Percentage of registered voters
Cape Province	29.5
Cape Peninsular	11.1
Western Cape rural	35.4
Natal	26.9
Orange Free State	61.4
Transvaal	43.4
National	32.5

Source: Johnson and Schlemmer 1996: 117.

African political organisations across the spectrum, including Chief Buthelezi's Inkatha movement, opposed the proposals. The coloured and Indian communities were divided, hence the low turnout in the elections, but some voters were persuaded by the argument that this first constitutional reform could initiate a process of fundamental change that would benefit all Africans. Certainly, the turnout of 61.4 per cent in the Orange Free State was quite large. The National Party attracted support from some coloured people living in the Cape, a tendency that continued in the 1994 elections and has been the subject of much study. The Coloured Labour Party also received considerable support. But the elections were divisive, with Indian and coloured groups being regarded as 'beneficiaries' of the apartheid state. Black consciousness groups and other non-white communities campaigned for an election boycott, as did the Inkatha movement and the ANC. On the other hand, the Coloured Labour Party and the Indian National People's Party joined the government in calling for a big vote of approval. As part of the government's policy of co-opting the coloured and Indian communities, funds were made available for local development projects and programmes aimed at improving their economic conditions (see Box 3.2). A period of embourgeoisement of coloured and Indian South Africans began, which created further socio-economic polarisation between Africans and other ethnic groups.

The new constitution came into effect in September 1984, and although it was a departure from the former all-white model it had been designed to ensure that

Box 3.2 Impact of the tricameral system on coloured communities

- Over 100,000 houses were built, 60,000 in the Cape Town area.
- The number of coloured children in secondary schools increased by one-third.
- The number of coloured graduates increased by 100 per cent.

Source: Johnson and Schlemmer 1996: 115.

policy could be made and implemented regardless of the behaviour of the coloured and Indian chambers (see Figure 3.2). Measures designed to achieve this included:

- the ability of the President's Council, which had a built-in majority of whites, to break deadlocks between the parliamentary chambers;
- the white House of Assembly's capacity to act as parliament if the other two chambers failed to function;
- a fixed 4:2:1 numerical ratio of white, coloured and Indian representation in parliament, which entrenched white hegemony and made it impossible for genuine cross-racial coalitions to develop.

Botha became president and the old cabinet was retained, although one coloured and one Indian minister were added. However, all key positions in government were still held by Afrikaners. One political reform to emerge from the new constitution was the removal of the ban on racially mixed parties. Theoretically, the new system provided some leverage for the coloured and Indian chambers, since the constitution required a large degree of consensus on legislation. In practice, however, coloured and Indian politicians used their time bargaining for more money for health, education, housing and so forth. Although they campaigned for the abolition of pass laws, many critics complained that they confined themselves to socio-economic issues, for which they were rewarded, rather than pressing for fundamental political change.

The United Democratic Front's campaign

The United Democratic Front (UDF) was at the forefront of the campaign against the government during the 1980s. It has been described as a pivotal movement against apartheid: 'In the history of black resistance to white rule in South Africa, the United Democratic Front was a movement of unprecedented pervasiveness and depth.'[31] The UDF was a heterogeneous movement comprising a variety of groups and organisations, e.g. students, women, youth congresses, civic associations, church societies and trade unions. At its peak, with a total membership of over 2 million, it claimed the adherence of around 700 affiliates, embracing every major centre of population in the country.[32] The UDF was originally created to coordinate the activities of organisations opposed to the government's 1984 constitution, and although its affiliates were ideologically diverse, they were united in their opposition to the government. A basic triumvirate supplied the UDF with its active popular following in most localities: civic association, women's group and youth congress. In many townships, the UDF core groups were supplemented by branches of the national schoolchildren's organisation. The UDF was generally concerned with the return of the liberation movements rather than operating as a political party itself. Although regarded as 'ideologically ambiguous', it was

---

[31] Lodge and Nasson 1991a: 34.
[32] *Ibid.*

committed to the armed struggle and supportive of revolutionary change. The UDF adhered to the principles enshrined in the ANC's Freedom Charter and favoured the exiled ANC's claims to leadership, while the ANC saw the UDF as a 'rebirth of a mass movement'.[33] Ideologically, the ANC was still dominated by the South African Communist Party and received an estimated $8 million from the Soviet Union during the early 1980s. The ANC also received money from European countries, including around $5 million from Sweden.[34]

Civic groups campaigned around basic local issues such as rent and township services. An estimated 54,000 non-governmental organisations (NGOs) were operating in areas ranging from non-formal education to community development projects, from feeding schemes to medical and scientific research institutes. There were 22,000 church and religious organisations engaged in some kind of community activity, and 20,000 organisations were concerned with development issues such as education and community-based services. The NGO sector raised over 6 billion rand (10 rand = 1 pound sterling) in donated funds: 1 billion rand from foreign agencies, 1 billion rand from business and at least 4 billion rand from individual donations.[35] Such financial support during the 1980s was crucial to the development of community activities, solidarity and opposition to government policies and actions. As Ann Bernstein asserts: 'often the funding was not motivated by an intrinsic and positive belief in the benefits of NGO activity as such, but rather in order to fill a gap or help defend community and individual interests in the face of an antagonistic state.'[36] Funding for NGOs came from the United States, the European Union, Britain and Denmark.

Youth activity was central to the UDF, and one of the biggest organisations formed in 1979 was the Congress of South African Students (COSAS), which had branches in towns and cities throughout South Africa. Some civic organisations actually grew out of parent–student committees that had been formed to support educational issues. COSAS and its equivalent organisation for university students, the Azanian Students' Organisation (AZASO), worked together to highlight the condition of education, and massive national school boycotts rocked the townships in 1980 and again in 1984–85. Unemployed young people began to join youth action. The post-Soweto young were at the centre of political radicalism, and their numbers boosted their significance. In 1980, 55 per cent of the African population was under the age of 20. As Lodge and Nasson assert, during the 1980s age and generational difference were 'as important in influencing black political behaviour as belonging to a particular social class or community'.[37] In 1986, the system of apartheid education almost collapsed when all black educational institutions throughout the country were affected by mass action aimed directly at challenging the system. However, the young were to pay a high price for their struggle against

[33] *Mzabalazo*, 21.
[34] Ellis 1992: 153; Lipton 1986: 347.
[35] Gumede 1996.
[36] Bernstein 1994.
[37] Lodge and Nasson 1991a: 38.

apartheid. The school boycott affected their educational attainment so badly that they barely managed to reach an elementary grade, the level of a 10-year-old. When political change came, many young people were found to be uneducated, unskilled and unemployed in Nelson Mandela's democratic South Africa.[38]

Worker organisation and power also took a major leap forward in the 1980s with the formation of the Congress of South African Trade Unions (COSATU) in 1986. COSATU was formed by the amalgamation of the Federation of South African Trade Unions and the community unions. Although relatively few strong unions affiliated themselves to the UDF, they did provide experienced leaders for local civic groups. The growth of unions also brought about a change in the nature of black politics by introducing a greater degree of leadership and organisational structure. A shift away from the racial exclusivity of black consciousness towards the non-racial ideology of the ANC began to be noticeable in the early 1980s. A 'release Mandela' petition was launched in 1980, and black consciousness supporters joined the ANC.[39] By 1983, many of the ingredients necessary for the establishment of a mass national organisation existed. For some, it offered the hope of becoming a 'non-racial, internal opposition to the government's reform programmes'.[40] As Lodge and Nasson explain:

> Black youth had been mobilised through struggles over the content and quality of education at schools and colleges. An unprecedentedly strong labour movement was beginning to provide a model and source of inspiration and leadership for township-based groups ... It is likely, therefore, that even without the catalyst provided by the government's new constitutional proposals, a nationwide opposition movement would have emerged.[41]

For despite the government's reforms, the primary pillars of the apartheid state still existed: the Group Areas Act, which was the cornerstone of segregated living; the Population Registration Act, which assigned everyone by racial grouping; and, above all, the segregated political system in which blacks had no electoral rights.[42]

Mobilisation against the government's proposed new constitution began in 1983. Public rallies marked the creation of UDF regional committees in Natal, the Transvaal and the Western Cape. A national secretariat began functioning in Johannesburg, and Cape Town, the seat of South Africa's parliament, was the place of launch. The UDF campaign used leaflets, 500,000 of which were printed and distributed, open-air meetings, house-to-house visits and other forms of publicity. Potential voters were called on to 'reject the new apartheid constitution'.[43] Public rallies with flags, logos, T-shirts and stickers proved to be effective ways of mobilising support against the government. Its campaign against the constitution and

---

[38] Febe Polgeiter, interview.
[39] Lodge and Nasson 1991a: 43.
[40] Johnson and Schlemmer 1996: 116.
[41] *Ibid.*: 45.
[42] Horowitz 1992: 18.
[43] Lodge and Nasson 1991a: 59.

the election boycott had been influential, not necessarily in stopping the policy or the elections but in raising the nature of the opposition. The UDF also campaigned against the municipal elections in the townships, but it was the policy of 'ungovernability' that highlighted the degree of resistance to the policies of the government. In 1985, township residents were called upon to destroy the black local authorities, and councillors were called on to resign. Municipal buildings and the homes of government collaborators were attacked. As administrative structures broke down, the ANC admitted that 'an atmosphere of mass insurrection prevailed in many townships and rural areas across the country'.[44] In Soweto, some areas 'bore all the marks of a war zone: streets were patrolled at night, fire was exchanged with fire, nobody could enter or leave hostels, money was collected from houses to finance the purchase of food and ammunition, women cooked collectively and fed the "troops" and young men walked about openly parading arms'.[45] Marxists claimed that the increased resistance of the black working class indicated that a revolutionary situation was maturing in South Africa: one that was directed at the heart of the exploitative racist system.[46] Some activists hoped that revolutionary change in the country would alter not only the face of southern Africa as a region but also the balance of forces on the entire continent. Ultimately, the events in Africa would lead to a shift in world power: 'A revolutionary government in South Africa could use the country's highly developed industrial base to provide significant material support to other African states.' A Marxist southern Africa would promote 'socialist construction' on the lines of the Soviet model.[47] Such ideas played to the government's fears of a 'communist onslaught' and also alarmed the business community.

Although the UDF supported the idea of unity, violence worsened in the eastern Cape townships as the UDF battled against the rival Azanian People's Organisation (AZAPO), which was loyal to black consciousness ideals and opposed to the UDF's acceptance of whites. Vigilante groups operated freely in this 'reign of terror', adopting a practice that would become notorious: people being burned with gasoline-filled tyres around their shoulders. This execution technique became known as 'the necklace'.[48] The situation became grave in 1985 as the government announced a state of emergency in parts of the country. The government asserted its intention to 'take steps' against 'those who promote violence and lawlessness'.[49] International pressures began to have an impact as foreign banks suspended credit and economic sanctions were imposed on the country by the United States. But if there was an expectation that the central government would fall, it was mistaken. The government was fully prepared to hit back at what it called 'terrorist savagery'.[50]

---

[44] *Mzabalazo*, 23.

[45] White 1995a: 11.

[46] Magubane 1983: 52.

[47] Bush 1983: 11.

[48] An interview with Mono Bandela in Lodge and Nasson 1991a: 238.

[49] *Hansard*, 25 January 1985.

[50] *Hansard*, 30 January 1987.

Chapter 4

The end of apartheid

Total strategy and the security forces

South African society was characterised by authoritarian control, yet the government's successive states of emergency during the 1980s contributed to an ethos of increasing lawlessness. The government had been in pursuit of order and control since the Soweto uprisings of 1976–77. After those events, the South African Defence Force (SADF) believed that the country needed an integrated social, economic, psychological and political programme in order to deal with opposition. A counter-insurgency war against opponents would be waged 'indirectly' by the government through various channels: propaganda, education, media, societal, and so on. The aim of such a campaign would be the restoration of state control. This programme was known as the 'total strategy'. As Gavin Cawthra explains: 'all aspects of life were viewed through the prism of security' and, consequently, all opposition was seen as part of a threat to the government and its policies.[1] In 1977, a Ministry of Defence white paper outlined the approach that the government would adopt in the face of what it called 'the total communist onslaught'. All opposition to the state was defined as 'pro-communist', including international pressures for sanctions and internal organisations campaigning for peaceful change. The government believed that South Africa faced the external threat of a violent transformation to a Marxist state. Equally, interference from the so-called 'action for peaceful change' from Western circles also contained the 'potential danger of a revolutionary transformation of the South and Southern African community'.[2] According to government propaganda, there was no legitimate opposition to the state; it all formed part of the wider communist conspiracy. In 1972, Vorster set up the State Security Council (SSC) to coordinate security strategy. Initially, it was a cabinet committee consisting of the police and military officers and selected senior ministers, including the president together with the ministers for law and order, defence, foreign affairs and justice. However, under President Botha, the SSC was upgraded, no longer subordinate to the cabinet but responsible for all major strategic and security decisions.

---

[1] Cawthra 1993: 21.

[2] cited in *Ibid*.: 22.

The most important sectors in South Africa's security apparatus were the South African Police (SAP) and the SADF. Under the total strategy, the operations of the SAP and SADF were closely integrated, with the SADF emerging as the dominant partner.[3] Political differences existed between the two organisations, with the members of the SAP firmly supporting extreme right-wing political parties, while the SADF generally supported the National Party. Nevertheless, General Magnus Malan, a veteran of the Security Branch and counter-insurgency operations, director of intelligence between 1979 and 1981 and defence minister, was a hard-line authoritarian. Malan headed a national security management system that established a network of local administrative bodies under military and police command that would act as 'security controls'. The SAP saw its primary function as the preservation of internal security, and it regularly patrolled the townships in paramilitary style, carrying weaponry and travelling in armoured cars. Before 1984, the policing of political activities in the black townships was largely the preserve of the security branch, which operated outside national police structures. This branch, formerly known as the Special Branch, was widely feared and was responsible for the infiltration and prosecution of anti-apartheid organisations. As Nicholas Haysom states:

> For many years, the relationship between the police and the black community was one of unconcealed enmity. South Africa's black citizens seldom saw the police as protectors of their rights but rather as enforcers of unjust laws they had no part in making.[4]

After Soweto, riot squads were introduced to manage crowd control in the townships, and the expenditure of the Department of Law and Order increased by 800 per cent between 1975 and 1986.

Total strategy was to run in tandem with P.W. Botha's political programme, which aimed to promote a black elite in the homelands and to coopt Indian and coloured communities in the tricameral parliament. Yet events took a different turn when revolts spread across the country in 1984. The SAP was entrusted with the task of suppressing the revolt with maximum-force policing. Subsequently, a state of emergency was declared and the police called on the military for assistance in fighting black opposition. Under the ensuing states of emergency, the police gained enhanced powers (see Box 4.1). The effect of the emergency regulations was to create an environment in which unsupervised and unaccountable behaviour on the part of the security forces was inevitable. According to Haysom, the security forces were given permission to 'pacify the townships by engaging in an undeclared war, unconstrained by conventional limits'.[5]

While the SADF led raids into neighbouring countries to destroy ANC bases and destabilise the governments of Marxist-leaning Mozambique and Angola, in South Africa secret security units killed activists and bombed their houses.[6] The

---

[3] Haysom 1992: 59.

[4] *Ibid*.: 63.

[5] *Ibid*.: 75.

[6] *Mzabalazo*, 24.

Box 4.1 1985: Additional powers granted to the South African police during the state of emergency

- The power to arrest and detain without trial was extended to any officer, however junior, of the security forces.
- Divisional police commissioners were given the power to govern black areas by decree.
- Judicial supervision of police powers was curtailed.
- Members of the security forces had an indemnity against the consequences of their unlawful actions.
- A ban on reporting on incidents of unrest and photographing police actions.
- All journalists reporting on security matters had to be accredited by the police or the government. Journalists who reported events could be deported or detained under emergency regulations. Some were not even permitted to be present in certain designated areas.

Sources: Dugard *et al.* 1992: 74–5; Schrire 1991: 89.

---

government accused the ANC/communist alliance of inciting black communities to racial violence and of encouraging a climate of 'bloodshed' and 'terrorist savagery', while the ANC claimed it was 'people's power' that 'shook the foundations of the apartheid system'.[7] The government attacked anyone who promoted 'violence and lawlessness'. For General P.J. Coetzee, commissioner of police, 'the revolutionary ANC terrorist' was an 'outlaw and a criminal' and it was the governnment's legal responsibility to treat all terrorist conspiracies as criminal offences.[8]

Vigilante groups and low-intensity warfare

Military approaches towards conflict varied, and by the mid-1980s the concept of 'low-intensity' warfare had been accepted by the government. Low-intensity conflict aimed to pacify the population not through the conventional use of military involvement but via covert grass-roots operations. Such activity became evident in policing and security responses to civil revolt in 1986. The strategy is outlined in Box 4.2.

Vigilante killings and covert assassination squads established a new pattern of aggressive violence. In the homelands, vigilantes received open state sponsorship, while in urban areas they created a self-sustaining cycle of violence and retaliation. The attraction of vigilante activity for the government was that it provided incidences of black-on-black violence that played to its propaganda campaign.

---

[7] *cf. Hansard*, 30 January 1987; *ibid.*: 26.

[8] cited in Cawthra 1993: 25.

Box 4.2 Low-intensity warfare tactics used by the South African government between 1986 and 1989

- Community leaders were detained, and vigilante groups and assassins were used to disrupt popular organisations.
- In some cases, potential 'troublemakers' were 'surgically removed', i.e. assassinated.
- Local groups were influenced to support the government through financial incentives.
- The government began a national programme to introduce black municipal guards and auxiliary police, so-called 'kitskonstabels'. The municipal guards were armed and placed at the government's service.

Source: Dugard *et al.* 1992: 80.

Vigilante killings created the impression that black communities were fighting among themselves and, therefore, an apartheid state was necessary to safeguard every person's security. As Table 4.1 indicates, 'black-on-black' violence accounted for a considerable number of killings, especially in Natal. The vigilantes, who received money and equipment through the security apparatus, could target specific black township residents in a far more accessible way than could the police or military units. Equally, this form of violence and terror seemed not to be associated with the state and therefore attracted less international condemnation. The government's Bureau of Information blamed activists for the 'necklace murders', which resulted in 220 deaths in a six-month period in 1986. Although 'neck-

Table 4.1 Black deaths in political violence, 1984–1988

Year	How died	Number	Total
1984			175
1985			879
1986	Shot by police	412	
	Killed by other blacks	265	
	Burned bodies found	231	
	Other	390	1298
1987			661
1988	Shot by police	34	
	Killed by other blacks outside Natal	15	
	Burned bodies found	5	
	Killed in Natal conflict	912	
	Other	183	1149

Source: South African Institute of Race Relations, annual surveys 1985–1989.

Box 4.3 The story of 'Stompie'

In Tumahole, a children's army was under the leadership of the 'Little General', 13-year-old James 'Stompie' Moeketsi Seipei, who had been the youngest detainee in the country. Refused admission to school after emerging from the police cells, he taught himself. He could recite by heart the entire text of the Freedom Charter and reputedly could also repeat whole 'chunks of writing by Karl Marx'. He carried a black briefcase stuffed with newspapers that he read enthusiastically every day. Stompie hated TV, loved political discussion and looked forward to the day when he could own a BMX bike and have enough to eat. Stompie was murdered in Soweto in 1989; one of Winnie Mandela's bodyguards was later convicted of the crime.

Source: cited in Lodge and Nasson 1991a: 102.

lacing' was used by several different groups, it was popularly associated with the youthful followers of the UDF, particularly after its misplaced endorsement by Winnie Mandela and her bodyguards. Winnie Mandela's role in the political violence was later to be explored when her bodyguards were convicted of murdering a 13-year-old boy, 'Stompie' Seipei (see Box 4.3).[9]

Violence flared in Natal between Inkatha supporters and members of the United Democratic Front (UDF). At the time, although the ANC recognised that some conflict between these two black organisations could be the result of competition over community groups, by 1990 it sensed that the violence was organised and had deeper roots than simply 'black-on-black' aggression.[10] The ANC suspected the government of encouraging violence in the expectation that it would weaken the liberation movement. In 1986, when Inkatha members led a parade against the ANC-backed Congress of South African Trade Unions (COSATU) and launched its own trade union movement, the United Workers' Union of South Africa, violence erupted. Later, it was discovered that the rally had been secretly organised and funded by South African military intelligence. The government regularly gave money to Inkatha in order to continue its fight against ANC-supporting groups.[11] The security forces secretly trained Inkatha members and resourced their activities. Several hundred Inkatha supporters were taken for military induction by the SADF to covert counter-insurgency bases in Namibia and Natal, all of which was funded by military intelligence. The trained men were later involved in assassination units targeting anti-apartheid campaigners and ultimately became part of the 'loose network of security force hit squads'.[12] It was

---

[9] See Chapter 7 for details of atrocities reported to the Truth and Reconciliation Commission.
[10] ANC 1994b.
[11] *Mzabalazo*, 27.
[12] Cawthra 1993: 122.

subsequently revealed that leading religious figures critical of apartheid were targets of the government-backed assassination squads.[13] Through collusion with Inkatha and the covert use of police and security forces, the government was actually promoting violence.[14] Certainly, the SAP and the KwaZulu police furthered the bitter war between Inkatha and the UDF, yet despite attempts to exercise control over the population the government continued to face spiralling levels of opposition. The security strategy had many inherent contradictions that the government seemed not to have foreseen. It damaged the economy and so generated wider opposition, and as the involvement of the state became more obvious the legitimacy of government was further undermined.

Between 1977 and 1989, forty-nine activists were assassinated. The homes of anti-apartheid campaigners were ransacked or fire-bombed, and the offices of the Congress of South African Trade Unions (COSATU), the headquarters of the South African Council of Churches and the Southern African Catholic Bishops' Conference were all demolished by bombs. Covert elements within the security forces were held responsible for these acts. With networks of spies and informers collecting information on ANC sympathisers, low-intensity warfare was effective 'in its repressive and disorganising components' but could only really create a situation of 'violent stability'.[15] However, other analysts believe that the activities of the security forces only served to enhance the 'spectre of anarchy'.[16] The submissions to the Truth and Reconciliation Commission in 1996 recall the widespread terror and suspicion of communities caught in a climate of lawlessness.[17]

A report issued by the Institute of Criminology at the University of Cape Town in 1985 revealed that of '176 people who had been held in custody, 75% reported having been beaten, 25% reported having been subjected to electric shock, 18% claimed they had been subjected to strangulation and 14% alleged they had been suspended on a pole and spun around [the 'helicopter']'.[18] Numerous reports of physical abuse and torture emerged during the time of the total strategy, and the figures for 1986 alone reveal that 624 adults and ninety-two children were killed by the police. Funeral processions were attacked, black protesters were shot in the back and many people suffered human rights violations. The appalling levels of political violence that occurred in South Africa between 1960 and 1994 were later investigated by the Truth and Reconciliation Commission (TRC). The TRC was established in 1995 in an attempt to help the country's population come to terms with its recent past.[19] The term 'gross violation of human rights' was defined by the TRC as the 'killing, abduction, torture or severe ill-treatment of any person'. The TRC gave voice to the experiences of victims, witnesses and per-

---

[13] Schrire 1991: 86.
[14] Saxena 1992: 64.
[15] Human Rights Commission 1992, cited in Haysom 1992: 89.
[16] Cawthra 1993: 36.
[17] See Chapter 7 for details.
[18] Cawthra 1993: 66.
[19] See Chapter 7 for details of the TRC and information about human rights abuses.

petrators of acts of violence during the last three decades of apartheid policies: 21,000 people came to speak at its public sessions, and 38,000 incidents of gross violations of human rights were reported. Of those people who came forward, 90 per cent were black, and most were women speaking on behalf of their dead male relatives.[20] The TRC sessions cast a long and painful shadow over South Africa's recent history, yet even by the late 1980s it was clear that low-intensity warfare could not continue indefinitely without the country sliding into chaos, socially, economically and politically. As F.W. de Klerk stated: 'You cannot simply have a counter-insurgency approach, because the enemy is the majority of the population.'[21] The government's counter-revolutionary strategy brought the country to the brink of civil war. It was clear that the situation could not continue.

The emergence of F.W. de Klerk

'The season of violence is over,' declared F.W. de Klerk in 1990, but the legacy of lawlessness continued and the polarisation in the country widened. Botha's attempts to win the support of the coloured and Indian communities in the tricameral parliament had highlighted the plight of the disenfranchised black majority and caused uprisings against the government. As Robert Schrire states ironically: 'By excluding the African majority from the tricameral system, Botha inadvertently made it clear that African political rights were the central issue in the political debate.'[22] Although Botha had claimed that 'apartheid is dead', he never rejected the policy of white supremacy. His understanding of apartheid was steeped in the policies of separate development and segregation introduced by Dr Verwoerd. Although he had introduced reforms, he could not accept the full democratisation of society and always dismissed the principle of 'one person, one vote'. As Schrire puts it: 'To Botha apartheid did not mean the power structure in South Africa but rather the obsolete socio-economic policies of previous governments.'[23] Consequently, white rule would always be upheld.

The 1989 election took place amid the shock of Botha's resignation as president and leader of the National Party. F.W. de Klerk was thrust into the political limelight as the new party leader in February 1989. He was not Botha's choice of successor, and relations between the two men were difficult. De Klerk believed that the National Party had to make a fundamental change of course, particularly as the mounting crisis was engulfing the country. He made speeches about the need to remove obstacles to negotiation with opponents and singled out five critical areas for attention: 'bridging the gap of distrust, initiating the process of negotiation, opening the door to economic prosperity, setting up a new political dispensation to accommodate everyone in the country and dealing firmly with violence.'[24]

---

[20] Hamber and Kibble 1999: 6.
[21] cited in Cawthra 1993: 37.
[22] Schrire 1991: 123.
[23] *Ibid.*: 118.
[24] cited in W. de Klerk 1994: 15.

Although de Klerk served in Botha's cabinet, he was not identified with any of the powerful bureaucracies that helped to define the policies of his predecessors, and he was also regarded as flexible with a good sense of tactics. Botha had in fact conducted a meeting with Nelson Mandela, but it was still unclear as to the direction of future policies at the time of the 1989 election. The results of the election are outlined in Table 4.2, and it can be seen that the position of the National Party had started to weaken with support polarising in favour of organisations to its left and right. A total of 52 per cent of the electorate voted for the right-wing Conservative Party or the left-leaning Democratic Party, against 48 per cent for the National Party. The majority of the electorate cast their votes against the party of government. In terms of voting patterns, Table 4.3 reveals the political preferences of English-speaking and Afrikaans-speaking voters. The Conservative Party campaigned on the issue of political unrest in the country, playing on security fears and improving its share of the vote among Afrikaners. Its major policies included an expanded programme of territorial separation between whites and Africans that would ultimately lead to partition, together with a return to the all-white pre-1984 parliamentary system. English-speaking voters shifted their support from the National Party to the liberal Democratic Party, which was an amalgamation of the Progressive Federal Party, the Independent Party and the National Democratic Movement. Yet perhaps the most significant aspect of the 1989 election, largely unknown to the wider population at the time, was that it was to be the last restricted election to take place in South Africa.

Table 4.2 Voter support by party in the South African elections of 1987 and 1989

	1987	1989
National Party	1,083,575 (53%)	1,053,523 (48%)
Conservative Party	549,916 (27%)	685,250 (31%)
Democratic Party	343,017 (17%)	451,544 (21%)
Herstigte Nasionale Party	62,888 (3%)	5,536 (0.25%)
Total votes	2,039,396	2,195,853

Source: Schrire 1991: 128.

Table 4.3 Voting patterns in the 1989 election

	English-speaking voters % of voter support	Afrikaans-speaking voters % of voter support
National Party	25	55
Conservative Party	5	40
Democratic Party	70	5

Source: Schrire 1991: 129.

de Klerk's reforms

President de Klerk took office in September 1989 and immediately announced that he would seek a political solution to the demands of black opponents rather than a military one. Although under de Klerk security remained a prerequisite for reform, the balance began to shift as security action took into account a broader political agenda. De Klerk downgraded the influence of the security forces in determining national strategies and emphasised the role that the police would play. The functions of the South African Police (SAP) were to 'monitor opposition organisations, contain them and aid the government in its negotiations with them'.[25] The police were instructed to adopt a different approach to demonstrations and public gatherings. By the end of 1989, political rallies and marches took place in all major cities without overt police intervention. The police force hoped to improve its image, but sections of the security police and the army continued to wage a secret campaign to destabilise and disorganise the ANC and its allies. The campaign came to be referred to as the 'third force'. Although the SAP denied that its officers would support a right-wing coup, a white revolt against any potential reforms was feared. Many policemen resigned from the SAP as the force confronted its recent practices and activities. In early 1990, de Klerk instituted

---

Box 4.4 Accounts of terror and violence

In April 1991 a survivor of the March 27 1991 night vigil massacre in Alexandra, 18 years old Oupa Sehume claimed that he was forced by members of the SAP into a hostel. White policemen wearing camouflage uniforms put a knife in his hands and warned him that he would be kicked if he put it down. The police then started to call out 'here's a member of the ANC, come and get him'. Sehume claims he was told to fight Inkatha with the knife. He was later returned home as the hostel-dwellers refused to attack for fear of it being a trap.

In April 1992 a civic association chairperson, Weston Shabangu said that he had received information from an eye-witness that a young boy had been abducted by a policeman and taken to the hostel. We rushed to the hostel and arrived just as the boy was being assaulted by hostel dwellers. If we had not arrived at that time the boy would have been killed.

15 July 1991: Police allegedly stood by and watched while more than 300 armed men from the KwaMadala hostel attacked residents in the nearby town. Residents claim that one man was killed during the attack and that afterwards members of the SAP escorted the group back to the hostel.

Source: verbatim accounts from the Independent Board of Inquiry report, *Fortresses of Fear*, Johannesburg, 1992.

---

[25] Cawthra 1993: 38.

Box 4.5 The unbanning of the African National Congress

F.W. de Klerk's Opening Address to Parliament on 2 February 1990

- The prohibition of the African National Congress, the Pan Africanist Congress, the South African Communist Party and a number of subsidiary organisations is being rescinded.
- People serving prison sentences merely because they were members of one of these organisations or because they committed some other offence which was merely an offence because a prohibition on one of the organisations was in force, will be identified and released.
- The media emergency regulations as well as the education emergency regulations are being abolished in their entirety.
- The restrictions in terms of the emergency regulations of 33 organisations are being rescinded. These organisations include: the United Democratic Front, Congress of South African Trade Unions, the South African National Students' Congress, the National Education Crisis Committee.
- The conditions imposed in terms of the security emergency regulations on 374 people upon their release are being rescinded and the regulations that provide for such conditions are being abolished.
- The period of detention in terms of the security emergency regulations will be limited to six months. Detainees will acquire the right to legal representation and a medical practitioner of their choosing.

Verbatim report of F.W. de Klerk's speech, cited in W. de Klerk 1991 (see Appendix 2).

---

the Harms Commission to investigate the activities of the death squads, and although it produced findings critical of the security forces it concluded, wrongly as was later revealed, that assassination squads did not exist.[26] Anthony Sampson referred to the report as a 'whitewash', but the government decided to accept the commission's findings. Nelson Mandela found Harms's report 'unbelievable' and thought that de Klerk and others in the government had chosen 'to look the other way or ignore what they knew was going on under their noses'.[27] The rift between Mandela and de Klerk widened, but with levels of violence escalating between 1990 and 1993, it became clear that other agencies were involved in the terror. From 1990 to 1993, over 10,000 people were killed in circumstances that were described as 'political'[28] (see Box 4.4). De Klerk attempted to distance himself from these events by rearranging his cabinet in favour of more conciliatory min-

---

[26] *cf.* Haysom 1992: 91; Ottoway 1993: 34.
[27] Sampson 1999: 439.
[28] Johnson amd Schlemmer 1996: 24.

isters. He also accused Mandela of hypocrisy as the ANC had its own 'trouble-makers', but the issue of security was not to go away.[29]

On 2 February 1990, de Klerk made a speech to parliament that was to dramatically change South Africa's political scene (see Appendix 2). He announced the unbanning of the African National Congress, the South African Communist Party, the Pan Africanist Congress and a range of subsidiary organisations (see Box 4.5). It was the government's intention to normalise the political process in the country, and its aim was to negotiate 'a just constitutional dispensation in which every inhabitant will enjoy equal rights, treatment and opportunity in every sphere of endeavour – constitutional, social and economic'.[30] For the first time in South Africa's history, de Klerk declared that the government accepted the principle of the recognition and protection of fundamental individual rights and that its task was directed at the protection of human rights in a future constitution

International factors and the question of reform

Although de Klerk's speech came as a surprise to many, contacts had been established with the exiled ANC and Nelson Mandela since the mid-1980s. The Institute for Democratic Alternatives, led by Frederik van Zyl Slabbert, a former leader of the Progressive Federal Party, had instigated meetings with opposition groups in 1986. The imprisoned Nelson Mandela had written a letter to the government in 1988 calling for the institution of a process of negotiation, and Botha had met Mandela in prison in 1989. These attempts at some form of rapprochement prepared the way for de Klerk's later dialogue with the ANC. The question is why these meetings took place when the violence in South Africa was at its peak. Part of the answer rests in the radically changing international political scene. After 1986, the relationship between the West and the Soviet Union was overtly softening, and during US–Soviet summit meetings it became clear that the USSR wanted to reach an agreement about its aims in southern Africa. Mikhail Gorbachev, leader of the USSR, was busy introducing reforming programmes in the Soviet Union and wanted an agreed settlement with the West over Angola and Namibia (see Figure 4.1). The potential framework for a common US–Soviet response towards southern Africa had initially been developed during a series of bi-national discussions involving academics, government officials and other concerned persons between 1983 and 1987. A series of 'implicit agreements' emerged from those meetings:

- that both the United States and the Soviet Union had important interests in southern Africa but neither had vital interests there;
- that neither superpower had the ability to shape the political and economic future of the region unilaterally;

[29] Sampson 1999: 440.
[30] cited in W. de Klerk 1994: 34.

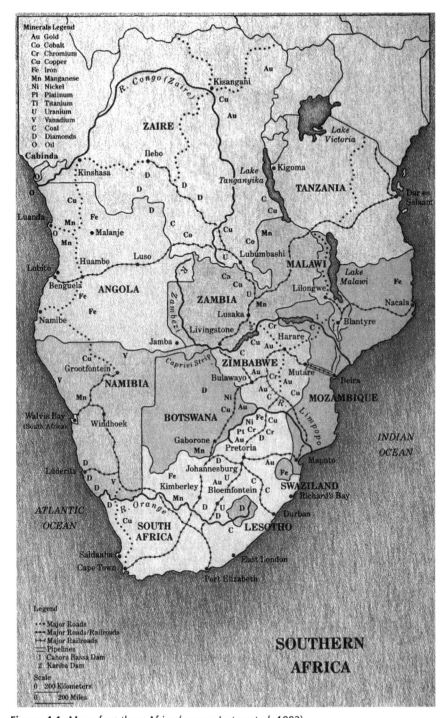

Figure 4.1 Map of southern Africa (source: Jaster *et al.* 1992)

- that regional conflicts must ultimately be resolved through political and not military means; and
- that both nations had an interest in seeing a more rapid, less violent, negotiated transition to majority rule in South Africa.[31]

One interesting point that Jaster *et al.* make is that these agreements between the USA and the USSR had begun to take shape well before Mikhail Gorbachev's rise to power. They argue that irrespective of who emerged as leader of the Soviet Union, regional realities in southern Africa and the constant drain on resources would have forced the USSR to change its policy towards the area.[32] This is especially intriguing if we consider what was actually happening in South Africa during that period. The adoption of the 'total strategy' in the face of the 'total communist onslaught', which resulted in such devastating levels of violence and brought the country to the brink of civil war, seems at variance with the potentiality of Soviet disengagement in the region. Certainly, Soviet and, by proxy, Cuban involvement in Mozambique and Angola on their independence in 1976 raised the threat of a 'communist attack', but a decade later the situation had changed considerably. As Marina Ottoway states:

> If negotiations between the ANC and National Party had started after the 1976 Soweto uprising, any subsequent transition would have been exposed to a totally different set of circumstances, with the Soviet Union deeply involved in southern Africa and the United States concerned about Soviet expansionism.[33]

At that time, both parties were caught up in the mutual hostilities of the Cold War.

South Africa's crackdown on domestic opposition and its continued regional belligerence during the mid-1980s began to embarrass and frustrate America. Apartheid was becoming a major domestic issue in the United States, and the Republican government of President Ronald Reagan did not wish to appear 'soft' on South Africa's racist policies. Consequently, in 1986 the US Congress passed the comprehensive Anti-Apartheid Act, which introduced economic sanctions. During 1988, the South African government took advantage of the easing of hostilities between the West and the USSR and made contact with its neighbouring countries. Without the threat of Soviet expansionism in the region, South Africa's central rationale that it was fighting the threat of communism began to seem hollow and self-serving. As Central and Eastern European member states of the old Soviet bloc gained independence through the power of non-violent forms of protest, it became clear that the old anti-capitalist, revolutionary rhetoric of the ANC and the SACP would also have to change. In any case, with the collapse of the Soviet Union starting in 1989 all funding for liberation movements was at an end, and the ANC could no longer rely on this source of external funding for its

---

[31] Jaster *et al.* 1992: 122–3.
[32] *Ibid.*
[33] Ottoway 1993: 205.

survival. Notwithstanding the appalling levels of violence in South Africa, the international scene seemed to be pushing the combatants towards some form of negotiation. As de Klerk put it in his 1990 speech: 'The dynamic developments in international politics have created new opportunities for South Africa.' He was right. The old Soviet model of politics once upheld by radicals as an ideal society was now deemed repressive and dysfunctional. The world had moved on, and one-party ideological politics was considered both undesirable and restrictive. Events moved rapidly, and the Cold War, only a few years earlier such a potent and menacing threat to peaceful coexistence, had vanished. The ANC also recognised that political negotiations took place at a time 'when the end of the Cold War shifted the balance of forces internationally decisively in favour of the resolution of regional conflicts through negotiations'.[34] The South African Communist Party, however, continued to adhere blindly to old-fashioned Marxism–Leninism. In June 1989, only a matter of months before the fall of the Berlin Wall and the absolute collapse of the Soviet system, the party adopted a manifesto looking forward to the 'sweeping of socialism across the world'. The SACP predicted the eventual demise of capitalism, yet in reality, it was the heralded Soviet socialist experiment that had crashed by the end of the year.[35] In a strange irony, the unbanning of the SACP presented the party with a clear and uncomfortable challenge to its future ideological direction, one that it is yet to fully resolve.

Within the region, contacts with other African states were established under Botha's presidency, but while individual countries were prepared to hold discussions with the South African government, their collective entity, the Organisation of African Unity (OAU) was deeply concerned about the continuation of apartheid. In fact, African representatives at the United Nations called for 'the total abolition of apartheid'. In 1989, the OAU issued a statement on South Africa that later became known as the 'Harare Declaration'. It called for the release of political prisoners, the unbanning of political parties, the removal of troops from the townships, the end of the state of emergency and the cessation of political executions.[36] The OAU looked towards the 'speedy end of the apartheid system', which denied 'justice and human dignity' to black Africans. The declaration urged the people of South Africa to 'get together to negotiate an end to apartheid' and to agree on a formula that would transform South Africa into 'a non-racial democracy'. Guidelines for the process of negotiation were laid down and are outlined in Box 4.6 (see Appendix 1 for the full text of the Harare Declaration). The declaration was adopted by the United Nations in December 1989.

The guidelines for negotiation contained in the Harare Declaration assumed that South Africa's future would be a democratic one. Only a matter of months after de Klerk made his momentous speech, some white South Africans began to

---

[34] ANC 1994b: 5.

[35] Ellis 1992: 154.

[36] Declaration on the question of South Africa by the *ad hoc* Committee on Southern Africa of the Organisation of African Unity, Harare, Zimbabwe, 21 August 1989.

Box 4.6 Guidelines for the South African process of negotiation

The process of negotiations between the government and opposition groups should commence along the following lines:

(1) Discussions should take place between the liberation movement and the South African regime to achieve the suspension of hostilities on both sides by agreeing to a mutually binding cease-fire.

(2) Negotiations should then proceed to establish the basis for the adoption of a new constitution by agreeing on the following principles:
- South Africa shall become a united, democratic and non-racial state.
- All its people shall enjoy common and equal citizenship and nationality regardless of race, colour, sex or creed.
- All its people shall have the right to participate in the government on the basis of a universal suffrage, exercised through the one-person, one-vote system.
- All shall have the right to form and join any political party of their choice, provided that this is not a furtherance of racism
- All shall enjoy universally recognised human rights, freedoms and civil liberties, protected under a Bill of Rights.
- There will be a new legal system which shall guarantee equality of all before the law.
- There shall be an economic order which shall promote and advance the well-being of all South Africans.
- A democratic South Africa shall respect the rights, sovereignty and territorial integrity of all countries.

(3) Having agreed to these principles, the parties should then negotiate the necessary mechanisms for drawing up the new constitution.

(4) The parties shall define and agree on the role to be played by the international community in ensuring a successful transition to a democratic order.

(5) The parties shall agree on the formation of an interim government to supervise the process of the drawing up and adoption of a new constitution, govern and administer the country, as well as effect the transition to a democratic order, including the holding of elections.

(6) After the adoption of the new constitution, all armed hostilities will be deemed to have formally terminated.

(7) For its part the international community would lift the sanctions that have been imposed against apartheid South Africa. The new South Africa shall qualify for membership of the Organisation of African Unity.

(see also Appendix 1).

discuss the possibilities for 'genuine and lasting democracy' in South Africa. Yet they were becoming aware of the enormous disparities in wealth, education, income, access to resources and so on that existed between the different communities. As one commentator put it: 'Our lack of serious attention to black socio-economic development in the past has come home to roost with a vengeance.'[37] It was clear that political changes would have to be paralleled with economic opportunities. Democracy required far more than giving everyone the vote; there had to be some form of development in order to redress the country's huge inequalities. With the demise of the socialist command economy as a role model, the only viable economic system would be that of a liberal free market. As the ANC moved into the formal political arena as a legitimate participant, its own socialist views had to be confronted.

Nelson Mandela and the ANC

On 11 February 1990, Nelson Mandela was released from jail after twenty-seven years of imprisonment (see Appendix 3 for the text of his speech following his release). Oliver Tambo stood down as president of the ANC on the grounds of ill-health, and Nelson Mandela assumed the role. The first formal talks between the ANC and the government took place in May 1990, and thereafter Mandela undertook a world tour that included a visit to the United States to meet President George Bush and to address Congress. Later, de Klerk conducted a similar trip to America. By August, the ANC announced a ceasefire, which effectively ended its thirty-year armed struggle against apartheid. The liberation movement continued to uphold the democratic principles contained in the Freedom Charter of 1956 and included those principles in its 1988 constitutional guidelines for a democratic South Africa. The OAU had included the basic democratic sentiments of the ANC in its Harare Declaration, but the ANC guidelines considered more closely issues such as the economy and affirmative action. The economy would be a mixed one, with public, private, cooperative and small-scale family sectors. The private

---

Box 4.7 Robben Island

Robben Island had been used for many years as a prison by the Dutch and the British. However, it became known as 'the Island' after the South African government turned it into a maximum security prison in 1961. The prison was built to help to incarcerate the large numbers of black political activists arrested after the African National Congress and the Pan Africanist Congress were declared unlawful in 1960. In 1964, an isolation section was created to separate those prisoners that the authorities considered 'ringleaders'. The island became a symbol of black resistance to white rule. Serving time there gave stature, dignity and political credibility to its inmates.

---

[37] Speech given by J.H. Steyn, chairman of the Urban Foundation, Johannesburg, May 1990.

sector of the economy would be 'obliged to cooperate with the state in realising the objectives of the Freedom Charter in promoting social well-being'. Equally, the 'state and all social institutions would be under a constitutional duty to eradicate economic and social inequalities', which had been the product of racial discrimination.[38] Land reform programmes would be devised that took into account the status of victims of forced removals, and workers' trade union rights would be protected. Women would have equal rights in all spheres of public and private life, and the state would take affirmative action measures to eliminate inequalities and discrimination between the sexes. A democratic South Africa would have a constitution and a bill of rights that eradicated all forms of racial discrimination (see Appendix 4 for democratic South Africa's Bill of Rights 1996).

However, primarily, the ANC had to reform its own undemocratic structures. Organisationally, at the time of its unbanning, the ANC was described as 'an exiled insurgent body' that had a 'disciplined and autocratic character'.[39] No leadership elections had been held for twenty-six years, between 1959 and 1985, and the South African Communist Party continued to play a central role in the movement. According to Tom Lodge, the ANC exiles 'returned home with a well-developed set of authoritarian and bureaucratic reflexes'. Yet a very different form of political socialisation had taken place in South Africa itself.[40] A deep network of voluntary organisations had developed during the resistance of the 1970s and 1980s, with the trade union movement, COSATU, often spearheading community action and workplace-related concerns. The ANC recognised the need to reconsider its own framework and constitution, and when Nelson Mandela was elected president at the ANC's 1991 National Conference a commitment was made to amend the movement's constitution. The main amendments were concerned with the structures and functioning of the organisation. References to Umkhonto we Sizwe (MK) and overseas branches were removed from the new constitution. The ANC was democratised, with the National Conferences becoming its 'supreme ruling and controlling body'.[41]

The ANC justified its early negotiations with the National Party on the grounds that they were the two major players in South African politics: one, 'the premier liberation movement' and the other, the party of government.[42] Nelson Mandela interpeted the negotiations:

> The situation had to be handled in such a manner that we could tactfully persuade the leading forces within the National Party that the transition was also in their interests. Transition with the minimum of disruption required their co-operation. And this helped pave the way for the final settlement.[43]

---

[38] ANC 1988.
[39] Lodge 1996: 191.
[40] *Ibid.*
[41] Deegan 1998.
[42] ANC 1994b: 6.
[43] Nelson Mandela, cited in *ibid*.

The first phase of negotiations between the ANC and the government lasted until the end of 1991 and focused on the return of political exiles and the release of political prisoners. As part of the process of negotiation, a National Peace Convention was held in September 1991, and that event led to the emergence of a National Peace Accord (NPA).

The National Peace Accord and the Convention for a Democratic South Africa

The accord, signed by the leaders of all major parties, was intended to be a step towards national conflict resolution. Its objective was to bring political violence to an end in the country, and it set out the codes of conduct, procedures and mechanisms to achieve that goal. It instituted regional and local peace committees, which were charged with the investigatation of incidents and the causes of violence and intimidation. A section of the accord was devoted to how political parties could help to minimise conflict and encourage a climate of democratic tolerance. In a statement that highlighted the appalling nature of political life in South Africa, the accord demanded that no party or organisation should 'kill, injure, apply violence to, intimidate or threaten any other person in connection with that person's political beliefs, words, writings or actions'.[44] All political organisations were called to refrain from 'incitement to violence or hatred' and to conduct any public meeting, rally or march in a peaceful manner. Although the NPA was well intentioned, critics complained that it lacked grass-roots support and was dominated by predominantly white professionals who could speak no African languages. This rather compromised the effectiveness of the local committees. Equally, although the ANC, the Inkatha Freedom Party and the government realised that a joint peace effort was required, 'none of the political leaders was in a position to facilitate a peace agreement because of distrust and suspicions about political agendas'.[45] Mandela was beginning to distrust de Klerk's commitment to reform, while de Klerk hoped for Inkatha's support as a counterweight to the ANC but found Buthelezi 'awkward and contradictory'.[46] Levels of violence escalated and ultimately threatened to derail any political negotiations.

In December 1991, the multi-party Convention for a Democratic South Africa (CODESA) was held in Johannesburg. Delegations from nineteen political organisations, supported by teams of advisers, prepared to negotiate the future of the country. The convention marked the beginning of the formal process of negotiation, which many hoped would lead to some form of compromise. Such expectations were always overambitious and CODESA came to a halt only six months later. It did, however, set up five working groups that would report back to a sec-

---

[44] National Peace Accord, 14 September 1991, chapter 2, 'code of conduct for political parties and organisations'.
[45] Gastrow 1995: 93.
[46] Sampson 1999: 440.

ond CODESA general meeting. The working groups were given certain issues to discuss: the creation of an environment for free political participation; general constitutional principles; transitional arrangements; interim government; the future of the homelands; and an agreed time frame. Trade unions and civic organisations were not regarded as political organisations and consequently were excluded from the convention. The Conservative Party refused to attend, as did the leftist PAC and AZAPO.

Although de Klerk had instigated the negotiating process, there was a lack of clarity about the nature of the country's political future. At CODESA, he announced the government's willingness to negotiate an amendment to the existing constitution so that an interim power-sharing model could be created, but no details were presented. The situation was difficult for the National Party because the Conservative Party (CP), which was strictly opposed to any negotiated settlement, was becoming more popular, and many feared that white militancy would turn into a right-wing attack on the negotiating process. The CP claimed that it represented the majority of whites and that the NP had no mandate for its policy. In response, de Klerk decided to call a referendum on whether negotiations should go ahead or not, which resulted in a 68.5 per cent vote in favour of continuing the process. However, there was still no certainty as to where the negotiations would lead. Many analysts believe that the government was prepared to drag out the proceedings for as long as possible: 'It is quite possible to suppose that the government wanted the kudos that went with having negotiations in progress without the discomfort of actually having to change anything in a radical way.'[47] Nelson Mandela endorsed this view: 'the government feared the advent of democracy and was worried about the pace of change.' As far as Mandela was concerned, de Klerk was 'dragging out the talks, to frustrate majority rule'. De Klerk was looking for a 'power sharing arrangement, on the lines of a rotating presidency and a senate of regional representatives that would uphold minority interests'.[48] So confident of its popularity, the National Party calculated that it could 'delay the process and in the intervening period, disorganise, weaken and discredit the ANC'.[49] ANC members believed that the security services were operating a 'third force' military campaign and that de Klerk had failed to control these forces. Assassinations, sophisticated bombings, vehicles with armed gunmen stalking the townships, and armed white men in balaclavas involved in Inkatha killings were all evidence pointing to the continuation of the government's total strategy. ANC officials reported cases of harassment and threats, with many continually moving to avoid violence. Assassinations perpetrated in the early 1990s, a human rights commission reported, were directed against anti-apartheid campaigners as they had been during the 1980s.[50] De Klerk, meanwhile, claimed that he did not have the power to prevent violent activities.

---

[47] Johnson and Schlemmer 1996: 26–7; Ottoway 1993: 107; Sampson 1999: 460.
[48] *Ibid.*
[49] Mandela, in ANC 1994b: 5.
[50] Human Rights Commission 1992.

Relations between de Klerk and Mandela were cool during the first sessions of CODESA, and any thoughts of a quick deal being struck between the two leaders were unrealistic. Perhaps inevitably, by the second session of CODESA (known as CODESA II), which took place on 16/17 May 1992, negotiating positions had hardened. The NP confronted the ANC with a set of principles, including:

- domination and abuse of power must be prevented;
- there should be maximum devolution of power;
- a phased approach must be followed during the transition;
- unrealistic time scales must be abolished; and
- a provisional constitution must already entrench the principles of a final constitution.[51]

The ANC retorted by accusing the government of deliberately slowing down the process and of operating a hidden agenda. The ANC suspended its involvement in negotiations following a massacre in Boipatong in June 1992, when ANC squatters were murdered by IFP-supporting dwellers, allegedly supported by the police.[52] The wider population was called upon to demonstrate through direct action, and the newly formed Campaign for Peace and Democracy intended to mobilise the general public. During the second half of 1992, the whole negotiating process reached its nadir with the prospect of any form of agreed settlement seeming remote. The ANC blamed the government for failing to stop the violence, while the NP saw the ANC as an organisation only interested in seizing power. The ANC believed that its campaign was instructive in that the organisation 'learnt the need for tighter discipline and a better assessment of situations'. Other commentators, however, viewed the mass action as either unsuccessful or a contributory factor in the breakdown of law and order in the country.[53] Nevertheless, if there was one issue on which everyone agreed it was the important role played by external actors. The international community's intense pressure on both the government and the ANC to resume negotiations was critical at this stage. Mandela claims that the ANC sought increased international involvement through the UN, the OAU and the Commonwealth to help to 'reinforce initiatives'. Certainly, a catalyst for returning to negotiations occurred when all parties were invited to New York to speak to the Security Council of the United Nations. Meanwhile, the Commonwealth Observer Mission to South Africa (COMSA) urged the parties not to allow violence in the country to continually delay negotiations, which, in the end, could only fuel more violence.[54] De Klerk's position started to weaken as reports indicated that there had been collusion between Inkatha and the government and their relationship seemed unwholesome

---

[51] W. de Klerk 1994.

[52] Johnson and Schlemmer 1996: 27.

[53] cf. Mandela, in ANC 1994b: 6; ibid.; W. de Klerk 1994.

[54] Commonwealth Observer Mission to South Africa 1994: 7.

and covert. The ANC refused to shift from its request for majority rule, and the government was ultimately obliged to accept the possibility of an ANC government. On 26 September 1992, Mandela and de Klerk agreed to a Minute of Understanding, which set in process new multi-party talks. Anthony Sampson maintains that once this document had been signed by both leaders, 'a fundamental realignment' took place. 'It not only ended de Klerk's political alliance with Buthelezi it also rapidly reduced the political violence outside KwaZulu Natal.'[55] In November 1992, President de Klerk proposed a prospective time scale for change:

- A large number of bilateral talks and a multi-party negotiation conference would be held by the end of March 1993.
- A transitional executive council and an electoral commission would be established by June 1993.
- The adoption by September 1993 of an interim constitution that made provision for a constitution-writing body.
- A general election to be held in March/April 1994.
- The institution of a government of national unity by the middle of 1994.

Return to negotiations

Lessons had been learned from the failure of CODESA, and the Multi-Party Negotiating Process (MPNP) had a different structure. The working groups of CODESA had consisted of around eighty people, an unwieldy arrangement far too large to lead to negotiation and even less to compromise. Also, CODESA had no central negotiating body that would have provided a compromise-seeking mechanism when parties failed to agree with each other. It had become over-politicised and generally lacked adequate 'technical' input, that is, the benefit of impartial advice or guidance of experts. The MPNP did not intend to replicate this situation.

In April 1993, twenty-six political parties and interest groups gathered at the World Trade Centre in Johannesburg in a renewed effort to resolve the political future of South Africa. The structure of the MPNP was designed to facilitate agreement, because this time 'there could be no failure'. The Negotiating Forum initially referred specific issues to the technical committees, but once the Negotiating Council expanded and was opened to the media, the forum was not required and it delegated its powers to the council (see Figure 4.2). The council, which was the representative negotiating body, received reports from the Planning Committee. Although the Planning Committee was not mandated to take any decisions on substantive matters, it played an important role in pre-empting and averting problems and was considered fundamental to the success of the MPNP. Essentially, it acted as a 'guardian' over the process. Reports from the technical

---

[55] Sampson 1999: 464.

	PLENARY 10 members per party	
	NEGOTIATING FORUM	
	NEGOTIATING COUNCIL	
	▲ ▲ ▲ ▲ ▲ ▲ ▲ ▲	
	PLANNING COMMITTEE	
COMMISSION FOR THE DEMARCATION OF PROVINCES		COMMISSION ON NATIONAL SYMBOLS
Technical committees		Technical committees
	Administration	

Figure 4.2 Summary of the Multi-Party Negotiating Process structures (source: Eloff 1994)

committees, which comprised non-party specialists and lawyers, were also sent to the council. Most of these reports 'contained the seeds of compromise'. If the technical committees failed to reach agreement, the problem was referred to the Planning Committee or dealt with by an *ad hoc* task group. Both the commissions shown in Figure 4.2 were non-partisan but were acceptable across the spectrum of political organisations. According to one analyst, the continual 'flow of reports and referrals between the Committees and the Council led to increased clarity and consensus'.[56] Equally, the policy of alternating chairpersons, selected from a panel of eight, ensured that participants could trust the impartiality of the proceedings. Although admittedly this process was regarded as cumbersome and inefficient at times, it did give each group a chance to steer the talks at some point.[57] On 15 June 1993, the Negotiating Council agreed by a 'sufficient consensus' to hold elections on 27 April 1994. Within only ten months, black South Africans would be able to vote for the first time in their lives.

---

[56] Eloff 1994: 17.
[57] Commonwealth Observer Mission to South Africa 1994: 11.

Part III

The nation in transition

Chapter 5

1994 – The new South Africa

The build-up to the election

Although the Inkatha Freedom Party and the Conservative Party withdrew from the negotiating talks, by 24 September 1993, the 'four pillars of the transition' had been agreed by the Negotiating Council. These were the Transitional Executive Council (TEC), the Independent Electoral Commission (IEC), the Independent Media Commission (IMC) and the Independent Broadcasting Authority (IBA). The existing parliament enacted these bodies, which are outlined in Figure 5.1.

The institution of these bodies, just seven months before the elections were due to be held, marked 'the irreversibility of the ending of apartheid'.[1] Yet none of the legislation could become operational until the Negotiating Council had agreed upon an entire package of reforms. By 19 November 1993, the council had finally negotiated an interim constitution, an Electoral Act and the removal of all apartheid laws, and they were presented for endorsement at the Multi-Party Negotiating Process (MPNP) plenary session. South Africa's tricameral parliament sat for the last time at the end of 1993 and ended its existence with the repeal of remaining apartheid legislation and the adoption of the interim constitution and the Electoral Act. As the Commonwealth secretary-general stated: the occasion marked 'an historic watershed'.[2]

Of the original twenty-six organisations that attended the first meeting of the MPNP in April 1993, twenty-two political parties and groups remained to the end. Later, some parties regretted leaving the negotiations. The deputy provincial secretary of the IFP declared in 1996 that doubts had existed within the organisation as to whether it had been correct to withdraw from the negotiations.[3] Johnson and Schlemmer believe that the establishment of such transitional administrative arrangements was critical in ensuring that 'the government did not use its superior resources to rig the first election'. The TEC was a 'broadly representative body with the power to make authoritative rulings on any matter required for the "levelling of the playing fields" prior to the

---

[1] Commonwealth Observer Mission to South Africa 1994: 9.
[2] *Ibid.*
[3] Sam Razak, interview.

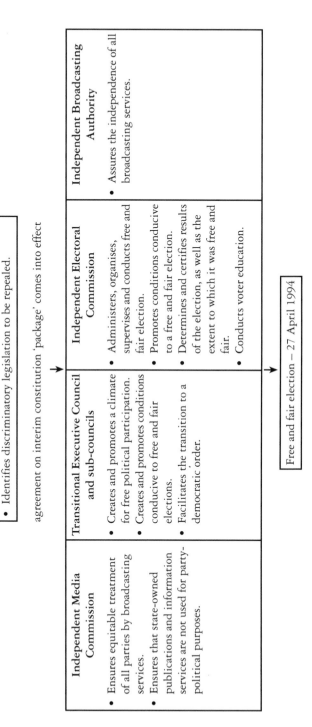

Negotiating Council
- Adopts draft bills on IEC, IMC, IBA and TEC.
- Establishes transitional structures.
- Negotiates interim constitution, including a bill of rights.
- Identifies discriminatory legislation to be repealed.

agreement on interim constitution 'package' comes into effect

Independent Media Commission	Transitional Executive Council and sub-councils	Independent Electoral Commission	Independent Broadcasting Authority
• Ensures equitable treatment of all parties by broadcasting services. • Ensures that state-owned publications and information services are not used for party-political purposes.	• Creates and promotes a climate for free political participation. • Creates and promotes conditions conducive to free and fair elections. • Facilitates the transition to a democratic order.	• Administers, organises, supervises and conducts free and fair election. • Promotes conditions conducive to a free and fair election. • Determines and certifies results of the election, as well as the extent to which it was free and fair. • Conducts voter education.	• Assures the independence of all broadcasting services.

Free and fair election – 27 April 1994

Figure 5.1 The negotiating process leading up to the election

election'.[4] Each participant in the MPNP was entitled to one representative member on the Executive Council. As Figure 5.2 demonstrates, a great deal of the TEC's work was performed by seven multi-party sub-councils, all of which operated under its control and liaised with the relevant government department.

The TEC could obtain any information that had a direct bearing on the holding of free and fair elections. Yet it was neither a 'super-government' nor a parallel government. It was, in essence, an advisory and monitoring council that had the power of veto over any policy of the existing government of President de Klerk. The Conservative Party criticised the council on the grounds that it effectively denuded the role of the cabinet and parliament in favour of a non-elected body.[5] Yet it is very difficult to see what other option would have been more appropriate at such a critical time. As commentators make clear:

> What South Africa did not have during the transitional phase was a nuanced and normal democratic political practice. The practice of political power was still premised on threats of mass action, violence and counter-violence. In many ways it was still a militarised and polarised political culture.[6]

The objectives of the Executive Council were to minimise and contain the pervading culture of violence and political intolerance. Its aims were to:

- eliminate any impediments to legitimate political activity and intimidation;
- ensure that political parties were free to canvass support and hold meetings;
- ensure the full participation of women;
- ensure that no government or administration used any of its power to either advantage or prejudice any political party.[7]

The transitional institutions had to work because the wider population, irrespective of political alignment or racial category, possessed a stake in South Africa's future. Through the negotiations, South Africans had been forced to 'confront each other and each other's worst fears'.[8] The ANC and the NP were bound together in 'antagonistic cooperation', with both fully recognising that the only alternative to negotiation was civil war.[9] The ANC believed that the National Party also had an interest in ensuring that the transitional arrangements contributed towards moving the country away from its years of apartheid. Although such moves would close 'a treacherous chapter in South Africa's history', there were great anxieties in the NP that de Klerk was 'giving the country away'.[10] James Barber believes that de Klerk was especially vulnerable to such charges

---

[4] Johnson and Schlemmer 1996: 28.
[5] *Hansard*, 20 September 1993, col. 13223.
[6] Johnson and Schlemmer 1996: 29.
[7] Commonwealth Observer Mission to South Africa 1994: 14.
[8] *Ibid.*: 11.
[9] Welsh 1994b: 24.
[10] Sampson 1999: 472.

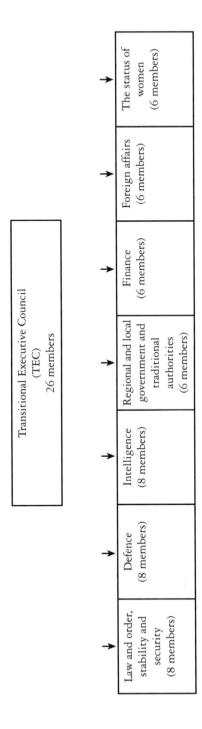

Figure 5.2 The Transitional Executive Council and sub-councils (source: COMSA 1994)

because he appeared to be acting against the interests of Afrikaners. Equally, in earlier statements de Klerk had not anticipated the complete relinquishment of Afrikaner power; rather, he favoured a power-sharing arrangement that would keep the National Party in control. For Barber, de Klerk was a pragmatist: 'Had he harboured the ideological convictions of a Verwoerd, or been afraid to split Afrikanerdom like Vorster, or baulked at the consequences of change as had P.W. Botha, a negotiated settlement could not have been achieved.'[11] However, if negotiations were to continue the cooperation of the National Party was required. According to Mandela, it was this acknowledgement that helped define the principles contained in the interim constitution.[12]

The interim constitution

In July 1993, the Negotiating Council accepted a package of constitutional principles with which the transitional constitution would have to comply. The new transitional constitution was adopted in December 1993 but, as it had not been the product of a democratic legislature, it would serve for a period of only two years. The document's central achievements were the thirty-four principles it enshrined that sought to protect democratic norms and prevent their being overruled by a subsequent dominant party government. In other words, an elected majority government could not simply rewrite the constitution to suit itself.[13] Clause VI of the constitution stated: 'There shall be a separation of powers between the legislature, executive and judiciary, with appropriate checks and balances to ensure accountability, responsiveness and openness.' And Clause VIII pronounced: 'There shall be representative government embracing multi-party democracy, regular elections, universal adult suffrage, a common voters' roll and, in general, proportional representation.'[14]

The basic values underpinning the essentially liberal democratic 1993 constitution included the rule of law, freedom and equality, and the independence of the judiciary. A number of commentators have pointed to the apparent incongruity of the major parties involved in the negotiations accepting liberal democracy. The acceptance of democratic principles, Bertus de Villiers argues, was not 'part of a general philosophical plan that the various parties had agreed to beforehand', while Johnson and Schlemmer maintain that the NP, the ANC and the IFP had never been completely enamoured of liberal democracy:

> The NP had spent its whole period in power up until 1990 attempting to resist international pressure for such a constitution. The IFP, in its governance of Kwa-Zulu, had shown itself to be a party of conservative chiefly oligarchs. The ANC, for its part,

---

[11] Barber 1999: 314.
[12] Nelson Mandela, in ANC 1994b: 6.
[13] Peter Leon, interview.
[14] Interim constitution of the Republic of South Africa 1993.

had for a generation espoused the language of populist Marxism and had always taken as its goal a revolutionary (and thus presumably single-party) seizure of power.[15]

Yet both the ANC and the IFP had supported some democratic principles in the past. The ANC's Freedom Charter of 1956 had upheld equal rights of freedom of speech, assembly and the rule of law, together with universal suffrage (see Chapter 2). In 1988, the Freedom Charter became the basis of the ANC constitutional guidelines, which were recommended as the framework for a future 'free, democratic and non-racial South Africa' (see Box 5.1)

Equally, during the 1980s, Inkatha had proclaimed an 'Indaba' or bill of rights, which upheld 'the right to life and liberty; the right to own and occupy property; equality before the law and the principle of administrative justice'.[16] So, regardless of the rhetoric of the ANC and the IFP, both organisations had raised some democratic principles before the establishment of the interim constitution. In fact, the 1993 constitution upheld many of the clauses that were contained in the

---

Box 5.1 ANC constitutional guidelines for a democratic South Africa, 1988

- South Africa shall be an independent, unitary, democratic and non-racial state.
- Sovereignty shall belong to the people as a whole and shall be exercised through one central legislature, executive and administration.
- All organs of government, including justice, security and armed forces, shall be representative of the people as a whole, democratic in their structure and functioning and dedicated to defending the principles of the constitution.
- The people shall have the right to vote under a system of universal suffrage based on the principle of one person, one vote.
- Every voter shall have the right to stand for election and be elected to all legislative bodies.
- The constitution shall include a bill of rights based on the Freedom Charter and guaranteeing fundamental human rights of all citizens irrespective of race, colour, sex or creed.
- The economy shall be a mixed one, with a public sector, a private sector, a co-operative sector and a small-scale family sector.
- Property for personal use and consumption shall be constitutionally protected.
- Workers' trade union rights should be protected.
- Women shall have equal rights in all spheres of public and private life, and the state shall take affirmative action to eliminate inequalities and discrimination between the sexes.

---

[15] Johnson and Schlemmer 1996: 9–10.
[16] Inkatha Freedom Party 1987.

ANC's 1988 guidelines. There was, of course, very little credible alternative to a constitutional liberal democratic agenda. If South Africa was to declare itself a democracy, there was barely any choice as to the form that democracy would take. Socialist democracy as defined by a dominant party had been undermined by the collapse of the Soviet Union and was generally viewed as a system that denied human rights. Authoritarian or traditional rule was deemed intrinsically undemocratic, the iniquities of the former repressive apartheid political structure being precisely the system from which South Africa was escaping. In a country where the majority of the population had been denied the most basic human rights, it was inevitable that any new constitution would have to include a bill of rights in order to demonstrate that people's dignity could never be undermined again (see Appendix 4). The constitutional values of the new South Africa, then, had to be viewed against the background of 'apartheid, exclusion and domination'.[17]

The 1993 constitution established the Constitutional Court as the highest legal authority in the country. Such a move was important as distrust of the courts was widespread because of their support for apartheid. The court had jurisdiction over any dispute of a constitutional nature.[18] After the election, it was agreed that a representative constitutional assembly would draft a final constitution, inclusive of the thirty-four democratic principles, to be approved by a two-thirds majority. In a sense, all constitutions are historical documents attempting to redress past injustices and grievances while simultaneously defining a politico-legal framework for the future. Yet South Africa was not emerging as an independent state following a process of decolonisation. Neither had it completely severed links with past political actors. The negotiated transition inevitably had implications for the manner in which the 1993 constitution was drafted. At that time, a number of factors had to be taken into account: the white community was entrenched in a strong economic and bureaucratic position; polarised and socially disparate groups had their own political agendas; and political violence was raging across the country. There could be no absolute certainty about the future stability of a post-apartheid South Africa. The constitutional principles were a way of attempting to ensure that democratic practices could not easily be hijacked. 'No constitution is entirely resistant to the machinations of power-hungry politicians', asserted David Welsh, but the 1993 constitution was mindful of any subsequent abuse of power.[19]

One of the interesting features of the transitional period was the government of national unity (GNU), which was designed to last for a period of five years, from April 1994 to June 1999. The idea was originally conceived by Joe Slovo of the South African Communist Party, who introduced what became known as the 'sunset clause' that led to the birth of the GNU. Slovo argued that as the sun was setting on apartheid, the ANC should accept a power-sharing formula for five years

---

[17] Erasmus 1994: 8.

[18] Peter Leon, inteview.

[19] Welsh 1994b: 32.

to enable those who supported the former government to make a dignified exit from power.[20] This compromise agreement allowed for any party that gained at least twenty seats in the National Assembly to proportionate seats in the cabinet. The cabinet would consist of the president, the deputy presidents and no more than twenty-seven ministers to be appointed by the president. The underlying spirit of the GNU was intended to be one of compromise, yet the arrangements were really designed to 'reassure many of those who were still apprehensive about majority rule'.[21] The ANC admitted that compromises had to be made and acknowledged that a government of national unity was necessary because of 'the particular balance of forces' that existed in the country.[22] Although Nelson Mandela had been sceptical about the idea at first, he recognised that a coalition was a way of 'keeping the country together and defusing the threat of civil war'.[23] As Anthony Sampson asserts, both the ANC and the NP made concessions and moved to the centre ground, yet Mandela's and de Klerk's relationship was caustic and steeped in 'vitriol and suspicion'.[24] Both men were joint winners of the Nobel Peace Prize in 1993 for their role in steering the country towards democratic rule. Sampson, in summing up the qualities of the two leaders, found Mandela to have 'unique credentials and a history of sacrifice', while de Klerk 'took risks without losing his nerve'. In the final analysis, though, Mandela's pursuit of universal suffrage and majority rule provided the 'goal that unified his movement'.[25]

The relationship between the central and regional governments proved to be one of the most controversial in the negotiations, driven primarily by the demands of different groups. Opinions on the form of state, whether it should be unitary, federal or regional, remained the greatest stumbling block in the negotiating process. Some parties, united under the umbrella title the Freedom Alliance, including the Conservative Party, the Inkatha Freedom Party and the ruling party of the homeland of Bophuthatswana, looked towards different constitutional configurations for the future South Africa. The Conservative Party wanted an independent Afrikaner state, while the IFP preferred a devolved system of government.[26] The Freedom Alliance opted out of the formal negotiations, yet discussions continued between the ANC, the government and the alliance in order that some form of provincial arrangement could be decided upon. Ultimately, the recommendations resulted in the effective redrawing of the map of South Africa. The constitution made recommendations that nine provinces be created: Eastern Cape, Eastern Transvaal (later renamed Mpumalanga), KwaZulu Natal, Northern Cape, Northern Transvaal (later renamed Northern), North West, Orange Free State

---

[20] Jeremy Cronin, inteview.
[21] Commonwealth Observer Mission to South Africa 1994: 15.
[22] ANC 1994b: 5.
[23] Sampson 1999: 467.
[24] *Ibid.*
[25] *Ibid.*: 475.
[26] Sam Razak, interview.

(later renamed Free State), Pretoria-Witwatersrand-Vereeniging (later renamed Gauteng) and Western Cape[27] (see Figures 5.3 and 5.4). The boundaries were provisionally outlined by the Delimitation Commission for the purposes of the elections, although provision was made for changes to take place either by consensus before the elections or by referendum afterwards.

Under the interim constitution, each province had its own legislature, an executive council of not more than ten persons and a regional head of government or premier. Each party with more than 10 per cent of the provincial vote was entitled to seats in the cabinet, on a proportional basis. National and provincial governments had concurrent powers in areas such as culture, education, health, welfare, housing, local government, transport, tourism, urban and rural development, and trade, although the IFP later complained that only foreign policy, defence and macro-economics should have been placed within the sphere of central government, with regional government taking care of everything else.[28] The most appropriate policy for the former 'homeland' territories of Bophuthatswana, Ciskei, Transkei and Venda was to be their full reincorporation into South Africa before the elections.

Preparing for the elections

Few elections have been awaited with greater anticipation than those that took place in South Africa on 27 April 1994. Yet even politicians later admitted their apprehension and lack of certainty as to whether or not they would go ahead.[29] In a communiqué of October 1993, the Commonwealth heads of government looked forward to the 'historic significance' of the future elections but also cautioned that considerable difficulties stood in the way of 'holding free and fair elections'. The prevailing circumstances in the country created a potentially destabilising environment, and it was agreed that a sizeable international observer presence would be indispensable if confidence in the process was to be assured and the 'people of South Africa enabled to cast a valid ballot'.[30] A Commonwealth elections observer group (COMSA) took a close interest in the development of arrangements for the elections.

Two major pieces of electoral legislation were agreed by the Negotiating Council: the Independent Electoral Commission (IEC) Act was passed by parliament in September 1993, and the Electoral Act was passed three months later. The structure of the IEC is outlined in Figure 5.5. The IEC comprised between seven and eleven South African members, who were appointed by President de Klerk on the advice of the Transitional Council. The International Advisory Committee was allowed up to five members, also chosen by de Klerk, but the

[27] de Villiers 1994: 67.

[28] Sam Razak, interview.

[29] Cheryl Carolus, interview.

[30] Commonwealth Observer Mission to South Africa 1994: 54.

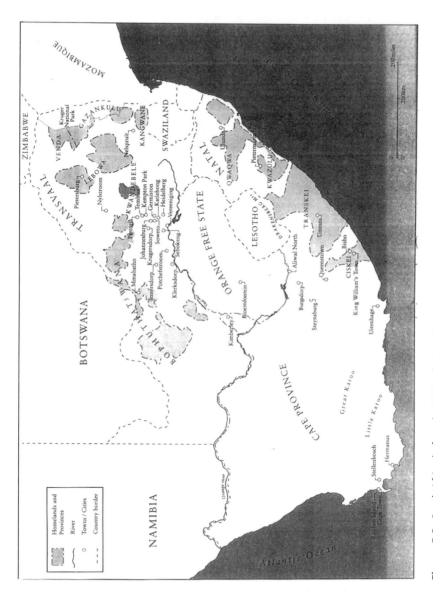

Figure 5.3 South Africa before the 1994 election (source: Barber 1999)

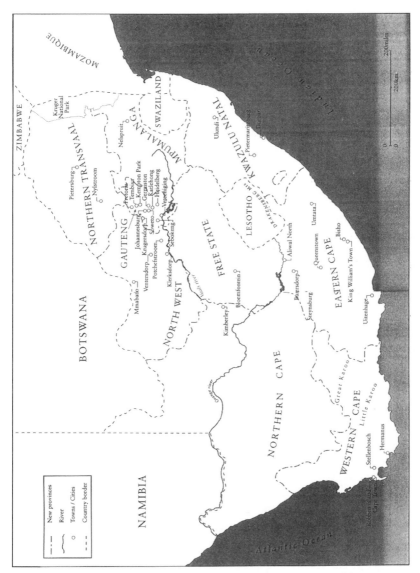

Figure 5.4 South Africa after the 1994 election (source: Barber 1999)

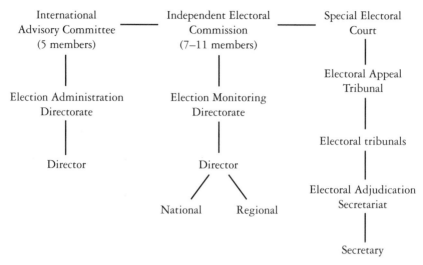

Figure 5.5 The structure of the Independent Electoral Commission

monitoring directorate appointed and coordinated election monitors. Electoral tribunals with authority to investigate electoral infringements and irregularities were established across the country. The staffing of the IEC was problematic, for although South Africa had considerable resources and personnel with experience of elections, the nature of those former racially exclusive events prohibited the formation of a representative group that would truly reflect the composition of the population. It was decided, therefore, that a number of IEC staff would have to be drawn from outside the existing bureaucracy.

The country's first non-racial elections were conducted under a form of proportional representation that the negotiators believed was the most appropriate electoral system for the country. The electorate voted for political parties rather than individual candidates, and the successful candidates were chosen from individual party lists. Each party applied to the IEC for registration and affirmed its commitment to the electoral code of conduct. The object of the code was to promote the conduct of free and fair elections and the creation of a climate of political tolerance. Box 5.2 outlines the electoral code of conduct. In such a politically and socio-economically polarised country, such a code was vital. It also had some powers of sanction for breaches of the code, including formal warnings, fines, forfeiture of electoral deposits, withdrawal of the right to campaign and ultimately, cancellation of the right to contest the elections. These provisions were taken further by the Electoral Act, which set out a range of offences relating especially to intimidation, bribery, impersonation and interference with canvassing and campaigning. Such offences resulted in fines or imprisonment. Demonstrations and marches were prohibited within 48 hours of polling day, and no public meetings could be held within 12 hours.

The franchise was extended to all citizens and permanent residents of South Africa over the age of 18 years. Children and spouses of citizens and former citizens of South Africa were entitled to vote provided that they intended to reside

---

Box 5.2 The 1993 electoral code of conduct

- Political parties, groups and individuals must respect the rights of others to express divergent political opinions, canvass support and campaign for the election.
- Commits political organisations to ensuring that voters are not intimidated or coerced; to repudiate bribery, incitement of hatred and false allegations; to comply with electoral processes and cooperate with the Independent Electoral Commission.
- Further commits political organisations to avoid discrimination on the grounds of race, sex, ethnicity, class, gender or religion, and to promote the role of women in the electoral process.
- Ensures parties and candidates accept the outcome of the elections and the Independent Electoral Commission's certification of the results.

Source: Commonwealth Observer Mission to South Africa, 1994

---

permanently in the country. There were a limited number of exclusions, notably the mentally ill, those dependent on drugs and prisoners convicted of major offences. Yet there was one essential feature upon which the introduction of electoral suffrage depended: voter education. It is worth remembering that while electoral knowledge is often taken for granted, the newly enfranchised citizens of South Africa had to be educated in the practical mechanisms of how to vote.

Learning how to vote and party identification

The media played an important role in bringing voter education messages to a large number of potential voters throughout the country. The headlines in the 1994 *Let's Vote* voter education manual were: 'Find out what is going on/Listen to the radio/Watch television/Read the newspapers/Go to meetings/Ask people to explain things to you.'[31] The information from TV and radio reached different groups of voters. Radio broadcasts were heard more often by black voters, while television was more successful in attracting coloured, Indian and white voters. Perhaps inevitably, radio programmes in African languages reached more black voters than broadcasts in English or Afrikaans. Table 5.1 shows the percentage of voters reached by radio, TV and newspapers. As Table 5.2 indicates, newspapers brought voter education to a small total number of voters, 41 per cent, which was partly related to high illiteracy levels in the country as a whole.

Voter education materials took different forms. Oral presentations and pamphlets were the most widespread methods of communicating voter information to more than 60 per cent of the electorate. A variety of films, videos, role playing,

---

[31] Moller and Hanf 1995: 7.

Table 5.1 Voters reached by radio, TV and the press before the April 1994 elections

	All South Africans (%)	Black South Africans (%)
Radio	68	78
Radio and TV	87	90
Radio, TV and press	88	91

Source: Moller and Hanf 1995: 8.

Table 5.2 Sources of voter information (all voters) before the April 1994 elections

Media	Total (%)	Black (%)	Coloured (%)	Indian (%)	White (%)
Radio	68	76	51	66	49
African Languages	51	77	11	8	4
English/Afrikaans	31	20	50	65	47
TV	66	61	79	89	72
English/Afrikaans	46	31	75	88	70
African Languages	41	57	26	22	10
Watch TV on weekdays	72	61	86	92	95
Newspapers	41	37	42	70	46
Read daily newspapers	39	34	50	58	49
Personal network					
Family	57	63	60	60	39
Friends/neighbours	54	64	61	55	26
Work/school	25	28	26	27	16
Church	22	28	21	12	6
Extended network					
Political party	43	54	36	28	18
Voter education	36	49	26	13	9
Trade union	6	8	6	6	1

Source: Moller and Hanf 1995.

mock elections and workshops were presented. Comic books and picture books were widely used, especially among black audiences. Yet more active forms of media presentation were favoured by younger and better-educated black voters, while comic books on voting found greater appeal among illiterate voters. Political parties played a role in the education campaign, although the ANC was considered to be the most active political agency. Figures 5.6 and 5.7 show the posters used by the ANC. Nelson Mandela announced to the post-electoral 1994 ANC National Conference that the party's 'emphasis on voter education had served the ANC well in the elections'.[32] Certainly, as Table 5.3 makes clear, when

---

[32] ANC 1994b: 8.

Figure 5.6 A 'Mandela for president' poster

Figure 5.7 An ANC election poster

respondents were asked whether they had received voter information from political parties, the 78 per cent registered for the ANC far exceeds the percentage for the other parties. Yet voter education should be distanced from political

Table 5.3 Voter education by political parties before the April 1994 elections

African National Congress	78%
National Party	10%
Inkatha Freedom Party	5%
Democratic Party	2%

Source: Moller and Hanf 1995.

Table 5.4 Useful voter information (all voters)

	Total (%)	Black (%)	Coloured (%)	Indian (%)	White (%)
My vote is secret	80	94	78	78	45
I can vote for whom I please	76	83	83	79	54
My right to vote or not	68	75	77	64	48
How to vote: procedures at polling station	64	79	74	65	21
Which documents entitle me to vote and how to get them	54	69	70	62	11
The difference between the first and second ballot	49	61	43	65	20
I can vote for the same or different parties on the two ballots	42	46	41	56	29

Source: Moller and Hanf 1995: 17.

mobilisation and indoctrination. In Moller and Hanf's study, all respondents were asked the question: 'Of what you learned about voting, which information was very important or useful to you?' The responses are outlined in Table 5.4. The secrecy of voting procedures was identified by all South Africans as a particularly important factor in the electoral arrangement, while among black voters it was the most significant factor in the voter education programme and rated a massive 94 per cent. The responses of the black community reflected the high level of political volatility in the country. The *Let's Vote* manual emphasised electoral secrecy in order to reassure the new electorate they had nothing to fear from reprisals. Irrespective of the electoral code of conduct, reported levels of intimidation were running very high, and secrecy was of the utmost importance in terms of voters' safety.[33] The instructions from the voter education campaign are outlined here:

[33] Gertrude Mzizi, interview.

REMEMBER: Your vote is a secret. Nobody will know who you vote for. Nobody can see who you vote for. You can vote for any party you want. If people ask you who you are going to vote for, you do not have to tell them (*Let's Vote* manual, voter education information).

Voter education took on a specific quality in the context of the South African elections, with political information assuming certain features. In an important analysis of the 1994 elections, Robert Mattes argues that racially differentiated experiences of apartheid, the liberation struggle and the transition all combined to inform voters of the party best suited to represent their interests. Because of the decades of separate development, information based on the past had different racially segregated sources. For example, as Mattes explains:

> White voters' perceptions of previous political events and party performance were heavily shaped by their understanding of their own economic and political interests, the threats to those interests and a particular interpretation of those past events conveyed by Christian National Education, the South African Broadcasting Corporation, the conservative Afrikaans national press or the liberal English print media.[34]

Equally, African voters had different political and economic expectations, and their experiences of the past were very different from those of the white community. Indian and coloured interpretations of the past straddled both African and white experiences. The effects of separate development meant that party identification corresponded with racial grouping. As Table 5.5 demonstrates, when party identification was aligned with racial grouping, the ANC, IFP and PAC were predominantly African parties, while the DP and the FF were supported mainly by whites. Ironically, during the 1994 election, 'only the NP, the creator of apartheid, had a multi-racial support base nationally'. Although over half its supporters were white, nearly 40 per cent were coloured and Indian and just under 8 per cent were black.[35]

Public perceptions of the various parties also revealed interesting aspects. The non-governmental organisation IDASA conducted a range of interviews with voters in order to identify how the public regarded the main political parties in terms of performance and their ability to engender change. The interviews hoped

Table 5.5 Racial breakdown of party supporters, 1994

	ANC	NP	IFP	FF	DP	PAC
African	94.4	7.8	88.0	–	2.2	94.4
White	0.2	52.3	11.7	100.00	88.8	–
Coloured	4.3	31.1	0.3	–	9.0	5.6
Indian	1.0	8.8	–	–	–	–

Source: Mattes 1995.

---

[34] Mattes 1995: 16.

[35] *Ibid.*: 24.

to reveal popular perceptions of the parties' effectiveness either in government or as extra-parliamentary agents of opposition. As majority political rights were denied under apartheid, a general analysis of how specific parties performed in a democratic partliament was not possible, and the general framework had to be expanded. Certain key issues were identified – political rights, political violence, law and order, and education – and respondents were asked to judge the performance of political parties by awarding them positive or negative ratings. Tables 5.6 to 5.9 record the responses.

The responses to the issue of violence are interesting in that more African respondents identified the IFP as an organisation that encouraged violence than the National Party, 53 and 24 per cent, respectively, while over half the white community and nearly one-third of coloureds felt that the ANC encouraged violence. However, marginally more whites believed that the ANC worked for rather than against freedom, 31 and 29 per cent, respectively. African perceptions of the ANC reached the highest percentage on the issue of freedom, with 79 per cent registering a positive performance. On balance, African perceptions of the NP were more positive than those accorded to the ANC by the white community.

Table 5.6 Voter perceptions of the ANC, 1994 (%)

	African	White	Coloured	Indian
Discouraged violence	67	8	27	40
Encouraged violence	12	52	32	15
Worked for freedom	79	31	43	78
Worked against freedom	4	29	15	5
Worked for law and order	68	7	31	52
Worked against law and order	7	41	24	8
Discouraged education	75	32	40	75
Encouraged education	7	17	20	5

Source: Mattes 1995.

Table 5.7 Voter perceptions of the National Party, 1994 (%)

	African	White	Coloured	Indian
Discouraged violence	13	61	50	52
Encouraged violence	24	4	7	2
Worked for freedom	6	37	44	43
Worked against freedom	33	9	10	5
Worked for law and order	18	68	58	75
Worked against law and order	18	1	6	2
Discouraged education	14	56	47	57
Encouraged education	23	3	6	2

Source Mattes 1995.

Table 5.8 Voter perceptions of the Inkatha Freedom Party, 1994 (%)

	African	White	Coloured	Indian
Discouraged violence	8	9	2	6
Encouraged violence	53	10	17	8
Worked for freedom	7	14	3	8
Worked against freedom	34	5	13	2
Worked for law and order	6	11	1	3
Worked against law and order	39	5	17	0
Discouraged education	9	10	1	20
Encouraged education	17	2	9	0

Source Mattes 1995.

Table 5.9 Voter perceptions of the Democratic Party, 1994 (%)

	African	White	Coloured	Indian
Discouraged violence	9	18	8	2
Encouraged violence	1	1	0	0
Worked for freedom	6	13	5	2
Worked against freedom	2	0	1	0
Worked for law and order	5	13	5	0
Worked against law and order	2	1	0	0
Discouraged education	4	13	5	5
Encouraged education	1	1	1	1

Source: Mattes 1995.

The voter education campaign took place during periods of violence and widespread intimidation in some regions. In fact, a month before the elections, 'operation access' was launched to ensure that voters could be reached in areas dominated by a single party.[36] As such, a pamphlet campaign was started in remote areas and in districts where there was political opposition to voter education. By April 1994, more than 90 per cent of the electorate had received some form of voter education. Some critics felt that the voter education campaign instructed voters on 'which party to vote for' rather than 'how to vote', and complaints of political bias were lodged with the Electoral Commission. Certainly, as Table 5.3 makes clear, the ANC devoted far greater resources to voter education than did other parties, and there was resistance to these activities in a number of localities. In fact, 165 areas were officially designated as 'no-go' areas, in which one party claimed total control over the population to the exclusion of all political

---

[36] Moller and Hanf 1995: 21.

Box 5.3 The method of voting in April 1994

- The voting officer examined the voter's eligibility document and confirmed the voter's identity.
- The voter's right hand was checked to see whether it carried the identification mark, which indicated that he/she had already voted.
- The voter's right hand and identity document were marked.
- The electoral officer handed the voter a ballot paper, having placed the official mark on the reverse.
- The voter took the ballot paper to a voting compartment and voted by placing a cross or other mark in the space next to the party of his/her choice.
- The voter displayed the official mark to the voting officer and placed the ballot paper in the ballot box.
- Signs were used to distinguish parties for those voters who were illiterate.

---

rivals. No-go areas were a reality of political life in 1994 and had to be accepted, but restrictions on campaigning were not the only worries confronting South Africa. The country was beset by bomb scares, racial violence and killings. In fact, the four-year transition period from February 1990 to April 1994 was a time of 'unprecedented political violence', and many voters anticipated the election with 'worry and anxiety'. Archbishop Desmond Tutu believes that the country came very close to the threatened 'bloodbath' that some had predicted.[37] For the Commonwealth Observer Mission, the setting of an election date, desirable though it was, simply created 'a different sort of battlefield'.[38]

Security arrangements

March and April 1994 were the most violent months in the history of political violence in KwaZulu Natal. The highest number of politically related deaths, 709, took place in August 1990, the moment when the government and the ANC agreed to negotiate and the time when the ANC agreed to the suspension of its armed struggle. In July 1993, the month when multi-party negotiators agreed on a date for the election, the number of politically related deaths totalled 581. And the Natal office of the Human Rights Committee of South Africa registered 429 deaths in March 1994. These killings took place a matter of weeks before the election was due to take place. In response to the crisis, on 31 March 1994, President de Klerk declared a state of emergency in KwaZulu and Natal under the powers

---

[37] Archbishop Desmond Tutu, address in St Paul's Cathedral, London, 1 November 1999; see also Guelke 1999 and Johnston 1996.
[38] *Africa World Review* 1994: 5; Johnson and Schlemmer 1996: 106; Cheryl Carolus interview; Commonwealth Observer Mission to South Africa 1994: 7.

of the 1960 Public Safety Act.[39] Under the state of emergency, security forces were given extraordinary powers of arrest, detention, search and seizure; military training by non-state parties was prohibited; the public display of weapons was forbidden; and any gatherings or processions had to gain authorisation before they were held. Deployment of the South African Defence Force in the region was increased from 1000 to 3000, which represented 14.6 per cent of the number of troops deployed nationally. By contrast with previous states of emergency, detainees were supposed to be given protection against ill-treatment, with lawyers appointed to visit and monitor their treatment. However, allegations of assault by the police continued to be made. Forty-six ANC members, who had been conducting military training, reported incidents of torture and the use of electric shocks.[40] An international observer group, appointed to monitor the actions of the security forces during the state of emergency, highlighted the dilemma facing the country:

> Many of the killings during the first week of the emergency could probably have been prevented by exercising the powers given to the security forces to go ahead with the preventative detention of individuals known to be disposed to kill or to organise killings for political reasons. But the political backlash of this measure could have generated even more violence, for the simple reason that many of those warranting preventative detention were political leaders.[41]

The reasons for the continued violence in KwaZulu Natal, Human Rights Watch Africa believed, resulted from the fact that the election did not 'settle the competition for political and physical territory between the ANC and the IFP'.[42] Adrian Guelke provides an interesting synthesis of the various interpretations of violence during South Africa's transition. Allegations of the existence of 'third force' activity destabilising society were made by the ANC, and such claims were later investigated by the Truth and Reconciliation Commission.[43] The violent actions between the ANC and the IFP were seen as evidence of strong racial and ethnic antagonisms within the country. While local rivalry often facilitated violent outbursts, as did the competing interests of the different parties, on some occasions acts of terror and random killings took place that seemed almost anarchic in character.

Whatever the nature of the violence, the events threatened to undermine the imminent elections. As part of its close interest in the preparations for the elections, the Commonwealth Observer Mission followed the debate regarding the creation of a national peacekeeping force. Members of the police, the military, political leaders and the ANC's defence organisation, Umkhonto we Sizwe, participated in a series of discussions and secret meetings about the proposal. The

---

[39] *Human Rights Watch Africa* 1995.
[40] *Ibid.*: 17.
[41] *Ibid.*: 18.
[42] *Ibid.*: 20.
[43] Guelke 1999; see Chapter 7.

need for such a force was demonstrated by the apparent lack of confidence of many South Africans in the police and the military. Yet as Mark Shaw maintains, political parties had to take some responsibility for preventing violence as most of it was 'fundamentally political' in origin.[44] Finally, the Independent Electoral Commission (IEC) called on the South African Defence Force (SADF) to assist in managing the elections. The SADF helped to transport ballot papers and equipment. When the polling period arrived, there was a great deal of apprehension in all spheres of the political environment. It was feared that extreme right-wing white groups would stage destructive protests against the elections and that the black community would riot. Rumours of impending action ranged from strikes and acts of sabotage that would close down electricity supplies to fears that incendiary devices would be placed inside ballot boxes. Although there were some incidents of right-wing activity, and the Electoral Commission monitors reported thirty-seven incidents of violence at polling stations, in general the electoral exercise was a peaceful and dignified event.

The 1994 election

Some new voters cried when they voted for the first time in their lives; pensioners, factory workers, ordinary people queued, walked or both for hours in order to vote. The patience, and the widely reported good humour in the queues, were the products of a deep desire to vote.

Figure 5.8 Voters waiting to vote
Source: *Election Talk*, Johannesburg, April 1999

---

[44] Shaw 1994: 190.

Table 5.10 Motivations to vote in the April 1994 elections (%)

	All voters	Black voters	White voters
I wanted to support my party	97	98	94
I felt proud to take part in the first elections for all South Africans	91	97	74
I am sure my vote was secret	91	92	87
When you get the opportunity to vote, you should use it	89	88	91
I knew the voting procedures well	84	81	92
There were enough monitors and security personnel at the voting station	89	81	88
There were many voters at the polling station and I had to wait a long time	63	77	32

Source: Moller and Hanf 1995: 34.

Around 86 per cent of the electorate participated in the historic 1994 elections, and as Table 5.10 demonstrates, for the vast majority of black voters pride in participating in their first elections was almost as important as the desire to support their respective parties. In effect, the elections ran over three days, with polling stations being opened on 26 April for 'special voters', e.g. the elderly, infirm and members of the security services on election duty, and 28 April being the last scheduled voting day. The Inkatha Freedom Party only agreed to enter the elections one week before polling took place, and a frantic rush ensued as ballot papers were amended to include the details of the organisation in order that voters could cast their ballots. According to R.W. Johnson, the IFP's decision 'transformed' the process and was responsible for 'the calm, even euphoric, spirit in which the election took place'.[45] One immediate effect was that it brought KwaZulu Natal into the electoral process, without which a democratic settlement could not have been fully contemplated. For the IFP, it was an astute move because the party captured over 10 per cent of the national vote, although around 90 per cent of that support was based in KwaZulu Natal. Yet the organisation did manage to gain over 170,000 votes in the Gauteng, formerly the industrial heartland of Johannesburg and its surrounding area. The number of political deaths in KwaZulu Natal fell significantly after the elections (see Table 5.11)

As Table 5.12 indicates, the ANC gained a huge electoral victory in the 1994 elections. Yet the National Party, together with the Inkatha Freedom Party, gained over 30 per cent of the total vote. The voting for the provincial legislatures resulted in the National Party gaining the largest share of the vote in the Western

[45] R.W. Johnson, in Johnson and Schlemmer 1996: 278.

Table 5.11 Political deaths in KwaZulu Natal during 1994

January	172	July	91
February	180	August	74
March	311	September	66
April	338	October	52
May	104	November	60
June	79	December	75

Source: *Human Rights Watch Africa.*

Table 5.12 Result of the 1994 election

	Percentage of vote	Seats in the National Assembly
African National Congress	62.6	252
National Party	20.4	82
Inkatha Freedom Party	10.5	43
Freedom Front	2.2	9
Democratic Party	1.7	7
Pan Africanist Congress	1.2	5
African Christian Democratic Party	0.4	2

Table 5.13 Result of the 1994 provincial election, Western Cape*

	Percentage of vote	Seats
National Party	53.3	23
African National Congress	33.0	14
Democratic Party	6.6	3
Freedom Front	2.1	1
African Christian Democratic Party	1.2	1
Others	3.8	0
Total	100.0	42

* formerly part of Cape Province.

Cape and the IFP attracting the largest percentage in KwaZulu Natal, 53.3 and 50.3 per cent, respectively. Of the nine new provinces, the ANC was in control of six and the NP and the IFP in control of one each, while the Northern Cape was equally balanced between the ANC and the combined opposition of the NP, the Freedom Front and the Democratic Party (see Figure 5.4; Tables 5.13–5.21).

Andrew Reynolds observed that when the ethnic distribution of voters was compared with the provinces in which the black population constituted over 80 per cent of the electorate, the ANC also won over 80 per cent of the popular vote.[46] In the Western Cape, the National Party was supported by both white and

---

[46] Reynolds 1994: 201.

Table 5.14 Result of the 1994 provincial election, Northern Cape

	Percentage of vote	Seats
African National Congress	49.7	15
National Party	40.5	12
Freedom Front	6.0	2
Democratic Party	1.9	1
Others	1.9	0
Total	100.0	30

Table 5.15 Result of the 1994 provincial election, Eastern Cape

	Percentage of vote	Seats
African National Congress	84.4	48
National Party	9.8	6
Democratic Party	2.1	1
Pan Africanist Congress	2.0	1
Others	1.7	0
Total	100.0	56

Table 5.16 Result of the 1994 provincial election, Free State*

	Percentage of vote	Seats
African National Congress	76.6	24
National Party	12.6	4
Freedom Front	6.0	2
Others	4.8	0
Total	100.0	30

* formerly Orange Free State.

Table 5.17 Result of the 1994 provincial election, North West

	Percentage of vote	Seats
African National Congress	83.3	26
National Party	8.8	3
Freedom Front	4.6	1
Others	3.3	0
Total	100.0	30

Table 5.18 Result of the 1994 provincial election, Gauteng*

	Percentage of vote	Seats
African National Congress	57.6	50
National Party	23.9	21
Freedom Front	6.2	5
Democratic Party	5.3	5
Inkatha Freedom Party	3.7	3
Pan Africanist Congress	1.5	1
African Christian Democratic Party	0.6	1
Others	1.2	0
Total	100.0	86

* formerly PWV province.

Table 5.19 Result of the 1994 provincial election, Northern Province

	Percentage of vote	Seats
African National Congress	91.6	38
National Party	3.3	1
Freedom Front	2.2	1
Others	2.9	0
Total	100.0	40

Table 5.20 Result of the 1994 provincial election, Mpumalanga*

	Percentage of vote	Seats
African National Congress	80.7	25
National Party	9.0	3
Freedom Front	5.7	2
Others	4.6	0
Total	100.0	30

* formerly Eastern Transvaal.

coloured voters. However, the ANC polled 33 per cent of the total vote, which represented a far greater percentage than the actual number of black voters in the province, around 19 per cent (see Table 5.22). Clearly, there was some transference of votes between different racial groups. The results in KwaZulu Natal were not surprising: the Zulu-based Inkatha Freedom Party won over half the popular vote. The number of seats allocated to each provincial legislature was based on the size of the population in those areas. At a national level, Reynolds analysed the extent to which party support was constituted on racial lines. Tables 5.23 and 5.24 illustrate that while support for the ANC was predominantly racially based, votes for

Table 5.21 Result of the 1994 provincial election, KwaZulu–Natal

	Percentage of vote	Seats
Inkatha Freedom Party	50.3	41
African National Congress	32.2	26
National Party	11.2	9
Democratic Party	2.2	2
Minority Front	1.3	1
Pan Africanist Congress	0.7	1
African Christian Democratic Party	0.7	1
Others	2.1	0
Total	100.0	81

Table 5.22 Ethnic distribution of voters within provinces (%)

	Black	White	Coloured	Indian
Western Cape	19	25	55	1.0
Northern Cape	31	18	51	0.2
Eastern Cape	84	8.2	7.5	0.3
North West	85	12	3	0.3
Free State	82	15	3	0
Gauteng	69	26	4	1.0
Northern	96	4	0.2	0.1
Mpumalanga	83	16	1	0.5
KwaZulu Natal	76	10	1.6	13.0

Source: Reynolds 1994.

the National Party cut across racial divides. Thus the constituency of the National Party in the 1994 election was racially mixed (see also Table 5.5 for the exact racial breakdown of party support). In the aftermath of the elections, much interest was shown in the fact that coloured voters gave 68 per cent of their votes to the National Party, 25 per cent to the ANC and 5 per cent to the Democratic Party.[47] Their overwhelming support for the NP was ascribed to the assumed 'traditional affinity' or 'conservatism' of coloured people.[48] It was also seen as irrational given the party's role in their oppression. Yet numerous opinion surveys pointed to disenchantment with the political process among the coloured community and feelings of marginalisation.[49] The issue of the 'coloured vote' was to return during the 1999 elections.[50]

---

[47] The coloured vote in the Western Cape, *EISA Update 15*, Johannesburg, 25 June 1999.

[48] *Ibid.*

[49] See Deegan 1998.

[50] See Chapter 8.

Table 5.23 How the ANC's vote was constituted

Community	Approximate vote
Black	11.5 million
Coloured	0.5 million
Indian	150,000
White	50,000
Total	12.2 million

Source: Reynolds 1994.

Table 5.24 How the National Party's vote was constituted

Community	Approximate vote
White	1.9 million
Coloured	1.2 million
Black	0.5 million
Indian	0.3 million
Total	3.9 million

Source: Reynolds 1994.

The Independent Electoral Commission's official pronouncement on the conduct of the elections was that, nothwithstanding organisational difficulties, they were largely free and fair. Although international observers recognised that campaigning by all political parties was 'impossible' in large parts of the country, they did acknowledge that South Africa's elections were taking place in a 'post-conflict' environment.[51] They were the 'elections of liberation' and were, therefore, unlikely to conform to democratic norms. The elections were the first step towards a new political climate and the 'celebration of freedom'. For the first time in the country's history, all people, irrespective of their racial origins were granted 'dignity' within the political arena. Inevitably, the elections represented not only the symbolic act of political freedom but also the 'historic moment in the course of the transfer of political power from the white minority to the democratic majority'.[52] The dreadful years of apartheid were finally over. The next task was to rebuild the country.

[51] ERIS interim report 1994.
[52] Cheryl Carolus, interview; ANC 1994b: 6.

Box 5.4 Excerpts from President Mandela's address to the nation at his inauguration on 10 May 1994

Out of the experience of an extraordinary human disaster that lasted too long, must be born a society of which all humanity will be proud. We, who were outlaws not so long ago, have today been given the rare privilege to be host to the nations of the world on our own soil.

We deeply appreciate the role that the masses of our people and their political, religious, women, youth, business, traditional and other leaders have played to bring about this conclusion. Not least among those is my second deputy president, the Honourable F.W. de Klerk.

The time for the healing of the wounds has come.

We have, at last, achieved our political emancipation. We pledge ourselves to liberate all our people from the continuing bondage of poverty, deprivation, suffering, gender and other discrimination.

We enter into a covenant that we shall build a society in which all South Africans, both black and white, will be able to walk tall, without any fear in their hearts, assured of their inalienable right to human dignity – a rainbow nation at peace with itself and the world. We are humbled and elevated by the honour and privilege that you, the people of South Africa, have bestowed on us, as the first president of a united, democratic, non-racial and non-sexist government.

We must, therefore, act together as a united people, for national reconciliation, for nation building, for the birth of a new world.

Let there be justice for all.

Let there be peace for all.

Let freedom reign.

God bless Africa.

Chapter 6

A time of change

Basic needs

With the elections over, the government of national unity (GNU) confronted the enormous difficulties facing the country. Together with the newly elected President Mandela, the former president, F.W. de Klerk, and Chief Buthelezi of the Inkatha Freedom Party sat in the cabinet. The National Party portfolios included the ministries of finance, mineral and energy affairs, environment, agriculture, welfare and population development, and provincial and constitutional development. The need for conciliation and consensus meant that the ANC alliance of the South African Communist Party (SACP) and the Congress of South African Trade Unions (COSATU) had to work in cooperation with other political organisations. Generally, the verdict on the GNU was that it was necessary and appropriate. It also operated adequately during an uneasy transitional period. The former ANC deputy secretary general felt that the government played a crucial mediatory role and acted as a force between conflicting interests.[1] The spirit of the government at that time was one of 'reconciliation' in providing a 'culture of negotiation'.[2] Even former president F.W. de Klerk admitted that for the first couple of years the new cabinet 'functioned surprisingly smoothly'.[3]

Most of the MPs who entered parliament in the aftermath of the April 1994 elections had not planned for it. Apart from those who served in the earlier tricameral structures, most came with no direct parliamentary experience, having not had the chance to participate in the political life of the country. Parliamentary experience was therefore limited to the National Party, the Democratic Party and other MPs drawn from previous institutions. The new democratic parliament was filled with people who had either returned from political exile or imprisonment, or fought in South Africa during the years of the struggle. Consequently, it was a very mixed environment in terms of members' political experience. Some worries were expressed that its great diversity might prevent it operating efficiently and effectively. Yet the government's strong emphasis on nation building and reconciliation forged a climate of 'co-operative law-making ahead of petty party

---

[1] Cheryl Carolus, interview.
[2] Mendi Msimang, interview; R. Meyer, speech, 1995.
[3] F.W. de Klerk 1999: 344.

differences'.[4] This transitional phase was essential in steadying the country, and parliament peformed well in terms of the quantity of laws it passed: 108 bills per session over the first three parliamentary sessions.

During the apartheid years, South Africa had little experience of consensual decision making, and the GNU was important in providing a framework for defusing potential problems. Yet tremendous challenges confronted all South Africans. The effects of the apartheid heritage were grim. The ANC had inherited a society that was characterised by deep socio-economic divides. Millions of people were victims of abject poverty, and the overwhelming majority were black. The condition of their lives was defined by 'joblessness, homelessness, landlessness with no access to education, health or opportunities for self-advancement'.[5] As outlined in Box 6.1, when the new democratic government assumed office, the basic needs in the country were formidable.

The asymmetrical nature of South Africa's development under apartheid produced a first/third world society: an industrialised, urban, technological society running in parallel with an impoverished rural hinterland. Fifty years of economic policies that favoured the white minority created an economy characterised by serious structural weaknesses. A deep divide had been created between the affluence of a privileged few alongside the extensive poverty and social deprivation of the majority. Until the early 1990s, four mining groups accounted for 80 per cent of the value of shares quoted on the Johannesburg Stock Exchange, with Anglo-American Corporation and De Beers accounting for half the value of shares quoted.[6] The economy and society had to be transformed if, as the ANC asserted, the country was to achieve non-racialism, development and equity.

Reconstruction and development

The Reconstruction and Development Programme (RDP) described itself as 'an integrated socio-economic framework aimed at building a democratic, non-racial and non-sexist community'.[7] It was originally the creation of the ANC, the South African Communist Party, the Congress of South African Trade Unions, the South African National Civics Organisation and the national Education Co-ordinating Committee, but it quickly became the centrepiece of the new government's programme for socio-economic transformation. The RDP contained six basic principles, which underpinned its political and economic philosophy:

(1) The programme had to be integrated and sustainable.
(2) Development was not about the delivery of goods to a passive citizenry. It was about active involvement and growing empowerment.

---

[4] James 1998.
[5] ANC 1996a.
[6] Overseas Development Institute 1994.
[7] Gauteng Provincial Government 1995.

Box 6.1 Profile of the basic needs in South Africa, 1993/94

Nutrition

- 25% of children under the age of 5 suffer from stunting as a result of chronic malnutrition, i.e. 3.37 million children.
- Malnutrition affects physical development as well as mental development, thus placing children at a disadvantage for the rest of their lives.

Water

- Nearly 25% of South African households do not have access to piped water, while only 40% actually have water laid on to their homes.
- Only 17.5% of all African households have access to piped water in their homes:
  - (a) 33% have to fetch water from other sources, such as rivers, streams, dams, springs or boreholes.
  - (b) 7.7% of African households in rural areas have piped water in their homes.
- 40% of African households in metropolitan areas have piped water in their homes.
- Over 99% of all white and Indian households have water laid on.

Energy

- 45% of all households in South Africa do not have access to grid electricity.
- 75% of African households in rural areas are not connected to the national grid.
- Many households in rural areas are experiencing serious energy shortages due to the depletion of fuel wood stocks and because alternative energy sources are unaffordable.

Housing

- Just under 1 million households live in shacks in South Africa.
- Around 500,000 households live in hostels.

Sanitation

50% of all households in South Africa have flush toilets:

- nearly all white and Indian households have toilets.
- 88% of coloured households have toilets.
- 34% of African households have flush toilets.
- 41% of African households have pit latrines.
- 6.5% of African households have bucket toilets.
- 16% of African households have no form of toilet.

▶

Health

Life expectancy

- 73 years for whites.
- 60 years for Africans.

Infant mortality rate for children under 5

- Range from 36.9 per 1000 births for all mothers 15–19 years of age to 81.1 per 1000 births for all mothers 45–49 years of age.
- For African mothers 30–34 years of age: 85.1 per 1000 births.
- For white mothers 30–34 years of age: 2.2 per 1000 births.

Source: Compiled from the South African Living Standards and Development Survey, 1994.

(3) It would ensure peace and security for all. There would be a national drive for peace, and endemic violence would be combated. Action would be taken against drug trafficking, gun running, lawlessness and the abuse of women.
(4) The RDP would embark on nation building and observe respect and protection for minorities. 'Unity in diversity' was the slogan.
(5) The programme would improve infrastructure and extend modern and effective services.
(6) Through democratisation, people would be enabled to participate in decision making.

The government would be accountable, and special attention would be paid to the empowerment of women in general and of rural black women in particular.[8]
The RDP grouped the following major policy areas:

- meeting the basic needs of the people;
- developing human resources;
- building the economy;
- democratising the state and South African society;
- implementing programmes.[9]

Meeting the basic needs of the people essentially implied the provision of jobs, houses, water, electricity, transportation, nutrition, health care and social welfare. The RDP hoped that people would be involved in regeneration programmes at the grass-roots level. Building the economy had to focus on growth, development, reconstruction, redistribution and reconciliation. Increased export capacity would

---

[8] *Ibid.*
[9] *Infospec* 1994.

be linked to industry, trade and commerce. The past policies of labour exploitation and repression were to be redressed and the imbalance of power between employers and workers corrected. The RDP intended to be involved with the economy, job creation, housing, public transport, health care, welfare and land reform. Initially, the programme attracted near-universal political support, but lack of progress towards the achievement of its aims soon undermined the initiative. The practical implementation of the programme's policies had been underestimated and undercosted. The financial resources necessary to improve disadvantaged communities were far beyond the 2.5 million rand (£250,000) budget that had been allocated initially. The population's basic needs, listed in Box 6.1, did not include other demands on the state, e.g. educational deficiencies, levels of unemployment, access to basic infrastructure such as roads and telecommunications, and access to basic services such as postage, refuse collection, street lighting and recreational facilities. The extent of poverty in the country was so great that 'it could easily absorb all the government's time and resources'.[10]

By 1996, it was clear that the RDP could not meet the wider needs of society and that it had failed to deliver its overambitious goals. Initially, the construction of 1 million houses within five years was the target, yet in two years only 15,000 houses had been built. However, some progress was made in areas such as electrification and water supply. The 1.3 million new electrical connections and 650,000 water extensions reached 6.4 million people. Additionally, private–public joint ventures were pioneered in various sectors: 550 clinics were built, 2358 were upgraded and free health care was made available to pregnant women and children under the age of 6.[11] In a sense, it was clear from the beginning that the programme could never fully reach its objectives. The problems and social divisions in the country were just too great. However, despite its difficulties the RDP served as a means of galvanising attention and interest in the economy and social redress during the post-election transitional period.

Economic challenges and unemployment

For many South Africans, the country's past racism was not purely a matter of attitudes and beliefs of white superiority and black inferiority; it was intrinsically linked to the acquisition of economic resources.[12] Yet when the ANC came into government in 1994 it was moving away from a policy of state intervention in the economy and towards a more market-oriented approach. In fact, one of the contradictory elements in the short-lived RDP was, on the one hand, its commitment to meet the population's needs, with its implication of strong state intervention and radical redistribution of wealth, and on the other hand, its affirmation of the free market. Policies of rapid industrial nationalisation and land appropriation

[10] Barberton 1995: 6.
[11] Maseko 1998.
[12] Hlope 1998.

were rejected in favour of privatisation and economic growth. F.W. de Klerk believes that the National Party's greatest contribution to the government of national unity was its promotion of a balanced economic policy framework that could 'assure growth and progress'.[13] Yet by the time the government changed its economic strategy, the National Party had decided to withdraw from the GNU. Party representatives claimed that its decision was influenced by the ANC's refusal to make concessions on power-sharing arrangements.[14] In June 1996, the government introduced a new economic policy, 'Growth, Employment and Redistribution' (GEAR), which set out specific targets:

- an economic growth rate of 6 per cent per annum;
- the creation of more than 1.3 million new jobs outside agriculture;
- an 11 per cent average growth in real manufactured exports;
- a 12 per cent average growth rate of real investment.

As Table 6.1 outlines, South Africa's major imports in 1994 were machinery and equipment, while base metals, gold and diamonds remained the country's major exports. This emphasises the country's dependence on commodities whose prices were fixed by international markets over which the government had no control.

The introduction of GEAR was controversial, predominantly because the tripartite alliance of the ANC, the Congress of South African Trade Unions and the South African Communist Party had not resolved its attitude towards the market economy. Although the 1997 ANC Conference passed a resolution upholding the basic objectives of GEAR, there were numerous arguments in the National Assembly between various ANC ministers. These divisions occurred because in certain quarters there had been no ideological shift away from the notion of some form of socialist, quasi-planned, egalitarian economy in which the government created jobs and was a major player in the economy. The National Party claimed that one of its functions in the government of national unity had been to steer a course away from the socialist tendencies of the ANC. But apart from the attitudes of the ANC alliance there was an intellectual climate in wider society that was

Table 6.1 Exports from and imports into South Africa, 1994

Major Exports	% of total	Major imports	% of total
Unclassified (gold)	36.2	Machinery and equipment	33.0
Base metals	13.2	Transport equipment	14.9
Jewellery (diamonds)	11.4	Base metals	4.5
Total	60.8	Total	52.4

Source: Economic Intelligence Unit 1996.

[13] F.W. de Klerk 1999: 345.

[14] Ray Radue, interview.

suspicious of capitalism. In part, this resulted from the historical experience of apartheid, which was seen as coterminous with capitalism and operating against the interests of ordinary people. Although Anthony Sampson claims that during the pre-electoral negotiations the ANC's 'settlement with international capitalism was as important as the settlement with de Klerk', there were still many South Africans who felt very uneasy about this situation.[15] For some commentators, the racial component in the early development of the mining industry still 'connected racism and the economy' in the new South Africa,[16] while the role played by the trade union movement in fighting the strictures of apartheid remained an important factor in its bargaining position.

One of the major criticisms of the 1994–1999 government has been that it reneged on its commitments to the 'working class', that is, organised trade unionists, in the interests of an emerging black bourgeoisie. The dynamics of the government's shift in economic policy has been explained as 'The growth of a black middle class with interests counter to that of the majority, and the seeming end of any discourse on alternatives to capitalism within the boundaries of the nation state'.[17] Quasi-Marxist class analyses have ignored the very real desires of the population to improve their lives and those of their children. Equally, they overlooked the vast employment inequality that existed in the business sector, with black representation in management statistics being desperately low (see Box 6.2). The link between race and economic inequality has been one of the greatest threats to South Africa's young democracy. For employment at managerial level to become more equal, black South Africans have to aspire to higher employment status in the labour market and should not be berated for doing so. In fact, it has been necessary for black workers to join management structures so that the personnel of corporate employers reflects the demographic balance of the country.

Box 6.2 Employment inequality: key management statistics, 1998/99

- 85% of all managers are white.
- 93% of all senior managers are white.
- 92% of all executive managers are white.
- Black Africans make up 15% of all management levels.
- Women make up 35% of all management levels.
- Black, coloured and Indian women make up 6% of junior and middle management.
- Black African women make up 6% of all women in management.

---

[15] Sampson 1999: 473.
[16] Ngwema 1997.
[17] *Ibid.*

In 1997, 9410 people, 1928 of whom were professionals, left South Africa. Surveys indicated that 75 per cent of newly qualified chartered accountants sought work abroad. These figures have reflected badly on South Africa's economy. The GEAR policy has had mixed results, with investment, savings and employment growth failing to reach targets. Although economic growth was 3.1 per cent in 1996 and 1.7 per cent in 1997, it fell short of its objectives of 3.6 and 2.9 per cent, respectively. Real private investment growth in 1996 and 1997 was 6.1 and 3 per cent, respectively.[18] In terms of the country's demographic structure, the highest percentage of the population is under 18 years of age (see Table 6.2).

Since 1994, unemployment has continually been a problem for the government and has been estimated at running between 33 and 36 per cent of the economically active population. Yet these figures have tended to underestimate the fact that many people are working in the informal sector. A study by the South African Institute of Race Relations revealed that although respondents were strictly unemployed, some money was earned informally (see Table 6.3). However, these findings have not minimised the problem of youth unemployment. In 1996, the unemployment level was 55 per cent among young male blacks. The ANC foresaw difficulties with the young, particularly those who had campaigned so strongly against apartheid. Its 1994 report made sobering reading:

> The young have been severely disadvantaged by the system of apartheid. As a result many young people face a bleak and hopeless future with little prospects of securing

Table 6.2 Demographic trends. Total population = 41.4 million (1995)

Age Profile	% of total population, 1994
0–18	47
18–64	45
65+	8

Source: Economic Intelligence Unit 1996.

Table 6.3 Unemployed household members earning more than 100 Rand (£10) per month (%)

African	35.0
Coloured	38.0
Indian	41.7
White	66.5
All unemployed	36.5

Source: South African Institute of Race Relations 1996.

---

[18] For greater detail, see Blumenfeld 1999: 44.

meaningful employment or overcoming a plethora of social and economic difficulties they have to contend with.[19]

The new democratic government of South Africa had to deal with the consequences of the youths' struggle against apartheid. Looking back, although 1976 was a momentous time for the young and a period of great politicisation, during the early 1990s there was much discussion about the so-called 'lost generation'. What had started as a struggle against an oppressive regime ended with accusations of 'undisciplined township youth' whom no political organisation could control. At the time, *The Sowetan* newspaper expressed anxiety about the effects of the deepening schooling crisis: 'The fruits of liberation and freedom, now within our grasp, will be extremely bitter if we produce another "lost generation" ... But this time we will have only ourselves to blame.'[20]

After the elections, the ANC commissioned research to discover whether or not there was a 'lost generation'. The findings revealed that young people had suffered a lack of education caused by the school boycott and the disruption of their struggle against apartheid. Consequently, their educational attainment was barely beyond that of an elementary grade, that is, the level of a 10-year-old. The ANC admitted that levels of educational attainment were so low that even if more jobs became available some sections of the black community would be unable to take them.[21] Therefore, training had to concentrate on basic literacy, numeracy and technical skills.

In order to redress the balance, a number of business organisations contributed to training programmes, including Johannesburg Consolidated Investments Limited Chairman's Fund, which made a donation of 260,000 rand (£26,000) to help to initiate training courses in self-employment. Much attention has focused on the development of black African entrepreneurship, and one of the strategies used to increase employment opportunities for young people has been the stimulation of self-employment and small business development. However, a World Bank report suggested that there were a number of complex constraints. Formerly, under apartheid, blacks were restricted to operating a narrow range of businesses, mainly township-based retail enterprises. They were prohibited from operating in white areas. Although the economic environment changed after 1994, certain factors continued to affect black businesses. Inadequate business premises and tenure arrangements were an inheritance of the apartheid years, when whites controlled the allocation of all formal business sites. Over 70 per cent of all small black businesses operated from the home. Equally, after 1994 black entrepreneurs faced institutional barriers, including a lack of access to finance. Large financial organisations were reluctant to provide the venture capital needed simply to start up a business. As Table 6.4 makes clear, over 70 per cent of the problems confronting black entrepreneurs have been concerned with lack of finance, inadequate premises

---

[19] ANC 1994b: 31.

[20] *The Sowetan*, 1993.

[21] Cheryl Carolus, interview.

Table 6.4 Most important problems facing black micro-enterprises* (%)

Constraints	At start-up	At time of survey
Crime and violence	4.4	7.2
Getting a licence	1.8	0.2
Inadequate premises	18.0	15.7
Lack of finance	22.5	9.4
Problems with law enforcement authorities	10.5	6.6
Unfavourable business conditions	32.0	51.2
Cost of doing business	12.7	20.3
Poor market conditions	19.3	30.9
Other	10.8	9.7

* Those employing less than five people.
Source: World Bank 1995.

Table 6.5 Black micro-enterprises in South Africa, 1994

Age in years	% of owners
16–20	2.0
21–30	33.2
31–40	32.9
41–50	18.2
51–60	8.6
61 and older	5.1

Source: World Bank 1995.

and unfavourable business conditions. Subjugated for so many years, it was not surprising to discover that the black community 'needed to know and understand more about the basics of business'.[22]

Although small enterprises in the informal sector had limited access to markets because business premises were scarce and poorly located, there was evidence of young black entrepreneurial activity. A World Bank study found that the owners of 'micro-enterprises', that is, those with five or fewer workers, tended to be concentrated in the lower age brackets, 35 per cent being less than 30 years of age. As Table 6.5 indicates, the highest percentage of small business owners is in the 21–30 age bracket. As unemployment is high among this group, the World Bank believes that the connection between unemployment and the creation of micro-businesses is reinforced. However, the report also raised the issue of educational deficiencies.[23] Around 30 to 40 per cent of entrepreneurs had too little education, less than Standard 4 – the level of a 10-year-old – to be functionally literate (see

---

[22] Molise 1996.
[23] World Bank 1995.

Table 6.6 Educational level and monthly turnover of black micro-enterprises in South Africa, 1994

Educational level	% of owners	Monthly turnover (rand)	Number of firms
No education	8.5	1106.38	48
Less than Standard 4	18.7	1111.96	102
Standards 4–6	33.8	1237.00	185
Standards 7–9	29.8	1540.52	163
Standard 10	7.6	2484.55	42
Post-school education	1.6	985.55	9

Note: The sample size was 549 firms. On average, children are 10 years old when they enter Standard 4; they have completed five years of schooling and are functionally literate. On completing Standard 8, children are 16 years old. Standard 10, also called Matric., represents the completion of formal education. The exchange rate in 1999 was around 10 rand = £1.
Source: World Bank 1995.

Table 6.6). Additionally, given that the quality of education in many areas in the late 1980s was very poor, the level of functional literacy could be even lower. Educational levels and turnover figures were closely associated. Entrepreneurs who had achieved a Standard 10 (level for an 18-year-old) level of education had an average turnover nearly twice that of those who had completed only Standard 8 (level for a 16-year-old).

However, it would be misleading to portray a depressing image of black entrepreneurship. Many black companies have been established in what has been referred to as a 'black economic empowerment boom', yet capability and competence are essential if they are to succeed. Although 'being black is good for business', black entrepreneurs fully recognise that most black companies stand little chance against their white counterparts in terms of experience and capacity. Under these conditions, black businesses have needed government help through enabling legislation in order 'to be in a better position to compete'.[24] White companies have adopted a policy of 'fronting' black partners in order to win government tenders. Some entrepreneurs have seen this approach as mutually advantageous in that the white company gets the business and the black partners share in the wealth. Yet others feel uncomfortable at being too closely associated with companies run by whites. In fact, the issues of black empowerment in general and ANC embourgeoisement in particular have been ridiculed and treated with contempt by white analysts. Commentators have sneered at ANC figures, accusing them of 'racing to catch up with the finer tastes of former leaders'. Much has also been made of a past socialist liberation movement now upholding capitalism and acquiring a taste for Mercedes and cellphones. R.W. Johnson recalls the past: 'It is hard to credit the heady days of 1990–1994 when men who are now besuited ministers marched in demonstrations declaring their faith in socialism and "people's

---

[24] Matshitse 1998: 23.

Box 6.3 President Mandela

It is true that we should not forget where we come from, but we must be careful not to be held hostage by the past, to the detriment of harnessing new energies of progress which are unleashed by the new situation.

Source: Interview, *Siyaya*, 1998.

---

power".[25] Although some people have enriched themselves, why should black business people not acquire the wealth that a number of the white community have enjoyed for decades? In the future, generations of black South Africans will be graduating from universities with aims of good employment rather than politicking against a repressive racist regime.

Transformation, affirmative action and gender

When commentators highlight the complexity of the transformational processes in South Africa, they point to the historical and demographic context of the country. For many, the impact of ingrained racial prejudice makes any speedy transformation of either the economy or society unlikely. As Pemmy Majodina, former treasurer-general of the ANC Youth League, asserts: 'Transformation will be a very slow progress.'[26] Yet the ANC has repeatedly placed a premium on transformation of the economy and has introduced employment equity legislation to ensure that employers introduce measures to reform their policies. The issue of the wage gap between racial groups, which was part of the heritage of apartheid, has focused attention on employment practices. South Africa's income distribution is among the most unequal in the world, with 20 per cent of income earners capturing only 1.5 per cent of national income while the wealthiest 10 per cent capture 50 per cent.[27] It became clear to former labour minister Tito Mboweni that inequalities could not be remedied by simply outlawing discrimination: 'Our constitution has already done that.' In order to give practical effect to the country's Bill of Rights, 'specific programmes were needed to redress imbalances'[28] (see Appendix 4).

One of the central difficulties of transforming employment practices has been the attitude of the business sector. A survey carried out in 1997 questioned the business community about its feelings towards transformation and received the following response: 'Asking us to support transformation is rather like asking a turkey to endorse Christmas.'[29] That remark raised many assumptions about change, how it would be enacted and what outcomes might result. Put simply, the 1998

---

[25] *cf.* Adam *et al.* 1998: 166; Johnson 1996.
[26] Pemmy Majodina, interview.
[27] *Transit* 1998.
[28] Mboweni 1998: 5.
[29] *Transit* 1998: 10.

Employment Equity Act promoted equal opportunity and fair treatment in employment through the elimination of unfair discrimination and through strategies of affirmative action. These strategies involved targeting actions to redress the disadvantages experienced by specific groups, e.g. African, coloured, Indian, female and the disabled, in the workforce. Any employer, irrespective of the number of people employed or the financial turnover of the company, was required to adhere to sections of the Act that prohibited unfair discrimination in employment policies and practices. Such discrimination could be on the basis of race, gender, sex, pregnancy, marital status, family responsibility, ethnic or social origin, colour, sexual orientation, age, disability, religion, HIV status, conscience, belief, political opinion, culture, language or birth. This extensive list accorded with the clauses upheld in the Bill of Rights. Discrimination was not regarded as unfair if affirmative action measures were taken or if there were inherent requirements of the job.

In respect of affirmative action, all employers of fifty or more workers had to adopt measures to ensure that suitably qualified people from designated groups had equal employment opportunities and were equitably represented in all occupational categories and levels of the workforce (see Box 6.4). The definition of 'suitably qualified' included any one or any combination of a person's formal qualifications, prior learning, relevant experience or the capacity to acquire, within a reasonable time, the ability to do the job.

Box 6.4 Affirmative action measures contained in the 1998 Employment Equity Act

Employers of over fifty workers should:

- introduce measures to identify and eliminate employment barriers, including unfair discrimination;
- adopt measures to ensure further diversity in the workplace;
- make reasonable accommodation for people from designated groups, e.g. African, coloured, Indian, female and the disabled, in order to ensure their representation in the workplace;
- introduce measures to retain and develop people from designated groups;
- consult with employees through trade union organisations or nominated representatives.

As Tables 6.7 and 6.8 indicate, the racial and gender disparities between income levels reflected the situation that prevailed during the apartheid years. When these figures are compared with the racial breakdown of the population it becomes clear that only radical policies could deal with these inequalities (see Table 6.9).

Companies, in consultation with their employees, would draw up employment equity plans to be published with their annual financial reports, thus ensuring a degree of accountability and transparency. Companies would no longer be able to

Table 6.7 Unemployment – race and gender, 1994 (%)

	African	Coloured	Indian	White
Women	44.2	24.7	16.6	5.5
Men	33.6	17.4	8.1	3.7

Source: SARDC 1997: 20.

Table 6.8 Income ratios by race, gender and education as a percentage of income of white men with similar education, 1994

Level of education	Black women	Black men	White women	White men
Standard 5–6 (elementary)	10	25	75	100
Standard 7–8 (elementary)	10	10	40	100
Standard 9–10 (matriculation level)	5	20	40	100
Diploma	35	45	55	100
Degree	n/a	65	45	100

Source: SARDC 1997: 25.

Table 6.9 Racial breakdown of the population, 1994

Population aged 2–64	Number	% of total population of working age
African women	6,169,658	34.9
African men	6,243,918	35.2
Coloured women	834,463	4.7
Coloured men	794,199	4.4
Indian women	272,501	1.5
Indian men	265,716	1.5
White women	1,563,408	8.9
White men	1,585,382	8.9
Total	17,729,245	100.00

Source: White 1995b: 13.

withhold information about their employment practices. The equity plans intended to clarify recruitment and selection procedures, salary, training, performance targets, promotions, and disciplinary measures. Equally, adequate timetables had to be established setting out realistic targets for recruitment, specifying affirmative action strategies and detailing any special measure that might need to be adopted.

The employment equity legislation intended to achieve fairness in employment and correct past discriminatory practices that systematically disadvantaged black people, women and the disabled. However, corporations have often responded with the assertion: 'We're in business to a make money, not to promote social welfare.'[30] In a national survey of some of the top 100 companies in South Africa, chief executive officers and human resource directors noted the following problems:

- a lack of trust and confidence between different racial groups;
- a breakdown in communication between groups;
- prejudice and stereotype assumptions;
- poor teamwork;
- decreased productivity;
- inter-group conflict; and
- a high staff turnover, especially among those previously disadvantaged people recruited.[31]

Some critics of the government's policy have referred to affirmative action as a policy of 'reverse discrimination' against the white community. Whites have feared replacement or non-promotion, the coloured and Indian communities have been apprehensive about increasing marginalisation, and some sections of the black community feel that the policy might suggest that they have been employed or promoted solely because they are black and not on the basis of merit. Businessmen like Peter Matshitse, a former communist and member of the South African Students' Organisation, argued strongly in favour of merit rather than preferment: 'I want to be recognised as a good businessman, not a charity case.'[32] The Inkatha Freedom Party felt that affirmative action should be concerned with abolishing obstacles to promotion:

> There should be a meritocracy not a quota system because standards will be lowered. There should be open and equal opportunities, but affirmative action can risk leading to a culture of entitlement and privilege. This must not happen to black people.[33]

In order for employment equity legislation to be successful, a climate of acceptance must exist within wider society.

Results from the case studies of fourteen South African companies, including Siemens, South African Breweries, Independent Newspapers and First National Bank, revealed that among those companies with employment equity plans, implementation was still uncertain. Management failed to take a strong lead, and the monitoring of moves towards equity was generally absent.[34] Although employees were sent on training courses, which appeared to be politically correct, no attention

---

[30] *Ibid.*: 4.
[31] *Ibid.*
[32] *Infospec* 1995; Matshitse 1998: 23.
[33] Gertrude Mzizi, interview.
[34] *Transit* 1998: 4.

was paid to career development. In essence, the business community has to be receptive to employment reform, and as one black corporate leader highlighted, 'transformation should not be a shorthand for merely redressing inherited racial imbalances'.[35] While the objective of reform was the creation of employment opportunity and progress for previously disadvantaged sections of society, it was important to look forward rather than reliving past injustices. Saki Macozoma cautions: 'The obvious pitfall in launching transformation is to simply castigate those who have been before, who represent the past. That must be avoided, because all you are doing is building resistance.' In looking to the future, the country has to shift away from the past. Macozoma urges: 'However dark the history, it doesn't help to be constantly reminding people of it. What you must do is focus on the good things, remind them of the good things they have done.'[36] However, this can be difficult when past practices intrude into present working realities.

The issue of the apartheid wage gap and the need for employers to supply details about salary structures for all employees has continued to affect labour relations. Equally, the legacy of the former coloured labour preference policy, in which jobs were reserved for coloureds rather than black Africans, is still apparent. As Andrea Weiss argues:

> The effects of the policy are still glaringly evident. For example, 12,000 people work for the Cape Town municipality yet only 1000 workers are Africans. Equally problematic was the resultant atmosphere of suspicion, with Coloureds regarding their jobs as threatened and Africans smarting over the degree to which they seemed deliberately obstructed in the job market.[37]

As Cape Town houses South Africa's parliament, it was deeply offensive 'to have black people running the country at one end of the town while, at the other, the most senior black person is probably a messenger'.[38] The situation in Cape Town is difficult to remedy in the short term and demonstrates that the pervasive and racially divisive policies of the apartheid years will take some years to redress. In a sense, government has to work with business in making employment equity and affirmative action function effectively. Inevitably, when the ANC promised its black African constituency 'visible social and economic change', the spectre of rapid improvement was envisioned. Yet these objectives could never be met immediately. As the business sector continued to need skilled, trained and educated workers, times of disequilibrium between government and business were bound to emerge. Clearly, if the process of socio-economic restructuring is to move forward it must be on an incremental basis. Transformation of business is not going to happen overnight: 'It should be a drawn out process that empowers, enriches and affirms people. That is a process, not an event.'[39]

---

[35] Macozoma 1998/99: 3.
[36] *Ibid.*; Cheryl Carolus, interview.
[37] Weiss 1998: 27.
[38] Hanekom 1998.
[39] Matshitse 1998.

One of the central planks of the post-1994 South African government has been to upgrade the role of womern in society. Women of all ages wanted their voices to be heard and regarded equal rights between women and men as vital in a changing society. As Thenjiwe Mtintso put it, 'the eradication of patriarchy depends on changing attitudes'.[40] In terms of the legal status of women, the common law rule whereby a husband obtained marital power over his wife and her property was repealed in 1993. The Guardianship Act of 1993 gave married couples equal guardianship rights over minors. Previously, only the father had been the natural guardian of a child born within marriage. The position of women, President Mandela repeatedly stressed, should be 'radically changed for the better'. The first White Paper on Reconstruction and Development referred to economic gender discrimination, such as employment obstacles in public works projects, unpaid labour, credit constraints for women with limited collateral, and inadequate resource allocation to child care and education.[41] Certainly, gender divisions existed within industry and agriculture, as Table 6.10 makes clear. Although given the preponderance of mining work these figures might not seem surprising, it should be remembered that women of all races were excluded from apprenticeships under apartheid.

In 1996, it was estimated that unemployment among young black women was around 70 per cent, yet it would be both wrong and misleading to presume that women were disinclined to work.[42] In fact, historically it is well documented that women in black South African society 'perform all the hard work, planting and tilling the earth, digging, and thrashing besides cooking and collecting water'. Recent studies have collated the time rural women spend collecting wood for fuel and found that it ranged from 90 minutes to three hours.[43] One sector in which participants are almost exclusively women is that of domestic service. During the 1970s, women only entered domestic service out of necessity as conditions were

Table 6.10 Agriculture and industry by gender, 1994 (%)

Occupation	Men	Women
Agriculture, forestry and fishing	77.8	22.2
Mining, quarrying	94.3	5.7
Manufacturing	68.4	31.6
Electricity	85.1	14.9
Construction	91.4	8.5
Transport, storage and communication	87.4	8.6

Note: these are the figures as originally published, although not all rows add up to 100%.
Source: SARDC 1997.

---

[40] Mtintso 1996.
[41] Gauteng Provincial Government 1995.
[42] Febe Polgeiter, interview.
[43] White 1995b: 25.

poor, with long hours and very little time off.[44] Low educational attainment has further hampered progress in the labour market. In 1991, of the 160,000 African girls who took examinations on leaving school only 14,675 passed. The segregated educational system and the denial of equal educational rights during the apartheid years restricted opportunities to men and women. Although the ANC-led government has reformed educational practices, the effects of the previous system manifest themselves in the low levels of literacy, low enrolments in primary, secondary and tertiary institutions, and high drop-out rates. Literacy rates are higher in urban areas than in rural localities, and since there are more women in the rural areas, this has gender implications. Literacy levels differ between women from different racial groups. Whereas 99 per cent of white women over 15 years of age are literate, a third of all black women in the Transkei have had no education at all.[45] Table 6.11 outlines the great differences between literacy levels in urban and rural areas and between racial groups.

At every level of the public tertiary educational sector, black women are underrepresented, with the exception of the correspondence university, the University of South Africa (UNISA). Yet their predominance in that institution is only in relation to black men. UNISA still had a largely white intake in 1995.[46] One principal of a private commercial college identifies lack of confidence as the major drawback for young women entering either higher education or the labour market.[47] But white women at lower educational levels earn far more than black women and men. The government has committed itself to promoting the advancement of women in non-traditional fields by encouraging women to train in scientific and technical areas, information technology, and communications. Resources have been made available to the Department of Education to develop gender-sensitive programmes, and the government has made the first ten years of schooling compulsory.

Another important factor that has led to discrimination against women in the labour market is child bearing and child rearing. The high fertility rate among

Table 6.11 Literacy in urban, rural and metropolitan areas by race, 1994 (%)

	African		Coloured		Indian		White	
	literate	illiterate	literate	illiterate	literate	illiterate	literate	illiterate
Rural	39	61	32	68	–	–	92	8
Urban	53	47	55	45	84	16	86	14
Metro	61	39	74	26	78	22	91	9

Source: SARDC 1997.

[44] *Ibid.*; Buijs 1995.
[45] SARDC 1997: 34.
[46] White 1995b.
[47] Helene Rubin, interview.

African women, an average of 4.6 births per lifetime with 49 per cent of preg-
nancies occurring before a woman is 20 years old, limits women's educational,
training and employment opportunities. Development workers have continually
emphasised the importance of support systems for women who want to study, but
few training or academic institutions offered child-care facilities. In 1996, legislation was passed that permitted abortion for young women without parental
permission. It was seen at the time as a radical attempt by the government to gain
some control over the increasing birth rate and to offer a choice to pregnant
women. However, it is the division between urban and rural men and women that
is most polarised: 70 per cent of rural women make a subsistence living from agriculture. Historically, because men worked away in the mines, women had to take
over agricultural production together with bringing up children and struggling
to find fuel. As Anthea Billy explains: 'Rural women were at the bottom of the
heap because of discrimination on grounds of race, class and gender.'[48] The legacy
of the system of migrant labour, which allowed men to be employed in urban
areas, but not women, and the constraints of influx control, which admitted men
under regulated circumstances but prohibited the movement of women into the
cities, is that an asymmetical demographic structure emerged. Men of working
age outnumber similarly aged women in urban areas, where there are some possibilities of employment, by 1.1 million, whereas women outnumber men by 1 million in the rural areas.

Many commentators suggest that traditional customary law remains a potent
force in the lives of rural women despite the Bill of Rights and the government's
commitment to gender equality.[49] In rural areas, a strong relationship exists
between land ownership and decision-making powers. Since land is traditionally
granted to the male head of household, it automatically means that males acquire
powers to be involved in the local community. Historically, women were not
allowed to attend community meetings unless specifically called upon to do so.
This situation has changed due to political reforms, but given the nature of rural
society and the restricted employment opportunities, the main resource for rural
women is land. A key factor that contributes to the failure of women to overcome
poverty has been their lack of access to and rights to own land. The government
recognised women's need for land ownership in its Communal Properties
Association Act of 1996, which formalised the communal tenure system and
encouraged women to join land ownership schemes. The ANC is generally
acknowledged to have taken the issue of gender seriously.

As Table 6.12 demonstrates, one-quarter of all members of the National
Assembly in 1994 were women. During the apartheid era there were few women
in elected positions. For example, in 1985 only 2.8 per cent of parliamentarians
were women. The percentage of women in parliament has increased substantially
since the 1994 elections, and this can be attributed to the ANC's decision to

---

[48] Billy 1996.
[49] *Ibid.*; White 1995a.

Table 6.12 Gender composition of the national government, 1994

National Government	Females	Males	Total
Ministers	2	25	27
Deputy ministers	3	9	12
National Assembly	100	300	400
Senate	16	74	90

Source: SARDC 1997.

include a 33.3 per cent quota of women on its party lists. The ANC Women's League, which has been in existence since 1950, ensures that women are adequately represented in all decision-making structures of the ANC. The 1995 local elections resulted in a number of women becoming councillors and mayors. These new political representatives provide role models for younger women. Women occupy just under 20 per cent of the seats in local government, and they come from very different backgrounds: some are university-educated, while others are domestic workers. The influx of women into councils has brought a new approach to issues, and female councillors are tackling basic needs: the provision of crèches, help and protection for battered women, homelessness, and squatter camps. Women have a big role to play in politics:

> The hard jobs are done by women. They must keep their kids safe and protected. Men look after their own needs first, not looking to the children, the community. Single-parent families are many and are headed by women. A women councillor understands their problems.[50]

Questions of personal identity usually centre on racial, ethnic, religious, linguistic, national and gender categories. In South Africa there are many different identities. The country has eleven formal languages and numerous informal ones. Under the 1996 constitution a special clause was devoted to languages; the official ones are Sepedi, Sesotho, Setswana, siSwati, Tshivenda, Itsonga, Afrikaans, English, isiNdebele, isiXhosa and isiZulu. There is still a tendency for people to define themselves under the old apartheid criteria; that is, coloureds regard themselves as non-black and non-white. The coloured community is an ethnic minority that tends to distinguish itself from the dominant national category. According to IDASA opinion polls, there exists 'a palpable sense of marginalisation' from the new political system among the coloured communities, particularly in the Cape.[51] In a sense, this distance is inherited from the divisive legacy of apartheid, which placed coloureds 'above' blacks and 'below' whites, with the effect that 'the resulting middle ground became home for the various coloured communities', a place where 'uncertainty and ambiguity dwells'. Other analysts are scathing in their assessment of the so-called 'beneficiaries' of the apartheid

---

[50] Sophie Masite, interview.
[51] James et al. 1996: 14–15; see also IDASA Public Opinion Survey No. 3, 1996.

Table 6.13 Negative views of government by racial/ethnic category, 1995 (% of respondents)

Question	Coloured	White	African
No contact with MPs	67	87	76
Government too complex	59	39	44
MPs not helpful	46	33	16
National government does not represent people like me	36	57	7

Source: Adapted from IDASA public opinion survey No. 8, May 1996: 15.

years including not only whites but also the coloured and Indian communities.[52] Surveys have indicated that the coloured community in the Western Cape has shown 'the least commitment to democracy', either because of political apathy or alienation.[53]

Although the attitude of white respondents in Table 6.13 might be considered predictable, the response of coloured interviewees is high with over one-third of the respondents feeling that the government did not represent their interests. The coloured community has felt ignored by the new government regardless of the fact that racial segregation has been abolished. As one coloured respondent put it: 'We used to be squeezed out by the whites now we are squeezed out by the blacks.'[54] These attitudes have been reflected in the political preferences of the coloured community in the Western Cape, who continued to support the National Party in

Table 6.14 Voter turnout in local elections, 1995 (%)

Province	Turnout of eligible voters
Western Cape	60
Northern Cape	55
Eastern Cape	35
North West	38
Free State	38
Gauteng	36
Northern Province	38
Mpumalanga	36
Total	38

Source: Adapted from IDASA 1996, No. 6.

---

[52] *Ibid.*; M. Mamdani, TRC Conference, University of Sussex, September 1998.

[53] IDASA 1996 No. 3: 1.

[54] Non-survey interviews conducted with stall holders, shop workers and taxi drivers, Cape Town, 22–4 September 1996.

both the 1994 national elections and the 1995 local elections. Although the turnout rate for the 1995 local elections was very low, 38 per cent compared with the 86 per cent turnout in 1994, the electoral procedures were different. In the local elections voters had to register initially to vote. Despite a strong media campaign, both registration and turnout were low for a variety of reasons: failures in voter education, fear of registration, concerns about the secrecy of the ballot, apathy, indifference and lack of knowledge.[55] Table 6.14 outlines the voter turnout in each province. Interestingly, the highest turnout rates were in the Western Cape, where nearly two-thirds of the electorate voted, thus indicating that coloured voters were sufficiently motivated to participate in elections that concerned them most.

---

[55] See Johnston and Spence 1995; Deegan 1998 for discussion of local elections.

Chapter 7

Coming to terms with the past: the Truth and Reconciliation Commission

> *One did not need to be a political activist to become a victim of apartheid; it was sufficient to be black, alive and seeking the basic necessities of life (Truth and Reconciliation Commission Report, Vol. 1, Chapter 2).*

> *The human rights violation hearings restored dignity and provided a ritual of telling and naming the dead (A. Krog, Truth and Reconciliation Commission, in* Pulse, *1998).*

In 1992, several South Africans visited countries in Eastern Europe to discover how they were coping with their democratic transitions. One specific issue continually re-emerged: how do emerging democracies deal with past violations of human rights?[1] The early 1990s were critical years for South Africa in that negotiations were beginning, but there was much uncertainty as to their progress. At that stage, no one could be sure that the country would move towards majority rule and away from oppression and violence. If the nation was to make that transition, particular problems had to be confronted. Analysts argued that it was time for 'issues of memory, forgetfulness and history to enter the public sphere'. Was it possible for the people of South Africa to deal with apartheid? To what extent could human atrocities be forgotten? Could communities reject hatred and potentially live in harmony?[2] South Africa's polarised society had created differentiated racial histories, all of which needed to be reclaimed and re-examined. Chief Justice Mahomed asserted:

> For decades South African history was dominated by a deep conflict between a minority which reserved for itself all control over the political instruments of the state and a majority who sought to resist that domination. Fundamental human rights became a major casualty of this conflict.[3]

---

[1] Boraine *et al.* 1994: ix.

[2] Duvenage 1995.

[3] Chief Justice D.P. Mahomed Final Report, Truth and Reconciliation Commission, Vol. 1, Chapter 2.

A process had to be found through which a collective memory of the country could engage in recognising the tragedy of the past. Only by looking back would the nation be able to move towards normalised multiracial coexistence.

In 1973, the United Nations defined apartheid as a crime against humanity. The framers of the new democratic constitution of 1993 had to deal with the country's 'brutal history', and a number of options were discussed.[4] South Africa could ignore the past and refuse to acknowledge individual or societal sufferings and institute a form of 'general amnesia'. According to Archbishop Desmond Tutu, who ultimately became chairman of the Truth and Reconciliation Commission, apartheid supporters wanted a process that let 'bygones be bygones'. However, F.W. de Klerk claimed that he always recognised that some mechanism was needed that 'promoted mutual understanding of one another's motives' and allowed for the 'closing of the book on the past'.[5] With the high levels of violence on the eve of the 1994 elections, this option seemed unlikely. In any case, as Tutu made clear, 'the negotiators were aware that unless our past was acknowledged and dealt with adequately it could blight our future'. He recalled philosopher George Santayana's phrase: 'Those who cannot remember the past are condemned to repeat it.'[6] These views militated against the adoption of another option, that of general amnesty. It was possible for the government to award a general amnesty to all those who had perpetrated human rights abuses. However, this option would deny the experiences of victims of apartheid by implying that 'what happened to you was of no consequence'. In effect, it would 'victimise the victims' by not acknowledging the pain and suffering inflicted by the years of apartheid.[7] Conversely, the government could introduce Nuremberg-type trials for those who had committed crimes against humanity. Such trials had been used effectively in post-Second World War Germany. But South Africa was not emerging vanquished from a war; rather, it had to negotiate with supporters of the former regime and attempt to establish a mutual accommodation. In any case, members of the previous administration were part of the negotiating committee and were destined to sit in government and hold important ministerial offices. The Nuremberg option was never viable and would have run the risk of the 'police or military subverting the process'. With 'cadres of arms all over South Africa', the country would have been propelled into civil war.[8] Given the scale of violence between 1990 and 1994, the nation was already on the verge of catastrophe and the holding of divisive Nuremberg-type trials could have pushed it over the edge. Far from promoting reconciliation, trials would have created great rancour and resentment among people with whom the new government had to cooperate.

A fourth possibility was to leave all prosecutions to the usual legal channels. The viability of this option depended on whether these procedures could deal with

---

[4] Boraine *et al.* 1994.
[5] Archbishop Desmond Tutu, St Paul's, London, speech, 1 November 1999; F.W. de Klerk 1999: 369.
[6] Tutu *ibid.*
[7] *Ibid.*
[8] *Ibid.*

complex cases, particularly when evidence was scarce. Fears also existed that the process would incur vast costs that the country simply could not sustain. Finally, the nation could opt for some kind of truth and reconciliation commission, which might help society to adjust to a changed political environment and contribute towards a relatively peaceful transition. This option also raised criticism and increased the contention surrounding the whole exercise. Many South Africans felt that the past had to be forgotten in the interest of political stability, while others believed that a form of retribution was necessary. F.W. de Klerk recalled that he wanted an appropriate process to deal with the conflict of the past, one that would put an end to 'destructive, aggressive debates and recriminations'.[9] But he too was ambivalent about a commission of inquiry without the benefit of amnesty. Nelson Mandela also feared that investigating the past and holding public accounts of human rights abuses would stir up hostility and resentment rather than forging reconciliation. Nevertheless, a decision had to be made if the negotiations were to continue. During the 1993 multi-party discussions, while the interim constitution was being drafted, a compromise decision was reached, which, Tutu argued, effectively 'opened the door to the holding of the 1994 elections'.[10] The Truth and Reconciliation Commission (TRC) would be established to provide public acknowledgement of and reparation to the victims of gross abuses. An amnesty clause was inserted in the 1993 interim constitution, and only afterwards did the parties 'sign the negotiations'.[11] It was agreed that conditional amnesty would be granted to the perpetrators of gross human rights violations.

The inclusion of the amnesty clause may have eased the negotiations, but where was the issue of justice? 'Can it ever be right for someone who has committed the most gruesome atrocities to be allowed to get off scot-free, simply by confessing what he or she has done?'[12] Desmond Tutu raised this question when considering the relationship between amnesty and justice. The justice to be gained by the TRC was of a restorative kind, more concerned with healing relationships through a process of admission rather than through retribution and punishment. In 1995, the National Assembly passed the Promotion of National Unity and Reconciliation Act, which established the Truth and Reconciliation Commission. The TRC was given a mandate to establish the causes, nature and extent of gross violations of human rights committed under apartheid between 1960 and 1994 through the medium of investigations and hearings. It was to compile as complete a picture as possible of these events. The time frame was limited in order to place in a historical context the country's struggle for independence. It was recognised that conflict had engulfed South Africa since the mid-seventeenth century and that atrocities committed during the specific period of the commission's remit must be placed in the context of a much longer time frame. The 1960 Sharpeville

---

[9] F.W. de Klerk 1999: 369.
[10] Tutu, 1 November 1999.
[11] *Ibid.*
[12] Tutu 1999: 47.

massacres, with which the mandate of the commission began, were 'simply the latest in a long line of similar killings of civilian protesters in South African history'.[13] But it became clear that it would be impossible for a commission to cover over 200 years of grievances and wrongdoing by various administrations. It had to concentrate on a manageable period, and one that citizens could easily recall.

One deeply contentious aspect of the Act was the arrangement for the granting of amnesty to perpetrators of violence. No expression of remorse, contrition or apology for actions committed was required. The conditions for gaining amnesty were as follows:

- Any action for which amnesty was sought had to have occurred between 1960 and 1994.
- The action had to be politically motivated. Perpetrators did not qualify for amnesty if they killed because of personal greed, but they did qualify if they committed actions in response to an order, or on behalf of a political organisation, or the state, or a recognised liberation movement.
- The applicant had to make a full disclosure of all the relevant facts relating to the offence for which amnesty was being sought.
- The rule of proportionality had to be observed, in that the manner in which an offence was carried out was proportionate to its objective.[14]

If these conditions were met amnesty was granted, and although victims could oppose applications for amnesty they had no right of veto. Those seeking amnesty had to admit guilt and be prepared for the glare of media and public attention. Tutu believed that the admission of guilt was a 'powerful means of reasserting human dignity, not only to victims but also to the perpetrators'.[15] The Act limited the commission's investigations to gross violations of human rights, defined as 'killing, abduction, torture or severe ill-treatment' or the 'attempt, conspiracy, incitement, instigation, command or procurement to commit' such acts. Thus the TRC was restricted to examining only a fraction of the totality of human rights violations that emanated from the policy of apartheid.[16] Millions of South Africans were subjected to racial and ethnic oppression and discrimination on a daily basis, which the commission described as 'systematic, all-pervading and evil'. For many, the policy of apartheid was itself a human rights violation in that an individual's civil and political rights were defined by a single unchangeable factor: skin colour. Yet the commission eschewed notions of vengeance or retribution by focusing not only on those violations committed by the former state but also on those committed by all parties to the conflict. In order to carry out its tasks, the commission, which ran for a period of two and a half years, was divided into three separate

---

[13] TRC Report Vol. 1.Ch. 2: http://www.polity.org.zan/govdocs/commissions
[14] Tutu 1999.
[15] Tutu, 1 November 1999.
[16] *Ibid.*

committees: the Human Rights Violations Committee, the Amnesty Committee and the Reparation and Rehabilitation Committee.

The Human Rights Violations Committee

The task of the Human Rights Violations Committee was to investigate gross violations of human rights in or outside South Africa and to record all allegations made by survivors and the families of victims. It was the committee's responsibility to establish how and why such violations took place and who were responsible; the identity of the victims; their fate or whereabouts; and the nature and extent of the injuries and harm they suffered. The committee also had to reveal whether or not the violations resulted from deliberate planning by the state or any other organisation, group or individual.[17] Representative and demonstrative cases were chosen from among the statements taken, and these were presented at public hearings. In selecting which persons would be granted a public hearing, the commission took certain considerations into account:

- The nature of abuse in the community or area. The commission selected a group of victims whose experiences represented the various forms of human rights abuse that had occurred in the area.
- The various groups that had experienced abuse. The commission selected a group that included victims from all sides of the conflict in order to present a picture of abuse from as many perspectives as possible. In many instances, the commission had to pro-actively seek out victims from particular communities.
- The cases had to be representative in relation to gender, race, age and geographical location in the area in which the hearing was to be held.[18]

The statement takers were especially selected for their ability to listen to stories told by people in their chosen language. They had to distil the essential facts and record them in English, the language of the commission. Equally important was their ability to listen with empathy and respect so that the interview itself became 'part of the therapeutic and healing work of the Commission'.[19] Interviews would often take several hours and involve both the interviewee and the statement taker in an intense process of reliving anguishing experiences. Both parties were often deeply affected by the interview. The commission admitted that statement takers were at the forefront in helping people to come to terms with the past and, as a result, many actually received counselling themselves.[20] Archbishop Desmond Tutu, as chairman of the TRC, believes that the process gave everyone, irrespective of their position or status, the 'opportunity to tell their story in their own

[17] Human Rights Violations Committee: http://www.truth.org.za/hrv.htm.
[18] TRC Report, Vol. 1, Ch. 6, 32–3.
[19] Ibid.: Vol. 5, Ch. 1, 5.
[20] TRC Conference, University of Sussex, September 1998.

Table 7.1 Will the Truth and Reconciliation Commission promote reconciliation?

Respondents	% Yes
African	70
Asian	59
Coloured	53
White	26

Source: question asked in an opinion poll conducted by the Human Sciences Research Council of South Africa, 1996.

words', and these sentiments were echoed during the official hearings.[21] From its inception the commission hoped to achieve national reconciliation, but initial public reactions to it were mixed and divided racially. In 1996, just as its hearings were about to start, an opinion poll was conducted by the Human Sciences Research Council on the question of whether the commission would promote reconciliation. Table 7.1 demonstrates that a strong positive response emerged from black South Africans, and more than 50 per cent of the Asian and coloured communities registered support. However, members of the white community were far more negative about the process, with around 74 per cent of respondents expecting the Commission to fail.

When statements had been taken and submitted to the information management team for perusal and collation, the Human Rights Committee in the region would select those to be included in the public hearings. At these hearings, survivors and families of victims told of how they had been victimised. More than fifty public hearings were held across the country, and 21,000 individual statements alleged human rights abuses; 7124 statements were made by people requesting amnesty for acts they had committed, authorised or failed to prevent.[22] The hearings soon became the public face of the commission, with some assuming a religious quality. Prayers often initiated a session, and memorial candles were lit. Despite criticism of these rituals in the media, it was quickly accepted that public participation in hymns and singing helped to assuage moments of 'extreme emotion and drama'.[23] The tension in halls, recalled Desmond Tutu, was 'palpable', with the atmosphere becoming almost 'holy' because of the 'depth of emotion'. 'The telling of the story was often cathartic. Truth emerged after so many years of obfuscation and denial.'[24] The stories were also harrowing, and many communities were shocked by what they heard (see Box 7.1).

The main strength of the TRC was in the human rights violations hearings:

---

[21] *Sanibona* 1998.
[22] From Truth to Transformation, CIIR 1999: 6.
[23] TRC Report, Vol. 5, Ch. 1, 4.
[24] Tutu, 1 November 1999.

Box 7.1 Statements recorded by the Truth and Reconciliation Commission

Recurring thoughts of traumas that have been experienced continued to invade the lives of many South Africans. Mr Madala Ndlazi's 16-year-old son was shot by the police on 16 June 1986. At the public hearing he told the Commission that memories of his son's death haunted him to that day:

> I found my child brought to the home. I found him in the dining room. He was lying dead there in the dining room. When I looked at him, it was very painful for me to see how injured he was. My wife and I knew he would die … but the way in which my son was injured, makes me very painful. I cannot forget this. It is almost ten years now.

At the Johannesburg hearing, Ms Hawa Timoi spoke of her pain after the death of her son, Ahmed Timoi, at the hands of the security forces:

> I told the police that if my body had a zip they could open the zip to see how I was aching inside.

Many members of the state forces, both conscripts and career officials, described their experiences of being caught up in and traumatised by situations over which they had no control.

> I was hyper-vigilant, I was having screaming nightmares every night for at least six months. Whenever I heard a loud noise, I would dive to the ground. When I heard helicopters, I would look for somewhere to hide.

Physical disabilities alter a victim's life. Ms Elizabeth Mduli was an 18-year-old student during the 1986 school boycotts in Nelspruit. During a protest gathering she was shot by the police. At the public hearing she told the commission:

> What worries me, and what actually made me feel very painful, is because I am not a member of any organisation and I am not actually a person who is affiliated to any movement. But today I am crippled because it is just that I was found at school. That was my sin.

The particularly grim situation in KwaZulu Natal was described by Ms Nosimelo Zama at the Durban hearings:

> The stress on family life created by the constant pressure of the violence in this province cannot be underestimated. Parents were separated in the violence, children ran away from home, some were taken by the police, others were never found.

Family members were regularly detained in order to extract information about the whereabouts of wanted persons. Three of Ms Edith Mjobo's sons were activists in the Cape in 1985:

> As they were looking for my sons, they used to arrest my husband. And they used to cover his face with black plastic bags and torture his genitals. He became sick because of this. He suffered a lot until he died.

Source: Truth and Reconciliation Commission Report, *Consequences of Gross Human Rights Violations on People's Lives*, Volume 5, Chapter 4, pp. 1–10.

For the first time, the country heard the previously silent voices ... High profile commissioners travelled to little towns throughout the country to hear the stories of those people who before had been marginalised and ignored ...The Commission's translation facilities allowed victims to testify with dignity, integrity and wisdom.[25]

A post-hearing workshop revealed that the Commission had given people the opportunity of a disclosure they had formerly been denied: 'by telling their story people have shared a burden.'[26]

> The Commission tried to listen, really to listen – not passively but actively – to voices that for so long had been stilled. And as it listened to stories of horror, of pathos and of tragic proportion, it became aware of the high cost that has been paid by so many for freedom. Commissioners were almost overwhelmed by the capacity of human beings to damage and destroy each other. Yet they listened, too, to stories of great courage, concluding often with an astonishing generosity of spirit, from those who had for so long carried the burden of loss and tragedy. It was often a deeply humbling experience (Report of the Truth and Reconciliation Commision, Volume 5, Chapter 8, p. 2).

Equally, during the amnesty hearings people heard the grim and painful truth for the first time. In determining the actions of the security forces against resistance and counter-actions by armed opponents of apartheid, categories of torture and killings were defined.

Killings and torture

The first 'political hangings' took place in 1959, a year before the beginning of the commission's mandate period. In 1961, approximately twenty people were sentenced to death after the Pondoland revolt. Subsequent acts of resistance resulted in further hangings. Between 1960 and 1994 there were thousands of incidents of public disorder. The creation of a specialised riot control function in South Africa's policing agencies was a reaction to the disorder and political unrest arising from resistance to apartheid. As the resistance grew, so the police wanted a specialised capacity to 'control unrest' and looked to new training methods and riot control units. The South African Police were not equipped to deal with a domestic uprising of the scale they faced in June 1976. The police who faced the massive protest marches at that time were ordinary officers drawn from nearby stations, with no special skills or training in crowd control. The then minister of police, Jimmy Kruger, reported at the cabinet meeting of 10 August 1976 that unrest in Soweto continued and that the children were 'well-trained'. He proposed that the resistance movement be broken and that the police act 'a bit more drastically and harshly, bringing about more deaths'. Minister Kruger's suggestions

---

[25] Krog 1998: 42.
[26] TRC Report, Vol. 5, Ch. 9, 1.

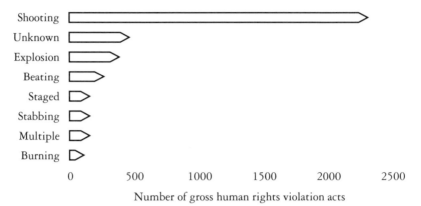

Figure 7.1 Number of gross human rights violation acts

Figure 7.1 Number of killings carried out by the South African security forces, 1960–1994 (source: TRC Report, Vol. 2, Ch. 3, p. 6)

were accepted.[27] During the 1980s, the riot policing function was expanded and separated from 'normal' police work, and resources were concentrated around what increasingly became a central police role. As Figure 7.1 illustrates, killing by shooting formed the overwhelming proportion of all deaths at the hands of the SAP, and the majority of those shootings occurred during the course of public order policing.

The minutes of a meeting held in May 1985 by the Joint Security Staff's intelligence structure read as follows:

> Recommendation: proposed action against the ringleaders (of resistance activity)
>
> (i)   Before a riot situation can be effectively defused, the ringleaders must be selectively eliminated
> (ii) The idea around elimination is twofold: (1) The physical gunning-down of leaders in riot situations who make themselves guilty of offences and (2) The removal of intimidators
>
> (In the latter case specific thought is given to schools and labour situations. The feeling here is that when ringleaders are removed, they also need to be restricted physically, to such an extent that they are removed from circulation and kept away.[28]

There were legal provisions for the use of force on crowds. Under the Riotous Assemblies Act (1956), the police were allowed to disperse a gathering by force, and that ruling was further strengthened by the Internal Security Act of 1982. On the basis of many hundreds of statements from victims of public order policing, the admissions of former government ministers and minutes of private meetings, the commission found the police culpable. Their crowd control actions displayed 'a gross disregard for the lives and physical well-being of both those engaged in

---

[27] *Ibid.*: Vol. 2 Ch. 3, 5.
[28] *Ibid.*: 6.

political activity and the general public'. The continued use of 'deadly force' resulted in deaths and injuries that 'constituted a systematic pattern of abuse'.[29]

A further area of concern to the commission was the incidence of torture and death in custody. The period 1960 to 1994 saw the systematic and extensive use of detention without trial. The Human Rights Committee estimated that the number of detentions between 1960 and 1990 was 80,000, 10,000 of whom were women and 15,000 children and youths under 18. The commission accepted the international definition of torture:

> The intentional infliction of severe pain and suffering, whether physical or mental, on a person for the purpose of:
> (1) obtaining from that or another person information or a confession, or
> (2) punishing him/her for an act that he/she or a third person committed or is suspected of having committed, or
> (3) intimidating him/her or a third person, or
> (4) for any reason based on discrimination of any kind.
> Pain or suffering that arises only from, inherent in, or accidental to, a lawful sanction does not qualify as torture.[30]

The cases of torture presented to the commission included a wide variety of physical and psychological forms. Figure 7.2 outlines the range of torture used by the security forces. The use of suffocation as a form of torture increased between 1975 and 1994. Forced postures or body positions were also used as torture, some of which involved forcing the detainee to stand on a piece of foolscap paper for hours, or to balance on a brick or sit in an imaginary chair. Other forms of torture included hanging detainees upside down for lengthy periods. Dreadful details emerged of Steve Biko's last days alive when five former security policemen

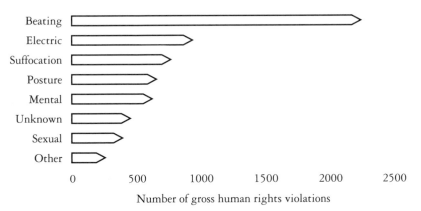

Number of gross human rights violations

Figure 7.2 Torture carried out by the South African security forces, 1960–1994 (source: TRC Report, Vol. 2, Ch. 3, p. 12)

---

[29] *Ibid.*: 8.
[30] *Ibid.*: 11.

applied for amnesty for their role in the killing. Biko had been severely beaten during interrogation and then chained in a 'crucified position' to a security grille.[31] Desmond Tutu recalled Minister of Police Jimmy Kruger's lack of interest in Biko's death and wondered what had happened to humanity in such a society: 'When one person is dehumanised, the perpetrator is dehumanised too. Brutality ultimately brutalises everyone.'[32] The artist Jane Alexander sought to represent South Africa's political environment through her impressive sculptures and photomontages (see Box 7.2).

Beating was the most commonly used form of torture. The TRC did not distinguish between beating detainees as torture and what appears to have been a routine practice of beating and assault at the point of arrest. The latter was used to instil terror and to 'soften people up' before questioning. Evidence presented to the commission confirmed that torture was used systematically by the security services as a means of 'obtaining information and terrorising detainees and activists'. Some political activists were aware of the possibility that they might be tortured: 'As freedom fighters, we were struggling; we knew the consequences. When we were fighting against the whites, the Boers, we knew we were going to be harassed.'[33] Yet many black detainees who experienced torture failed to make statements to the commission largely because of the shame and humiliation that was associated with the experience. Certainly, some organisations regarded 'a good comrade' as one who could withstand torture and not give information to the police, yet many detainees broke down and informed on their friends and associates. Informers were shunned in the community and in some instances tortured again. Winnie Mandela, the then wife of the imprisoned Nelson Mandela, was found to be operating a private vigilante unit, the Mandela United Football Club, which orchestrated 'killing, torture, assaults and arson in the community'.[34] The commission conducted an investigation into the activities of the 'football club' and found that those who opposed Mrs Mandela and the club, or disagreed with them, were branded as informers and killed. The labelling of opponents as 'informers' implied that they were legitimate targets.

The ANC was also held responsible for human rights abuses committed in exile. The ANC's military structures, responsible for the treatment and welfare of people in its camps, were found guilty of gross violations of human rights against suspected 'enemy agents' and mutineers. People who were suspected of being 'enemy agents' were 'routinely subjected to torture and other forms of severe ill treatment', including arbitrary execution. Although the use of torture was not ANC policy, its Security Department used torture to extract information and confessions from those being held in camps during the period 1979–1989. The torture took the form of the 'deliberate infliction of pain, solitary confinement,

---

[31] *The Star*, 27 October 1998.
[32] Tutu, 1 November 1999.
[33] Mike Basopu, TRC Report, Vol. 5, Ch. 4, 2.
[34] *Ibid*. Vol. 5, Ch. 6, 25.

Box 7.2

Jane Alexander won the Standard Bank Young Artist Award in 1995 for her powerful and haunting images of South Africa's political, social and racial inheritance (see Figures 7.3 and 7.4).

Butcher Boys (1985/86)

Three male figures sit upon a bench. Though they have been worked beyond the casting – bone has been inserted in the flesh and the flesh scraped away to reveal the bone – the bodies derive from casts made, compositely, from real people. But the heads are only half-human. Horns grow out from the skulls; the faces are distorted, pulled out of shape, flattened into snouts that do not open into mouths. It is, in one way, as though they are the mutant victims of some disaster. They are also sinister and malevolent. Personifications of evil, vengeance and retribution, deeply rooted in the history of South Africa.

The *Butcher Boys* are creatures that are not quite human, yet there is a strong implication that once they were human. Their mutation comes, in part at least, through mutilation – the spine shows through the flesh, the chests are split open. The heads of the figures have lost their features, begun to transform into the heads of animals. The *Butcher Boys* are images of brutalisation; they are the centre of malevolent and dehumanising forces. And what those forces are making them is inhuman. Mouthless, they can neither speak nor roar nor eat; they have gouged holes where they once had ears; it is only the searching ambivalent eyes that

Figure 7.3 *The Butcher Boys* (source: Jane Alexander sculpture and photomontage exhibition, Monument Gallery, Grahamstown, 1995, photographer Bob Cnoops)

remain intact. They are not even truly beasts. The horns are broken and useless, the spine is not properly welded. Where the reproductive organs should be there are protective boxes fused into the flesh.

They emerge from a specific time and place. They are personifications of the spiralling violence, the anarchy, the necklace killings, the police brutality, the child detentions, the burnings and lootings of South Africa in the 1980s.

Self Defence and Stability Unit (1994)

Self Defence and Stability Unit reads as though it is an evolution of *Butcher Boys*. It shows two male figures, their bodies tensed and anxious, positioned rather than seated on identical chairs. The black figure has over his head the more or less generic balaclava of the township revolutionary in the 1980s. On the head of the white figure is a canvas bag with holes cut for the eyes and mouth; it derives in general from a mask sometimes used by members of the Security Forces to disguise themselves during raids on township activists. But the device of the mask is used against itself. In *Self Defence and Stability Unit* the masks, instead of hiding the human face and disguising the human expression, serve to focus it – in the frightened eyes and the frozen, vulnerable mouths – into something like a distillation of anxiety and fear. By having both antagonists in the same space and naked, the artist makes them mirror images one of the other. They are both masked and exposed, aggressors and victims at the same time. Yet the masks echo the *Butcher Boys* in that the canvas bag fits on the Stability Unit figure's head as

Figure 7.4 *Self-Defence and Stability Unit*, 1994 (source: Jane Alexander sculpture and photomontage exhibition, Monument Gallery, Grahamstown, 1995, photographer Desmond Stewart)

if drawn over horns. Both figures are challenged by the social and political changes of 1994.

Exhibition by Jane Alexander, sculpture and photomontage, Monument Gallery, Grahamstown, July 1995. Text: Ivor Powell.[35]

withholding of food and water and/or medical care'.[36] The TRC found that during 1990–1994, after its unbanning, the ANC was responsible for killings, assaults and attacks on political opponents, including members of the IFP, PAC, AZAPO and the SAP. Its actions contributed to a spiral of violence in the country through the creation and arming of the self-defence units (SDUs). In the absence of adequate command structures and in a climate of general violence and political intolerance, SDU members often 'took the law into their own hands and committed gross violations of human rights'.[37]

The IFP was also found to have fostered the concept of paramilitary training, particularly among its youth movement. As a result, violence became institutionalised in KwaZulu with Inkatha supporters turning to militaristic methods. The commission received thousands of reports of attacks and massacres perpetrated by IFP supporters from April 1983, when Inkatha employed killer 'hit men', to 1994, when an IFP headman killed seven members of the Independent Electoral Commission for handing out pamphlets on how to vote.[38] During the period 1982–1994, the IFP was found responsible for gross violations of human rights in the former Transvaal, Natal and KwaZulu against persons who were perceived to be leaders, members or supporters of the UDF, ANC, South African Communist Party and the Congress of South African Trade Unions. In fact, any person identified as an opponent of Inkatha or suspected of disloyalty was under threat. The commission discovered that at a time when the IFP was portraying itself both nationally and internationally as a *bona fide* liberation movement, it was receiving direct financial and logistical assistance from the apartheid state's security apparatus. In effect, 'Inkatha's opposition to the South African government's policies changed to covert collaboration by the latter half of the 1980s, as both united against a common enemy, the UDF/ANC and their affiliates'.[39] Chief Mangosuthu Buthelezi served simultaneously as president of the IFP and chief minister in the KwaZulu government. He was also the only serving minister of police in the region. All three agencies were found responsible for human rights abuses and,

---

[35] The author attended the exhibition in Grahamstown.
[36] TRC Report Vol 5 Chap 6.25.
[37] *Ibid*.
[38] *Ibid*.: 19.
[39] *Ibid*.: 20.

Box 7.3 Statements and admissions of killings and torture

Former Security Branch member Jeffrey Benzien described and demonstrated one form of suffocation during his amnesty application:

> ... it would be a cloth bag that would be submerged in water to get it completely wet ... I get the person to lie down on the ground on his stomach ... with that person's hands handcuffed behind his back. Then I would take up a position in the small of the person's back, put my feet through between his arms to maintain my balance then pull the bag over the person's head and twist it close around the neck in that way, cutting off the air supply to the person ... On occasions people have, I presume, lost consciousness. They would go slack and every time that was done, I would release the bag.

Asked what the reactions of the person being suffocated were, Benzien replied:

> There would be movement, there would be head movement, distress. All the time there would be questions asked – 'Do you want to speak?' ... and as soon as an indication was given that this person wanted to speak, the air would be allowed back ... the person would moan, cry.

Benzien claimed that, with few exceptions, this method yielded results within half an hour.
(TRC Report, Volume 2, Chapter 3, p. 15)

General Andrew Masondo, national political commissar of the ANC between 1977 and 1985 and earlier a Robben Island prisoner:

> We were at war ... There might be times that I will use [the] third degree, in spite of the fact that it is not policy. People who were found to be enemy agents, we executed them. We were at war.

(TRC Report, Volume 5, Chapter 7, p. 2)

Cases of sexual torture included forcing detainees, both male and female, to undress; the deliberate targeting of genitals or breasts during torture; the threat of and, in some instances, actual rape of male and female detainees; and the insertion of objects such as batons or pistols into bodily orifices. One detainee, Ms Ntombizanele Zingxondo, testified:

> They unbuttoned my shirt, and pulled my breast out of my bra. They emptied one drawer and my breast was squeezed in the drawer. They did this several times.

14-year-old Patrick Mzathi recalled:

> They put my penis and my testicles into a drawer ... I went unconscious.

(TRC Report, Volume 2, Chapter 3, p. 15)

consequently, the commission held Chief Buthelezi accountable in his 'representative capacity' as leader, head and minister of the parties concerned.

The unprecedented levels of violence in the early 1990s led to suspicions that a so-called 'third force' was operating in the country. Numerous allegations were made of covert activities, including orchestrating and fomenting violence in order to derail the negotiation process. The commission investigated these claims and found evidence of:

- Involvement by members of the security forces in the provision of weapons and training to the IFP.
- An official plan to abduct or assassinate Chris Hani of the SACP.
- The existence of South African Police hit squads.
- Sustained efforts to conduct disinformation campaigns against both the liberation movements generally and particular individuals.

Little evidence was presented to the TRC that substantiated claims of a centrally directed, coherent and formally constituted 'third force' operating in the country. However, the commission found that 'a network of security and ex-security force operatives, often acting in conjunction with right-wing elements at a local level and/or sectors of the IFP, fomented, initiated, facilitated and engaged in violence that resulted in gross violations of human rights'.[40] Such networks functioned with the active collusion or knowledge of senior security force personnel. The former government, 'either deliberately or by omission, failed to take sufficient steps to put an end to such practices'. However, the success of 'third force' attempts to generate violence was at least in part a consequence of extremely high levels of political intolerance, for which both the liberation movements and the IFP were 'morally and politically accountable'.[41] The Pan Africanist Congress was also implicated in the pervading violence, particularly regarding its targeting and killing of civilians, especially white farmers. The United Democratic Front's campaign against the government during the 1980s was found to have created a climate in which violence was considered legitimate. Arbitrary killings of political opponents, often through the notorious 'necklace' method, and the burning and destruction of homes and properties all contributed to a sense of lawlessness over which the UDF leadership seemed to have little control. No disciplinary action was taken against members who were involved in such abuses. The UDF leadership accepted its 'political and moral responsibility' for the wrongdoing of its members: 'We concede that the language used by some of us from time to time could have provided the reasonable basis for some of our members to infer that violence or even killing was acceptable.'[42]

---

[40] *Ibid.*: 23.
[41] *Ibid.*
[42] Azhar Cachalia, Murphy Marobe, *ibid.*: 26.

Collective responsibility

In addition to the TRC's hearings on gross human rights violations, special hearings were held with various sections of society, including business, health, the media, religious organisations, civil society and the legal profession. It was not only the task of the security forces and liberation movements to examine themselves and their deeds but also for members of wider society to consider their actions. As one military contributor to the commission put it:

> Our weapons, ammunition, uniforms, vehicles, radios and other equipment were all developed and provided by industry. Our finances and banking were done by bankers who even gave us covert credit cards for covert operations. Our chaplains prayed for our victory, and our universities educated us in war. Our propaganda was carried by the media and our political masters were voted back in power time after time with ever-increasing majorities.[43]

The commission sought and received a number of submissions from organisations representing specific sectors of civil society. Although these sectors were not directly involved in abuses of human rights, they were part of an overall system that protected the rights and privileges of a racial minority. Many, such as those in the media and organised religion, were capable of defining the ideas and morals of society, while lawyers and doctors were highly regarded for their assumed impartiality and scientific knowledge. Consequently, their failure to oppose actively the injustice of apartheid society contributed to an overall ethos of public acceptance of racial injustice. A climate of acceptance, if not actual complicity, became the norm, and those who did speak out were often marginalised in their respective careers. The judiciary maintained that it was impotent in the face of a sovereign parliament's legislative power, but the commission held that judges had choices other than resignation:

> they could have resisted encroachments to basic rights and fairness ... A concerted stand by a significant number of judges could have moved the government formally to curtail the jurisdiction of the courts, thereby laying bare the degeneracy of its policies more devastatingly.[44]

The Commission found that religious communities, particularly the United Dutch Reformed Church, promoted the ideology of apartheid in a range of different ways through biblical and theological teaching and ecclesiastical practices. The churches failed to challenge the myth that apartheid was both a moral and a Christian initiative and as such were often seen as supportive of the former state. The media were also held responsible for following, at best, a policy of appeasement towards the government and, at worst, displaying direct support for apartheid and the activities of the security forces, although it has to be remembered that by the end of the 1980s there were more than 100 laws controlling the right to publish and broadcast within the country. The role of the business sector

---

[43] Craig Williamson, Armed Forces hearing, *ibid*.: 28.
[44] *Ibid*.: 31.

in sustaining the structures of the state again raised the critical and contentious issue of the relationship between capitalist enterprise and apartheid policies. The commission identified certain businesses, especially the mining industry, that 'were involved in helping to design and implement apartheid policies', while the white-owned agricultural industry benefited from its privileged access to land.[45] Inevitably, the TRC's economic hearings were viewed as 'contradictory' by businessmen and the financial community.[46] The charge against business was that it systematically underinvested in human social capital. Sections of the business community responded by asking what it could do under apartheid. As a general rule, business sought some accommodation with the political authority, but to what extent could this be defined as collaboration? Companies argued that 'business' had to be differentiated, as sectors of the mining industry had varied recruitment practices and there was little similarity between small firms and large conglomerates. Equally, there were different phases of apartheid, and whereas business might have been instrumental in supporting apartheid in the early period, by 1976 it had been forced to rethink. The establishment of the business-funded Urban Foundation in 1977 was presented as a sign that sections of the business community had shifted away from apartheid as its racial policies began to be seen as 'bad for business'.[47] In any case, from 1985 there was active lobbying between business groups and the ANC in exile.

During the hearings, the business sector refused to take responsibility for its involvement in state security initiatives. However, the commission found that the business community's denial of trade union rights to black workers constituted a violation of human rights. Actions taken against trade unions by the state, with the collusion of companies, frequently led to violence and abuse of workers. Sectors of the business community resisted responsibility partly on the grounds that no 'moral codes of conduct' existed in the pursuit of profit making. Therefore, they could not be judged on an ethical basis. The TRC did, however, manage to call them to account, and a business trust was launched in 1998. Under the trust's auspices, some prominent businesses have taken a lead in social and educational ventures that will prove beneficial to South Africans in the future. Yet, on balance, the whole relationship between the repressive apartheid state and the interests of major industrial enterprises needs much closer examination and revelation on an individual company basis.

Causes of and motives for violence

Many people rejected the findings of the TRC on the basis that the commission had failed to understand the complexities and historical realities of the time. In effect, it had not fully recognised the motives and perspectives of those who

---

[45] *Ibid.*: 30.
[46] Francis Antonie, Standard Bank of South Africa, TRC Conference, Sussex University, 1998.
[47] Merle Lipton, *ibid.*

perpetrated gross violations of human rights. The commission defended itself on the grounds that its function had been to expose the violations of all parties as it laid the basis for a culture in which human rights were respected. It had never been its intention to write the political history of South Africa. However, a number of contexts for the expression of violence existed, and the Commission referred to them: namely, the international backdrop of the Cold War and the liberation struggle against colonial rule. South Africa had been caught up in the Cold War, as were so many other African states, and a virulent form of anti-communism and anti-Marxism had taken root in the country since 1948. The former minister of law and order, Adriaan Vlok, asserted in a statement to the commission that violence by the state had to been seen in the context of the fight against communism:

> The ANC/PAC were seen with justification as fronts and tools of the Marxist–Communist threat against the country. I believed and still believe that if the forces of Communism and Marxism since the 1950s were allowed to take over South Africa, our country would today be destroyed, impoverished and a backward country with an atheist Communist ideology as the government policy ... I saw it as part of my duty to fight against such thoughts, programmes or initiatives and to ensure that these objectives were not successful.[48]

Members of the ANC and the SACP were both supported and trained by the Soviet Union, and it would by no means have been in the interests of the West had South Africa, rich in mineral resources and pre-eminent in the international commodity markets, fallen under the control of the Soviet Union.[49] The government regarded liberation organisations as the 'enemy' and a legitimate target for control. Similarly, some anti-colonial resistance movements regarded whites as the foe. As one member of the Pan Africanist Students' Organisation asserted: 'Speeches were closed with the slogan "one settler, one bullet". I understood this slogan to apply to every white person who came into the line of fire when we were assisting in making the country ungovernable.'[50] The claim that the country was at war was repeatedly made as a reason for the spiralling levels of violence and the loss of moral restraint.

Certainly, the country had suffered from racially based colonial subjugation under the British, and many Afrikaners felt that the Anglo-Afrikaner (Boer) War had forged a notion of apartheid based on the 'dangerous sentiments of a collective sense of injustice, discrimination and deprivation'.[51] Apartheid was rooted in colonialism and segregation, but as the years passed the struggle between the oppressor and the oppressed sharpened. Apartheid had been defined by the United Nations as a 'crime against humanity', while the National Party viewed 'separate development' as an acceptable and rational policy. Inevitably, the long-term denial of civil and political rights to Africans would result in opposition and violence.

---

[48] TRC Report, Vol. 5 Ch. 7, 10.
[49] Adam *et al.* 1998.
[50] *Ibid.*: 11.
[51] *Ibid.*

'The apartheid state left us no choice but to take up arms', proclaimed an ANC activist who was directly involved in Umkhonto we Sizwe's planned operations against police, embassy and state department targets in South Africa. The racist origins of apartheid could never be in doubt, and the ideological framework of the government reflected those concepts. In highlighting the differences and separateness of peoples, apartheid essentially graded ethnic groups hierarchically, or as the commission outlined: 'blacks required development, but at their own slower and different pace since, the rationale for apartheid assumed, they were essentially different from the more civilised, developed people of European origin.' It was this form of racism that served to dehumanise black Africans and prepared the way for violent revolt. Hatred, fear and distrust created an environment in which the violation of human rights could take place, with the result that all citizens became drawn into this 'fabric of abuse, as victims and perpetrators and, at times, as both'.[52]

The question of amnesty

In some quarters, the commission was regarded as a trade-off between truth and justice. The TRC's responsibility for the granting of amnesty aroused opposition from victims claiming that justice was not being done. The family of Steve Biko and others challenged the constitutionality of the amnesty provision, but the TRC's provisions were upheld. Other critics believed that the remit of the commission had been too narrowly defined and resulted in a distortion of the truth. Born of a political compromise, it had masked the real truth of apartheid.[53] Mahmoud Mamdani viewed the TRC's legalistic terms of reference as restrictive elements that narrowed the focus of its inquiry to torture and murder while ignoring wider societal constraints and forced removals, which were also features of apartheid policy. A much larger group of victims and beneficiaries of the apartheid system existed, which the commission ignored. Yet the TRC could never aim to solve all the ills of South Africa's past, and most of those who lived through the apartheid years were aware of the repression of the state, even if they chose, for one reason or another, to ignore it. As Merle Lipton states: 'most whites had readily closed their eyes to the appalling effects [of apartheid] while most blacks had kept their heads down and tried to get on with their own lives.'[54] The commission admitted that after 'so long a journey, with so many different and challenging experiences', all of South Africa, rural, urban, black, white, men, women and children had been caught up in oppression and resistance that 'left no one with clean hands'.[55] The granting of amnesty was not automatic (see Table 7.2); it could be given only where applicants made full disclosure of all relevant facts and of acts

---

[52] TRC Report, Vol. 5 Ch. 6, 33.

[53] Mahmoud Mamdani, TRC Conference, Sussex University, September 1998.

[54] Lipton 1999: 62.

[55] TRC Report, Vol. 5, Ch. 8, 2.

Table 7.2 Amnesty applications in figures to June 1998

Total applications received	7060
Total dealt with	4696
Amnesty granted at hearings	75
Amnesty refused at hearings	61
Amnesty granted in chambers	50
Amnesty refused administratively	4510

Source: CIIR, From Truth to Transformation 7.

'associated with a political objective committed in the course of the conflicts of the past'. The individual could not have acted on his/her own, or for private gain, or through personal malice, ill-will or spite. Rather, individuals had to be members of a publicly known political party or an employee of the state who 'on reasonable grounds believed that he/she was acting in the course and scope of his or her express or implied authority'.[56]

Those applicants who were granted amnesty were to be immune from prosecution and all criminal and civil liability. People responsible for politically motivated gross human rights abuses who acknowledged their crimes were allowed to go free. The amnesty provision 'thwarted many of the formal judicial possibilities for prosecuting former abusers of human rights'.[57] Although amnesty conditions undermined the ability of victims to gain restitution under the law, the Constitutional Court upheld amnesty on the grounds that without it, perpetrators of gross human rights violations simply would not have come forward and confessed to their misdeeds. The South African TRC, unlike similar commissions elsewhere, 'had the advantage of eliciting detailed accounts from perpetrators and institutions' of past abuses.[58] Regarding the issue of the trade-off between truth and justice, one TRC participant responded that if justice was defined as retribution, then the commission had operated at the expense of justice. However, if justice was interpreted in terms of societal openness and national peace of mind, truth and justice had been served by the commission.[59]

Although there was quite legitimate criticism of amnesty procedures at the inception of the TRC, few alternative procedures would have worked for the country. Certainly, for the former head of investigations at the TRC the criminal justice system would never have revealed the truth because it did not have full evidence of violations; it had only suspicions of killings of people in police custody. The families who had lost their relatives did not know the truth of events through inquest procedures. They discovered the facts only through the amnesty process. Information was revealed that criminality was not simply the acts of a

---

[56] CIIR From Truth to Transformation p. 7.
[57] *Ibid.*
[58] *Ibid.*
[59] C. Villa-Vicencio, South African Embassy, Dublin, March 1999.

'few bad eggs', as had been claimed by P.W. Botha, but was part of a systematic strategy against opponents of the state.[60] For Dumisa Ntsebeza, the amnesty procedure brought a disclosure of the truth not only by uncovering information from police and military sources but also through their clear admissions of guilt. On a personal level, the remains of the bodies of loved ones were returned to their families and buried with dignity. Some perpetrators felt deep sorrow and regret at their actions, and many victims were able to reject 'hatred, resentment, bitterness and revenge'. For Desmond Tutu, a spirit of forgiveness emerged in 'very different and polarised communities'.[61]

Reaction to the report

Irrespective of criticism, the TRC's strength was its exposure of facts about the country's history. Although its focus was narrow, it was no longer possible for any South African, of any racial group, to claim: 'I didn't know. My people would not do that.'[62] The sensitivity of the commission's findings together with its apportionment of blame drew strong and hostile reactions even before it was formally published. Just hours before the 3500-page report was due to be released, the ANC applied to the High Court to prevent it being placed in the public domain. The ANC believed that it had been treated unfairly on the grounds that it had had no time to rebut the commission's charges of gross human rights abuses. The TRC maintained that the ANC had been warned three months earlier that negative points would be included in the final report. A split occurred between Nelson Mandela and his deputy, Thabo Mbeki, as to how the ANC should respond to the report, with Mbeki favouring blocking publication. Desmond Tutu was incensed by the ANC's attitude: 'the ANC may be the ruling party in the country but that does not give it any special privilege.' The price of freedom is eternal vigilance, argued Tutu, as 'yesterday's oppressed may become tomorrow's oppressors'.[63] The response of the ANC highlighted differences between Mandela and Mbeki. While Mandela accepted the findings of the report, Mbeki believed, together with broad sections of the ANC, that the liberation struggle was being wrongly criminalised. Thabo Mbeki's communications director, Ronnie Mamoepa, argued that 'no member of the ANC can ever concur with the scurrilous attempts to criminalise the liberation struggle by characterising the heroic struggles of the people of South Africa as gross human rights violations'.[64] However, Mandela backed the release of the report, asserting:

---

[60] Dumisa Ntsebeza, TRC Conference, Sussex University, September 1998.
[61] Tutu, 1 November 1999.
[62] Villa-Vicencio, Dublin, March 1999.
[63] *The Johannesburg Star*, 2 November 1998.
[64] *The Sunday Times*, South Africa, 1 November 1998.

The ANC was fighting a just war, but in the course of fighting the just war, it committed gross violations of human rights. Nobody can deny that, because some people died in our camps and that's what the TRC said.[65]

Inevitably, those who struggled against apartheid were dismayed at finding themselves implicated in the atrocities together with the perpetrators, yet the findings of the commission had been uncomfortable for many different groups.[66] The ANC's legal moves had followed F.W. de Klerk's application to the court and his success in temporarily forcing the TRC to remove allegations implicating him in state-sponsored terrorism. Also Chief Buthelezi, on behalf of the IFP, threatened to sue the commission for defamation. The party placed an advertisement in a newspaper declaring that accusations against Buthelezi were 'legally obscene and morally repugnant'.[67] Notions of reconciliation were under threat as politicians and political parties raised contention about the findings of the TRC. As one newspaper commented, the commission's conclusions 'unleashed a storm of hypocrisy', but the High Court dismissed the ANC's bid to stop the report's publication (see Box 7.4).

The five-volume, 3500-page report was formally handed to President Mandela by Archbishop Tutu on 29 October 1998. Tutu acknowledged that while many were 'upset' by the findings, the report provided an insight into the country's past and the 'perspectives of those who supported apartheid and those who opposed it'. As a consequence of the commission's work, official documentation existed and provided formal acknowledgement that atrocities had occurred. A process of reconciliation and understanding had been set in motion that might eventually help people to come to terms with former acts of violence and abuse. The report served to remind the country of the capacity of individuals to disregard the dignity of human life. By undertaking the commission, Tutu asserted, 'We have been forced to deal with our horrendous past and with hope it will no longer keep us hostage'.[68] Mandela accepted the report graciously (see Box 7.5 for the text of Mandela's speech). Two years later, Tutu recalled how the prospect of confession and reconciliation had once seemed such a remote prospect in South Africa, a country with such a dreadful history. Yet the TRC process had demonstrated that although the nation had experienced 'devastating evil' it also had a 'great capacity for good; a capacity for compassion and forgiveness'.[69] Undoubtedly, Nelson Mandela helped to create an atmosphere of dignity and reconciliation, but many people had supported his lead.

[65] *Ibid.*

[66] Archbishop N. Ndungane, *The Johannesburg Star*, 9 November 1998.

[67] *The Sunday Times*, South Africa, 22 November 1998.

[68] *Ibid.*: 30 November 1998.

[69] Tutu, 1 November 1999.

Box 7.4 Highlights: The findings of the Truth and Reconciliation Commision report

- Between 1960 and 1994 the National government was responsible for perpe-trating a range of atrocities including torture of prisoners, unjustified use of force, judicial killings, incursions over South Africa's borders and deliberately manipulating social/racial divisions.
- The State Security Council was an institution involved in the perpetuation of gross human rights violations.
- The former government destroyed documents with the aim of denying the new government access to incriminating evidence.
- Former State President P.W. Botha was accountable for a wide range of human rights violations.
- General C. Viljeon and General P. Groenewald and Afrikaner Weers-tandsbeweging (AWB) leader E. Terreblanche were accountable for gross human rights violations committed by followers of their movements.
- The ANC and particularly its military structures were responsible for perpet-uating gross human rights violations in its camps and the organisation did not take adequate steps to ensure action against those responsible.
- The ANC contributed to a spiral of violence between 1990 and 1994 through the arming and creation of its self-defence units.
- Winnie Mandela was personally responsible for committing gross human rights violations and was politically and morally responsible for violations committed by members of the Mandela United Football Club.
- The Inkatha Freedom Party was guilty of human rights abuses and its leader, Chief Buthelezi, was accountable for its actions, as well as for atrocities com-mitted by the KwaZulu homeland government and its police force.

Towards reconciliation

In order for society to move away from past prejudices communal understanding between communities has to be initiated. In many ways this is one of the most dif-ficult objectives to achieve, particularly as segregation and separation meant that different peoples had very little contact with each other. As the TRC stated: 'rec-onciliation is a complex, long-term process with many dimensions.' Archbishop Tutu declared that 'confession, forgiveness, and reconciliation in the lives of nations are not just airy-fairy religious and spiritual things, nebulous and unreal-istic. They are the stuff of practical politics'.[70] Reconciliation was necessary for all because everyone needed to be healed, but it could not be achieved without the painful acceptance of past atrocities. Yet the commission had demanded neither

---

[70] TRC Report, Vol. 5, Ch. 9.

Box 7.5 Text of President Mandela's speech on receipt of the Truth and Reconciliation Commision report

We are extricating ourselves from a system that insulted our common humanity by dividing us from one another on the basis of race and setting us against each other as oppressor and oppressed. In doing so that system committed a crime against humanity, which shared humanity we celebrate today in a constitution that entrenches human rights and values. In denying us these things the Apartheid State generated the violent political conflict in the course of which human rights were violated. The wounds of the period of repression and resistance are too deep to have been healed by the TRC alone, however well it has encouraged us along that path. Consequently, the Report that today becomes the property of our nation should be a call to all of us to celebrate and to strengthen what we have done as a nation as we leave our terrible past behind us forever.

Let us celebrate our rich diversity as a people, the knowledge that when the TRC in its wisdom apportions blame, it points at previous state structures, political organisations, at institutions and individuals, but never at any community. Nor can any individual so identified claim that their brutal deeds were the result of some character inherent in any community or language group. All of us are now free to be who we really are, no longer forced to experience some of those things which are most precious to us – language, culture or religion – as walls within which we are imprisoned. Above all we should remember that it was when South Africans of all backgrounds came together for the good of all that we confounded the prophets of doom by bringing an end to this terrible period of our history.

Though the liberation movement was the primary agent of this change, it could not have done so on its own. Now the challenge is for all of us to protect our democratic gains like the apple of our eye. It is for those who have the means to contribute to the efforts to repair the damage wrought by the past. It is for those who have suffered losses of different kinds and magnitudes to be afforded reparation, proceeding from the premise that freedom and dignity are the real prize that our sacrifices were meant to attain. Free at last we are all masters of our destiny. A better future depends on all of us lending a hand – your hand, my hand.

State Theatre Building, Pretoria, 29 October 1998

national nor personal forgiveness as both seemed unrealistic goals. It had, however, looked towards the development of a strong human rights culture in the country. A democratic society needed to narrow the socio-economic gap that existed between communities. As economic marginalisation for the majority of South Africans had been a function of the apartheid years, the future had to hold promise of economic justice. In policy terms, this meant provision for training, empowerment and opportunity for the majority of the population.

The churches and non-governmental organisations could extend their services to communities and share their skills and knowledge. The government also had to play its part in committing itself to 'open, clean and transparent governance'. State institutions had to be strengthened and a process of transformation had to be achieved. The commission welcomed affirmative action and employment equity but also recognised that a culture of hard work and honesty had to be promoted. Yet it reminded the government that it had to ensure that the 'rule of law, human rights practice, transparency, accountability and the rooting out of corruption and other forms of criminality at all levels of society are seriously addressed'.[71] The commission also recommended that the business community should consider ways of redressing the continuing effects of apartheid discrimination by empowering the poor through a variety of schemes:

- a wealth tax;
- a one-off levy on corporate and private income;
- each company listed on the Johannesburg Stock Exchange to make a one-off donation of 1 per cent of its market capitalisation;
- a retrospective surchage on corporate profits;
- a surcharge on golden handshakes given to senior public servants since 1990; and
- the suspension of all taxes and other material donations to formerly disadvantaged communities.[72]

Some members of the business sector dismissed these recommendations on the grounds that business was not a social organisation and, therefore, could not put resources back into the country. Other industries, for example the South African wine industry, which had thrived under apartheid, agreed to a substantial payment to the government as a contribution to wider society.[73]

The commission fully accepted that reconciliation was a 'never-ending' process that needed a culture supportive of human rights together with a 'more decent, more caring and more just society'. Each individual had a role to play in committing himself/herself to the future of the country. Numerous criticisms of the TRC were aired at its inception, with some regarding it as a 'witch hunt' or biased and politically partisan and others questioning the exact 'meaning' of truth. But the angry reactions of the National Party, the IFP and the ANC to the commission's findings 'enhanced the credibility' of the TRC. It was not an 'ANC rubber stamp'.[74] Yet this interpretation was not apparent when the commission's report was discussed in the National Assembly in February 1999, when a bitter, lengthy and acrimonious debate ensued. Mandela emphasised that reconciliation had to be balanced with accountability. However, there was little reconciliation on display between the various parties, and the discussion often degenerated into name

---

[71] *Ibid.*: 5.
[72] *Ibid.*: Vol. 5 Ch. 8, 9.
[73] F. Antonie, Standard Bank of South Africa, TRC Conference, Sussex University, September 1998.
[74] Lipton 1999.

calling.[75] The New National Party (formerly the old National Party) attacked the TRC for its alleged bias in favour of the ANC, while Mbeki dismissed any suggestions of ANC human rights abuses during the liberation struggle. The white right-wing Freedom Front accused the commission of 'humiliating Afrikaners and former soldiers', while the Democratic Party and the Inkatha Freedom Party criticised the TRC for its narrow agenda. Mbeki's final remarks indicated that although reconciliation between the present generation might be problematic, future generations might begin anew: 'A beginning has been made. Like all beginnings, ours is also a prayer to the future. By our deeds, let us grant later generations the possibility to sing of unity and reconciliation among themselves.'[76]

Desmond Tutu's successor as Anglican Archbishop of Cape Town, Njongonkulu Ndungane, accepted that the work of the commission was never 'easy or comfortable' as it 'stumbled across many vested interests' in its search for the truth. In the event, Ndungane believes, an 'even-handedness' prevailed and to its 'lasting credit' the TRC managed to achieve so much within a limited time. The new archbishop understood the perspective of those sectors of society who fought a 'noble struggle against apartheid' yet found themselves 'lumped together in the Commission's report with the very perpetrators of this terrible era'. Sacrifices and mistakes were made in that struggle, but South Africans had to recognise that there were two levels on which the evil deeds of the past should be measured. The truth had been exposed and the fact that it had discomforted many was of benefit to society. Now the challenge facing the country was how to move forward towards reconstruction.[77] Other journalists suggested that a report that 'discomfited [sic] all, and not merely the obviously guilty', was more likely to promote reconciliation by limiting demands for retributive action.[78]

The TRC marked the first step towards an acknowledgement of the past, and each member of society had to bring about their own reconciliation; no committee or commission could achieve it for them. It was a rite of passage, a journey the country had to make in order to move forward. However, in the final analysis the 'yawning gap between the rich and the poor had to be bridged'.[79] As Alex Boraine, TRC vice-chairman, proclaimed: 'Unless health, homes, water, electricity and most importantly, jobs become part of the quest for reconciliation, we will remain the very deeply divided society we are.'[80] However, issues of economic justice, unemployment and poverty are difficult to resolve in the short term. Education, skills and training will take years to mature; poor rural communities cannot automatically become prosperous farms; social and demographic patterns will not be changed overnight. These developments are achievable only gradually. The depth

[75] One MP referred to his colleagues as 'bloodthirsty fascist braggarts' and another dismissed his opponent as a 'monkey-wrench'. cf. AFP 25 February 1999; Financial Mail 5 May 1999.

[76] Financial Mail, 5 March 1999.

[77] Archbishop Ndungane, quoted in The Johannesburg Star, 9 November 1998.

[78] Bell 1998.

[79] Villa-Vicencio, Dublin, March 1999.

[80] Alex Boraine, cited in CIIR Report 1999: 13.

of the problems facing the country was revealed by a series of poverty hearings that ran concurrently, but separately, with the TRC.

Poverty hearings

The Truth and Reconciliation Commission did not look at socio-economic assaults on human rights, that is, the economic degradation that people suffered under the apartheid system. The South African National NGO Coalition (SANNGO), supported by both the Human Rights Commission and the Gender Equality Commission, set up poverty hearings so that the very poor could speak for themselves. It gave those living in rural communities, a large percentage of whom were women, the opportunity to outline the issues that were of greatest concern in the locality. Initially, there was some scepticism from the ANC regarding the utility of such hearings, with some quarters believing that it would be 'one big whinge session'.[81] Perhaps more worrying for the ANC was the fact that the poverty hearings revealed that socio-economic benefits had not been gained by South Africa's wider society between 1994 and 1997. However, far from being a 'whinge session', most people spoke of possible solutions to their predicaments. Yet there was little media coverage in comparison with the reporting of the TRC hearings, although the process cost much less, 1 million rand as against 16 million rand for the Truth Commission.

Ultimately, the ANC supported the hearings, as did the Inkatha Freedom Party. The National Party and the Democratic Party tended to marginalise the process, with the NP arguing that the hearings raised expectations. This accusation was not true, as people repeatedly stated that they did not want 'handouts'. Political parties were consulted by SANNGO but were not permitted to speak at the hearings. Kami Naidoo was a commissioner in one of the poorest regions, Northern Province, and found the experience 'very moving' and was 'shocked' at the extent of poverty. Local communities were largely unaware of their rights but desperately wanted opportunities to work and to have shelter. Sometimes administrative structures were inefficient and people failed to receive legitimate payments such as pensions, while in certain areas traditional patterns of leadership restricted opportunities available to women. The general incidence of HIV infection was increasing, but some NGOs and local church organisations were contributing to the economic betterment of localities. There is little doubt that the poverty hearings highlighted the extent of the social and economic problems facing the country. Archbishop Tutu gave an especially positive response to the hearings and regarded them as complementary to the work of the TRC. Yet nobody should underestimate the enormity of the task confronting South Africa in finding economic justice for all its citizens.

The TRC and the poverty hearings have been a cathartic and humbling experience for many people, yet as Archbishop Tutu declared: 'Reconciliation is not

---

[81] Kumi Naidoo, interview.

about being cosy; it is not about pretending that things were other than they were. Reconciliation based on falsehood, or not facing up to reality, is not true reconciliation and will not last.'[82] South Africans have been urged to read the hearings of both the TRC and the poverty meetings on the grounds that the apartheid system affected everyone at a 'very deep level' and left a population that was deeply wounded. In a sense, Tutu saw the TRC as a microcosm of the wider community, reflecting its alienation, suspicion and lack of trust. It is still far too early to assess the long-term effects of the TRC, but the strength of any reconciliation must rest on the recognition of human rights, democracy and peaceful coexistence.

---

[82] Tutu 1998.

Part IV

Forward to the future

Chapter 8

The 1999 elections

Registration – gender and age

A few months before South Africa's second national and provincial elections took place, a newspaper editor called for a high voter turnout to ensure the legitimacy and accountability of those elected to office. 'Nothing could be more dangerous,' he argued, than 'an uninterested and uninvolved electorate.'[1] In 1999, the country faced the task of consolidating and building on the historic achievement of its first democratic elections in 1994. Yet the elections were arranged differently from those held in 1994. One major change was the constitutional arrangement governing elections. The new constitution of 1996 required the Independent Electoral Commission (IEC) to compile the country's first national voters' roll based on universal adult suffrage. The IEC, constitutionally upheld as a state institution whose function was to strengthen democracy, had to be independent and impartial. The commission carried the authority to manage elections to national, provincial and municipal legislative bodies in accordance with national legislation. Its duties included promoting conditions conducive to the holding of free and fair elections, the compiling and maintaining of the voters' roll, and the registration of parties. The IEC was also responsible for establishing and maintaining party liaison committees, reviewing electoral legislation and promoting voter education. Under the terms of the Electoral Commission Act (1996), the commission consisted of five members, one of whom was a judge, to be appointed by the president on the advice of a committee of the National Assembly.[2] Before the 1994 elections, the original IEC was the creation of the twenty-six parties that had negotiated South Africa's transition to democracy. The commission had held its inaugural meeting in December 1993 with Judge Johann Kriegler as chairman. Under the guidelines of the formalised constitution of 1996, Kriegler was reappointed as chairman but later resigned and was replaced by Dr Brigalia Bam and Judge Ismail Hussain.

Whereas in 1994 voters were only required to attend a polling station to cast their vote, in 1999 they were required to register to vote some time before the

---

[1] Kaizer Nyatsumba, editor of the *Independent on Saturday*, Durban, *The Johannesburg Star*, 11 November 1998.

[2] IEC 1999: 8.

actual day of the election. Their names had to be placed on a national common voters' roll. Citizens of South Africa who were 18 years or older had an identity book with a bar code under his/her ID number. This system was introduced in order to avoid duplication of voting, but the policy led to increased disagreements between the government and political parties. A survey carried out by the Human Science Research Council in August 1998 indicated that around 5.3 million people did not have bar-coded documents. Of these, 2.6 million held the old identity cards used during the apartheid years and carried by whites, Indians and coloureds, while 2.1 million black citizens were without any identity documents at all. The National Party and the Democratic Party decided to take legal action on the grounds that the bar-coded ID requirement was 'a deliberate ploy by the ANC to put opposition voters at a disadvantage'. Although this requirement had been agreed under the Electoral Act, both the NP and the DP argued that it should be amended.[3] The ANC claimed that the opposition parties were trying to discredit the country's democratic process. In any case, there was no clear evidence that the ANC would benefit from the way in which voter registration had been legislated for and organised.[4]

The first round of registration began in November and December 1998, and the response was disappointing. As Table 8.1 indicates, around one-third of the total census population actually registered to vote. Equally, there were large disparities between regions, with the lowest number, 25.54 per cent, registering in the Western Cape and the highest, 39.78 per cent, in the less populous Free State. In the Western Cape, opposition parties claimed that irregularities had occurred and people with old identity books without bar codes had registered at several places. Also, staffing shortages, heavy rains and inaccessible roads hampered progress on the first day of registration and at least 900 stations failed to open.[5]

Thabo Mbeki suggested that insufficient information about how and where to register had been available. Although information had been provided in the media, through the distribution of leaflets and via NGOs and churches, some rural communities were difficult to access efficiently[6] (see Figure 8.1). The whole country had been divided into voting districts, and voters could only register in the area in which they lived. The process was an arduous one, with the IEC admitting that when the project began in June 1998 the extent of the task had been largely unknown. Areas were mapped out, but the environment was complex, spatial databases were untested and the information technology was uncertain. The guidelines for voting districts were as follows:

- In urban areas, approximately 3000 voting-age persons were grouped within a 7.5 km travelling distance of each voting station.

[3] *Business Day*, 27 November 1998.
[4] Marius Steyn, interview.
[5] Bob Jones, interview.
[6] Marius Steyn, interview.

Table 8.1 National registration progress, December 1998/February 1999/April 1999

Province	Population (census)	% of population registered in December 1998 to vote in the June 1999 elections	% of population registered in February 1999 to vote in the June 1999 elections	% of population finally registered to vote in the June 1999 elections
Eastern Cape	3,819,371	27.22	51.79	76.84
Free State	1,726,080	39.78	55.83	81.74
Gauteng	5,512,651	36.04	58.54	89.94
KwaZulu Natal	5,440,536	27.80	50.08	74.12
Mpumalanga	1,685,322	36.74	59.68	83.54
Northern Cape	535,465	38.63	54.44	79.14
Northern Province	2,684,687	39.53	56.39	77.68
North West Province	2,174,893	28.77	57.56	81.17
Western Cape	2,776,108	25.54	44.96	80.64
Total	26,355,113	32.05	53.94	80.64

Source: Compiled from Independent Electoral Commission Progress Report, Pretoria, 11 December 1998; IEC statistics for second registration 12 February 1999 and final registration figures, 30 April 1999.

- In rural areas, approximately 1200 voting-age persons were grouped within a 10 km travelling distance of each voting station.
- Delimitation was carried out randomly and statistically, starting in turn from north, south, west and east.[7]

The geographical information system on which the formal boundaries of voting districts depended began work in February 1997. The intention was to map the whole country and its population in a single electronic system. In order to achieve a national common voters' roll, the entire eligible voting population had to be located geographically so that each individual's name would appear only once on the roll. It was an enormous project and called for staff working 24-hour shifts, seven days a week for extended periods to ensure that the process would be completed in time for the electoral timetable. The final delivery to the IEC of the first continuous geographical data set for the whole country took place in June 1998, an achievement that was regarded as 'close to a miracle'.[8]

However, despite the operation of a geographical database, the IEC's chief electoral officer, Mandla Mchunu, declared that there would be further registration exercises in order to increase the numbers of those eligible to vote. Registration was to be a 'process' rather than an 'event', but clearly problems with registration

---

[7] IEC 1999: 12–13.
[8] *Ibid.*

Figure 8.1 Voter educational material (source: Nazo Elections '99, 1999)

could threaten the very basis of the election. The registration process was undertaken in three distinct phases: November/December 1998, January 1999 and

March 1999. Although the commission later claimed that it was an 'overwhelming success', there was anxiety at the low level of registration in the first phase. The media viewed the low turnout for registration as 'shockingly poor' and effectively placing the future of the country's democracy in the balance.[9] Low registration was not in the interests of the country, the political parties or at the end of the day, the electorate. There had to be a surge in the registration figures during the early months of 1999. Generally, IEC officials and political spokespeople felt that the second drive for registration experienced fewer administrative hitches than the first. There had been considerable media publicity and the successful delivery of 10 million leaflets to households (see Figure 8.2). Political parties also made a more conspicuous contribution to voter education on the issue of registration. For example, in Gauteng (the area containing Johannesburg and Pretoria) the ANC spent, during the course of January 1999, 2.1 million rand (c. £200,000) on 150,000 posters and 1 million leaflets. Equally, the Democratic Party in Pretoria adopted a telephone campaign to encourage people to register to vote. These strategies were successful, and by the end of the second registration period, numbers had increased significantly. By the final registration deadline, the total percentage of the population registered was 80.64 per cent (see Table 8.1). These figures were later verified and revised to a total of 18,172,751 persons registered, representing 79.7 per cent of the population. The commission issued verified statistics for election day, 2 June 1999. They included the final breakdown of the registration figures into age, gender and rural/urban categories. These statistics revealed the divisions within the country, and Tables 8.2 and 8.3 outline the age/gender breakdown and urban/rural splits, respectively.

A number of women's organisations were active in monitoring the electoral process. These included the Commission on Gender Equality, the Gender Advocacy Programme, the Women's Development Foundation, the Women's Empowerment Unit and the Women's National Coalition. The organisations' collective aim was to increase the representation of women in the political process and to encourage female participation as both candidates and voters. Over 1.5 million more women registered than men. The high turnout may have resulted from the campaigns targeted at encouraging women to vote, although as women constitute a higher percentage of the population, 52 per cent, a greater number were eligible to register.[10] However, public opinion surveys conducted some months before the election indicated that a majority of women did not wish to vote. While women were aware of the need to register to vote, the survey claimed that 'their social environment tended to inhibit their participation'.[11] A so-called 'gender gap', that is, more males registering to vote than women, was expected. The actual

---

[9] cf. *The Sowetan*, 8 December 1998; *The Citizen*, 10 December 1998; *Business Day*, 8 December 1998.

[10] Ballington 1999.

[11] *Opinion 99*, IDASA.

Figure 8.2 Voter educational material (source: *The Power of Your Vote!* IEC 1999)

Table 8.2 Registration by age and gender, 2 June 1999

Age group	Male	Female	Total	% of age group registered
18–20	361,150	362,872	724,022	48.4
20–30	2,458,073	2,677,929	5,136,002	77.2
30–40	2,062,553	2,435,544	4,518,097	88.2
40–50	1,547,869	1,755,797	3,303,666	96.8
50–60	939,813	1,138,888	2,078,701	99.4
60–70	525,818	869,535	1,395,353	94.6
70–80	274,564	468,112	742,676	96.6
>80	87,542	186,692	274,234	97.0
Total	8,277,382	9,895,369	18,172,751	79.7

Source: Independent Electoral Commission, Pretoria, 2 June 1999.

Table 8.3 Rural/urban registration breakdown, 2 June 1999

Age group	Urban	Rural
18–20	436,226	287,796
20–30	3,414,873	1,721,129
30–40	3,138,876	1,379,221
40–50	2,250,528	1,053,138
50–60	1,350,209	728,492
60–70	797,507	597,846
70–80	400,841	341,835
>80	139,360	134,874
Total	11,928,420	6,244,331

Source: Independent Electoral Commission, Pretoria, 2 June 1999.

results completely reversed the 'gender gap' theory, and women have emerged as a dominant presence in the electorate.

Women had made significant gains in their levels of representation in the 1994 election. Of the 400 members elected to the National Assembly at that time, 111 were women, a development that was in large part due to the ANC's high representation of women. Of the 252 ANC representatives elected, ninety were women. Certainly, the country's form of proportional representation enabled parties to include women on their lists of candidates, but it is important to make a comparison between the numbers of women on parties' lists in 1994 and 1999. While there have been changes, the ANC is far ahead in the fielding of female candidates at both national and regional levels. The Democratic Party's position on gender equality assumes that 'women's rights are part and parcel of human rights, and any form of discrimination constitutes an infringement of the principles of equality

Table 8.4 Women's representation on party lists, 1994 and 1999 (%)

	1994		1999	
	National list	Regional list	National list	Regional list
African Christian Democratic Party	13	9	29	24
African National Congress	32	32	39	34
Democratic Party	31	19	n/a *	21
Freedom Front	12	7	16	17
Inkatha Freedom Party	10	15	22	28
New National Party	n/a	11	n/a *	18
Pan Africanist Congress of Azania	11	12	22	19
United Democratic Movement	n/a	n/a	23	19

* The New National Party and the Democratic Party did not compile national lists.
Source: Compiled from estimates EISA Election Update 99 No.13, 28/5/99, and *Government Gazette*, Pretoria, 11/5/99.

and dignity'.[12] The party is opposed to female quotas on the grounds that they 'disadvantage people from entering public life'. Julie Ballington points out that in 1994 the DP averaged 25 per cent representation of women on its national and regional lists, but with only one list submitted in 1999 this figure has fallen to 21 per cent (see Table 8.4). Despite the efforts of many women's organisations lobbying for a gender quota, none of the opposition parties followed the example set by the ANC and ensured that at least one-third of its candidates were women. However, as women become an increasingly important constituency in national and regional politics, parties who undervalue their interests will run the risk of losing women's votes. Given the disparity in male/female registration figures, no party can afford to ignore the question of women's representation.

One worrying feature of the registration was the exceptionally low figure for 18- to 20-year-olds. As Table 8.2 indicates, only 48.4 per cent of that age group registered to vote. There was also very little difference between male and female registration. The IEC made great attempts to target the young, and special literature on the electoral process was sent to schools and colleges. Youth organisations were contacted and rallies were organised in a bid to mobilise the young. This age group would have been 13–15 years old at the time of South Africa's first democratic elections and the commission considered their participation in 1999 to be important. Voter education literature emphasised the role of youth and its part at the forefront of the struggle to overthrow apartheid (see Figure 8.3). Educators

---

[12] J. Ballington in EISA *Election Update* No. 13.

Figure 8.3 Voter educational material (source: *The Power of Your Vote!* IEC 1999)

were encouraged to convince the young of the necessity of their votes in a new democracy.[13] Youth groups targeted festivals, and a free national youth telephone line was established to provide information about registration and the election. The IEC felt that it had exerted great efforts to mobilise the young.[14]

Yet participation rates remained stubbornly low. A number of reasons were advanced to account for the poor turnout. According to a poll many youngsters, 42 per cent, did not possess the requisite identity document to enable them to register as voters.[15] This deficiency suggests a lack of interest in the process, as the South African Youth Council, the IEC and sixty youth organisations had met in January 1999 and had agreed to work collectively to ensure that the maximum amount of information was made available to young people. The chief electoral officer of the IEC, Mandla Mchunu, warned that without the participation of the young, the country's democracy was not 'sustainable'. A registration drive was undertaken through the mass media and independent publicity, including posters and pamphlets. Young celebrities in music and the arts acted as role models in promoting registration, so excuses about lack of information were weak. A more convincing reason may be that many young people were not interested in the elections. Certainly, first-time voters were seen as politically unaware. Norman du Plessis, deputy electoral officer at the IEC, regarded their lack of participation as the result of apathy, while others asserted that the 'post-liberation baby-boomers were clearly not fired up'[16] (see Figure 8.4). Interestingly, registration figures for the 40-plus age range reached more than 90 per cent. Such high percentages reflect that elections are more significant for people who had experienced apartheid and remember their previous lack of political rights. In the 20- to 30-year-old age bracket, some voters would have been children at the height of the terror in the mid-1980s and adolescents when Nelson Mandela was released from jail. Yet their memories of the struggle during the closing years of apartheid motivated their participation in the election even though some would not have been old enough to vote in 1994. Certainly, a consensus emerged in the country that correlated maturity with political awareness. Those people who had been part of the liberation struggle were seen as far more politically alert. Nevertheless, if democracy is to be consolidated and sustained large swathes of the population must be encouraged to participate as part of their civil responsibility, rather than past activism. The 1999 voter education documents were right to stress that democracy takes 'active and informed effort' and critically depends on citizen participation[17] (see Figure 8.2).

[13] Make Yourself Heard 1999: 43; *Sondelani Sizovota*, 1999.

[14] Marius Steyne, interview.

[15] *Opinion 99* (SABC, IDASA, Markinor) 1999.

[16] Norman du Plessis, interview; EISA *Election Update* No. 4.

[17] Make Yourself Heard 1999.

Figure 8.4 A cartoon that appeared in *The Sowetan*, 8 December 1998 (source: Make Yourself Heard 1999)

The 1999 elections

The IEC finally completed its task of compiling a national voters' roll, and on 30 April 1999, Mandla Mchunu presented Deputy President Thabo Mbeki with the certified document, the first national electoral roll in South African history. It contained 960,000 pages and in Mchunu's words represented 'an heirloom of our democracy'.[18] It reflected the work of 14,500 voting districts, headed by 430 local electoral officers, and contained the names of a million more women than men, a predominance that was common to all age categories. On 2 June, election day, the Independent Electoral Commission had 14,650 voting stations divided into 34,799 voting areas. It allocated 96,597 pencils, 58,372 ballot boxes, 5986 sticks of sealing wax, 96,597 voting compartments and 50 million ballot papers to voting stations according to size, need and population. The commission also distributed 2 million paperclips, 1 million rubber bands, 245,965 ballpoint pens, 87,900 candles, and 108,348 tables and chairs. Although these figures might seem trivial, they were published by the IEC to ensure that the wider population knew that 'lots of people are making sure the polls are conducted properly'.[19]

---

[18] EISA *Election Update* No. 11.
[19] IEC 1999: 19.

Table 8.5 1999 national election result

	Votes gained	% of total votes cast
African Christian Democratic Party (ACDP)	228,975	1.43
African National Congress (ANC)	10,601,330	66.35
Afrikaner Eenheids Beweging (AEB)	46,292	0.29
Azanian People's Organisation (AZAPO)	27,257	0.17
Democratic Party (DP)	1,527,337	9.56
Federal Alliance (FA)	86,704	0.54
Inkatha Freedom Party (IFP)	1,371,477	8.58
Minority Front (MF)	48,277	0.30
New National Party (NNP)	1,098,215	6.87
Pan Africanist Congress of Azania (PAC)	113,125	0.71
The Government by the People Green Party (GPGP)	9,193	0.06
The Socialist Party of Azania (SOPA)	9,062	0.06
United Christian Democratic Party (UCDP)	125,280	0.78
United Democratic Movement (UDM)	546,790	3.42
Freedom Front (FF)	127,217	0.80
Abolition of Income Tax and Usury Party (AITUP)	10,611	0.07
Total valid ballots	15,977,142	
Total spoilt ballots	251,320	
Total ballots	16,228,462	
Total registered voters	18,172,751	

Source: Independent Electoral Commission, Pretoria, 1999.

There was much apprehension and tension about the extent to which the election would be conducted efficiently and effectively and considerable anxiety as to whether or not the ANC would achieve a two-thirds majority. The media continually asserted that if the ANC achieved such a majority it would be legally enabled to amend the constitution. The fact that the ANC indicated no inclination to drastically alter the constitution failed to calm the fears of opposition parties. In the event, when the final election results were released on 7 June, the ANC missed its two-thirds majority by just one seat in the National Assembly. It gained 266 seats out of 400 in parliament, one short of the 267 required to achieve a two-thirds majority. Tables 8.5 and 8.6 outline the 1999 national election results.

Sixteen parties participated in the national elections based on a proportional representation model known as the 'list system' (see Figure 8.5 on pages 180 and 181). The system was based not on constituencies but on percentages of the votes throughout the country. In this way, a party that received 10 per cent of the national vote would obtain 10 per cent of the seats in parliament. The candidates who occupy those seats are chosen from a list compiled by the individual party.

Table 8.6 Seats in National Assembly, June 1999 and April 1994

	1999	1994
African National Congress	266	252
Democratic Party	38	7
Inkatha Freedom Party	34	43
New National Party	28	82
United Democratic Movement	14	0
African Christian Democratic Party	6	2
Freedom Front	3	9
Pan Africanist Congress of Azania	3	5
United Christian Democratic Party	3	0
Federal Alliance	2	0
Azanian People's Organisation	1	0
Minority Front	1	0
Afrikaner Eenheids Beweging	1	0

Source: Independent Electoral Commission, Pretoria, 1999.

Table 8.7 Seats won in the provincial legislatures

	E. Cape	Free State	Gaut	KZN	Mpum	N. Cape	North.	North West	W. Cape
ACDP	0	0	1	1	0	0	1	0	1
ANC	47	25	50	32	26	20	44	27	18
DP	4	2	13	7	1	1	1	1	5
FA	0	0	1	0	0	0	0	0	0
IFP	0	0	3	34	0	0	0	0	0
MF	0	0	0	2	0	0	0	0	0
NNP	2	2	3	3	1	8	1	1	17
PAC	1	0	0	0	0	0	1	0	0
UCDP	0	0	0	0	0	0	0	3	0
UDM	9	0	1	1	1	0	1	0	1
FF	0	1	1	0	1	1	0	1	0

Source: Independent Electoral Commission, June 1999.

The proportional representation system ensures that minorities and smaller parties contribute to the passing of legislation and participate in parliamentary select committees (see Appendix 5). Such a system is a fair way of ensuring that a wide variety of political beliefs and cultures are represented.[20] Certainly, political parties and the IEC see the list system as preferable to a constituency-based electoral model.

---

[20] Marius Steyn, interview.

NATIONAL LIST OF PARTIES CONTESTING 2 JUNE ELECTION

  MINORITY FRONT (MF)

Committed to the recognition of minority rights in an emerging democracy and entrenching these rights in the Constitution. Promoting a non-racial, non-sexist, democratic society in which there exists a harmonious relationship between all communities.

  AFRIKANER UNITY MOVEMENT (AEB)

Strives to unite the Afrikaner, to empower him economically and otherwise to enable him to develop his full potential which can be utilised for the advantage of his nation, and the whole of South Africa. Supports free market principles and objects to discriminatory employment procedures, affirmative action and nepotism.

  AFRICAN NATIONAL CONGRESS (ANC)

"Together we've won our freedom and dignity. We've ended a government that served a minority only, and formed one that works for all citizens. We have brought electricity, water and other services to millions of people. Today 750 000 more families have a roof over their heads, on land that belongs to them. But much more work lies ahead. Together, we must step up the fight for a better life for all. And make change happen faster." Thabo Mbeki

  INKATHA FREEDOM PARTY (IFP)

"When we're elected the majority party in the government of South Africa, we'll make a real difference because first and foremost, we'll make the country governable. When we succeed, the country succeeds and you win. We must make the country governable. We have to succeed.

It's time for tough choices. And it's time for tough leadership. I urge you to cast your vote for governability." Mangosuthu Buthelezi

  DEMOCRATIC PARTY (DP)

The party commits itself to a true democracy which rejects race as its basis, protects the dignity and liberty of all its citizens, promotes the general interest and is founded on the principles which form the basis of liberal democracy. It believes in the protection of fundamental human rights and liberties.

It works towards a representative government on the basis of general adult franchise for all South African citizens, as one nation in which cultural groups can live in harmony.

Advocates an independent judiciary and promotes the maintenance of law, order and security.

  FEDERAL ALLIANCE (FA)

The Federal Alliance owes its existence to the need for a united opposition to form a broad-based alternative, effective government to a corrupt and incompetent ANC. As the highest priority the Federal Alliance will address the fundamental issues affecting all South Africans, namely crime, education and health.

The Federal Alliance also believes in the decisive resolution of unemployment, illegal immigrants and housing. The Federal Alliance believes in Christian principles but fully recognises diversity in the South African society.

  AFRICAN CHRISTIAN DEMOCRATIC PARTY (ACDP)

The party believes that South Africa is a nation under the almighty God and represents a fresh start for a new South Africa. It is a party uncontaminated by the past and consists of multi-racial leadership, united behind common principles to bring hope to the nation. It stands for Christian principles, freedom of religion, an open market economy, family values, community empowerment and human rights in a federal system.

  UNITED DEMOCRATIC MOVEMENT (UDM)

The party will unite South Africans from all communities in a new political home, built on the foundation of the principles and ideals of our national Constitution. Inspired by our unifying love of our country and her people, we will address poverty and imbalances in our society. We will cooperate with all stakeholders to ensure a quality life and individual freedom for every citizen. This will be based on good governance and civil order. Together we will build a winning nation.

Figure 8.5 Parties standing in the 1999 elections (source: Nazo Elections '99, 1999)

NATIONAL LIST OF PARTIES CONTESTING 2 JUNE ELECTION

NEW NATIONAL PARTY (N_{UWE}^{EW} NP)

It hopes to achieve its slogan, 'Let's Get South Africa Working' by: showing no mercy for criminals: ensuring economic growth that creates jobs through a flexible labour market: and an education system which allows access for everyone to good quality education.

PAN AFRICANIST CONGRESS OF AZANIA (PAC)

We are committed to a non-racial, gender affirming, Africanist and democratic Azania/South Africa where-in human potential is realised to it's fullest. We believe there is only one race, the human race. An African, for us, is one who, irrespective of colour, owes his/her only allegiance to Africa.

THE GOVERNMENT BY THE PEOPLE GREEN PARTY (GPGP)

Plans to immediately implement changes to all the many factors in this country that are destroying the systems that support life on earth. This includes: ending battery and factory farming; providing more food to feed people; introducing an environmental impact tax; ensuring producers get back product and packaging after use; using the media to change a consumer-minded society: creating an unemployment programme.

SOCIALIST PARTY OF AZANIA (SOPA)

The Socialist party stands by the principle that all forms of racism, sexism and capitalist exploitation (based on the theft of the creative human potential of workers) are fundamentally inhumane and degrading and must be strongly opposed. We dedicate ourselves to fighting such practices. A unified and composite social plan, involving all sectors of society and mobilising all of its citizens in vigorous and open debate is the best and most efficient way of securing our future and that of our children.

UNITED CHRISTIAN DEMOCRATIC PARTY (UCDP)

This party acknowledges the power of God and believes in the inalienable right of freedom and religion. It is committed to maximum provincial and local government autonomy and pursues the highest democratic ideal of having government as close to the people as possible. It is committed to the rule of law and the unconditional restoration and maintenance of law and order. It recognises the value of diversity. Education is placed above all else. It strongly believes in social welfare and is strongly committed to the free market system.

AZANIAN PEOPLE'S ORGANISATION (AZAPO)

AZAPO believes in a democratic order which entails the promotion of upholding the supremacy of the law, addressing the basic needs of all our people, providing free compulsory education from pre-school to grade 10 or age 16, promoting a relevant educational system, abolishing the right to bail for crimes such as murder, rape, drug-trafficking, armed robbery and child molestation and ensuring an efficient and expeditious justice system for the country.

VRYHEIDSFRONT/ FREEDOM FRONT (VF)

The party which believes in self-determination for the Afrikaner people. It proposes a constitutional model which provides for cultural self-determination, as well as for self-determination on a territorial base. Cultural self-determination should be facilitated by means of cultural councils (Afrikaner Councils), especially for Afrikaners not living in a proposed national home. Self-determination on a territorial base is to be achieved by negotiating for an area where Afrikaners could concentrate together, living and working to develop their own national home.

ABOLITION OF INCOME TAX AND USURY PARTY (AITUP)

It is ironic that despite technological advances there is such poverty amidst so much potential wealth. This is a result of usury which is not only the levying of excessive interest, but also the charging of interest on money or credit which has been created from nothing. The Abolition of Income Tax and Usury Party does not have pretensions to power in the short-term, but believes that if a number of representatives are elected, they could act as a catalyst to reform South Africa's monetary system and offer a more prosperous and secure life.

Produced by Lesley Hudson of EISA / Designed by Chakra Design (021) 762 1253

Figure 8.5 Continued

The campaign

The parties conducted vigorous campaigns in presenting their manifestos and programmes to the electorate. The ANC organised its activities around the principle of 'advance and consolidate' and intended to strengthen its position in its heartland areas and advance in regions where support was weaker. In practice, this required important party figures such as Thabo Mbeki to electioneer in marginal provinces, e.g. KwaZulu Natal and the Western Cape. Motorcades equipped with loudhailers and leaflets travelled through the countryside, culminating in the final weekend of May with joyous 'Siyanqoba' (we will triumph) rallies.[21] The ANC's message was upbeat and clear, outlining the government's achievements: 750,000 new houses, 500 clinics, clean water for 3 million citizens, electrification and telephones, as well as free health care for pregnant women and young children. The ANC's optimistic theme, based on 'our fight for change is showing results', was intended to create a mood of hope among poorer sections of society. This was important for the ANC, especially as a national survey of voter profiles conducted by the Human Sciences Research Council (HSRC) in March 1999 revealed that the party's average supporter was likely to be female, poorly educated and unemployed. Equally, the average ANC supporter was satisfied neither with the financial situation of his/her household nor with the general economic situation in the country. However, one positive feature emerged: the expectation that the situation would improve in the coming year (see Table 8.8). Given such a voter profile, the ANC's campaign slogan of promising a better life for all and particularly for 'women, workers, rural communities and people with disabilities' targeted its poorer constituency. 'Dealing with violent crimes against women and children is priority number one', its manifesto declared. The party emphasised its role in representing women by stressing that 39 per cent of candidates on its national list and 34 per cent on its regional and provincial lists were women. The ANC's programme was certainly the most progressive with regard to women.[22] Also, as

Table 8.8 African National Congress voter profile, 1999 (%)

	Black	Coloured	Indian	White
Male	39	2.6	0.6	0.1
Female	54	2.6	0.8	0.3
Household finances worse in last year		61		
Dissatisfied with SA economy		58		
Personal economic situation will improve		63		
Has full/part-time employment		40		

Note: Figures in this table refer to the percentage of all supporters of the party.
Source: Human Sciences Research Council, South Africa, March 1999.

---

[21] cf. EISA *Election Update* No. 12; *Evening Post*, Johannesburg, 6 May 1999.
[22] J. Ballington in EISA *Election Update* No. 12.

women represented a higher percentage of the total electorate and provided a significant constituency of support for the ANC, it was clearly to the party's advantage to highlight the role of women in the campaign. Yet to be fair to the ANC, the position of women in national, provincial and local government had increased dramatically, and a number of socio-economic policies had directly affected women voters.[23] The ANC's campaign was effective, according to opinion polls taken in September 1998 and again in April 1999. When respondents were asked which party they trusted most, the ANC scored 57 per cent in September 1998 and 65 per cent in April 1999.[24]

The ANC's campaign objectives were to speed up the provision of services to meet basic needs and to build the economy and create jobs. Crime and corruption would be combated by a strengthened criminal justice system, and education would be improved. Yet the party was firm against those who wanted 'rights without responsibilities' and engaged in 'selfishness and weak social discipline'. Working for a better South Africa did not imply soft options for those members of the population who disregarded law and order. Although the party did not make specific quantifiable promises, its campaign was generally regarded as positive and successful.

The Democratic Party's campaign was aggressive. Its leader, Tony Leon, wanted the party to be the country's formal opposition, but to achieve that role it had to displace both the New National Party and the Inkatha Freedom Party. The DP's manifesto slogan claimed that the party had the 'guts to fight back' against the government and stressed its resistance to affirmative action. The party looked to a society in which 'life chances for individuals are determined, not by arbitrary demographic criteria, such as race and sex, but by the ability and the will to work'. More jobs would be created through economic growth, and the party was firmly against 'compelling the private sector to move towards the use of demographic quotas in employment'. The party would also 'fight back' against violent crime. The elections, Tony Leon asserted, presented the electorate with a 'stark, simple but significant choice: the DP versus the ANC; right versus might; future versus past; non-racialism versus new racialism; fairness versus favouritism; merit versus mediocrity; people versus party; the individual versus the group'. All the ANC could do in the country was engender 'fear, race, resentment and division'.[25] It was not surprising that the New National Party leader, Marthinus van Schalkwyk, declared that the country had now 'arrived at the remarkable position that the Democratic Party is ideologically a more conservative political party than the National Party'.[26]

In the Western Cape, with 54 per cent of coloured voters, the Democratic Party played on racial scaremongering as it targeted that community with the assertion

---

[23] Refer to Chapter 6, 'Transformation, affirmative action and gender'.
[24] *Opinion 99*, IDASA.
[25] *Daily Dispatch*, 29 March 1999.
[26] Democratic Party Election Manifesto 1999; *The Star*, 6 May 1999.

'Your skin colour still matters'.[27] These electioneering tactics were especially sensitive among a community that regarded itself as marginalised and had since 1994 supported the National Party.[28] Equally, the province was beginning to have a reputation for regarding black Africans as outsiders.[29] Western Cape regional ANC leaders were incensed by the DP's 'fight back' slogan and countered it with the publication of their 'don't fight black' posters. Although the ANC was compelled to withdraw them after complaints to the Electoral Commission, there was an unpleasant undercurrent of racism in campaign tactics in the Western Cape. Even the media noted that the party's campaign 'exploited white fears, played on racial divisions and was completely off-key to the vast majority of black South Africans'.[30] Tony Leon claimed that he did not care who voted for the party as the DP would only be listened to if it gained electoral support. Certainly, in order to target the New National Party's Afrikaner constituency the DP had shifted to the right. Its voter profile was predominantly white, well educated and employed. However, as Table 8.9 indicates, although 57 per cent of DP voters were employed, widespread discontent still existed: 83 per cent were dissatisfied with the economy, and only a tiny 6 per cent believed that there would be personal economic improvement. These figures are in sharp contrast to ANC supporters, only 40 per cent of whom are employed, yet a relatively low 58 per cent are dissatisfied with the economy and nearly two-thirds believe it will improve. The profile of the DP's constituency has been increasingly viewed as a 'small group of wealthy, white supporters' disenchanted with the political changes in the new South Africa and largely pessimistic about their role in the country's future.[31]

The elections for the provincial parliament in the Western Cape resulted in the DP coming third with 11.91 per cent of the total vote (see Table 8.10). The ANC

Table 8.9 Democratic Party voter profile, 1999 (%)

	Black	Coloured	Indian	White
Male	7	5	3	37
Female	3	6	4	35
Household finances worse in last year		48		
Dissatisfied with SA economy		83		
Personal economic situation will improve		6		
Has full/part-time employment		57		

Source: Human Sciences Research Council, South Africa, March 1999.

---

[27] *Cape Argus*, 7 May 1999.

[28] See Deegan 1998 for an account of political preferences among the coloured community since 1994.

[29] See Chapter 6, 'Transformation, affirmative action and gender'.

[30] *Sunday Independent*, 6 June 1999.

[31] *Diamond Fields Advertiser*, 28 April 1999.

Table 8.10 1999 provincial election, Western Cape, and 1994 results

	Votes cast	1999 (%)	1994 (%)
African National Congress	668,106	42.07	33.01
New National Party	609,612	38.39	53.25
Democratic Party	189,183	11.91	6.64
African Christian Democratic Party	44,323	2.79	1.20
United Democratic Movement	9,513	2.40	–

Total registered voters: 1,864,019.
A total of 15 parties participated; 10 received more than 1% of the total vote. The United Democratic Movement did not exist in 1994.
Source: Independent Electoral Commission, 1999.

gained the largest share with 42.07 per cent, with the New National Party coming a close second with 38.39 per cent. Compared with the 1994 results there has been a marked shift in support for the main parties. The ANC increased its overall vote, but support for the New National Party slumped by nearly 15 per cent. The Democratic Party's support nearly doubled from that of 1994, suggesting that its abrasive campaign attracted some voters.

Before the election, the ANC joked that the New National Party was in 'intensive care and would die at any moment'.[32] Although such comments are the usual badinage of electoral competition, they contained an element of truth. The party was failing in the opinion polls. An analysis of party support trends between December 1998 and March 1999 revealed that the party's position had fallen by 4 per cent.[33] Although it was standing on a platform of 'no mercy for criminals', which emphasised law and order and a free market economy, it had begun to lose its core white, Afrikaner constituency. Eleven of its MPs resigned and reaffiliated to other parties in the run-up to the election. The NNP's leader, Marthinus van Schalkwyk, refrained from the ruthless partisanship adopted by his rivals and visited Sharpeville to lay a wreath. 'It is only when white South Africans understand the struggle of black South Africans to be free, that they will really be free' proclaimed van Schalkwyk in an act of symbolic reconciliation. Such acts failed to appeal to hard-line white voters, and one reason cited for their shift away from the party was that it no longer claimed to be an exclusively white party. The traditional ties between white voters and the party declined, with only 5 per cent of white South Africans claiming to identify with it, compared with 48 per cent in October 1994.[34] The NNP committed itself to a non-racial, non-sexist democracy and favoured the provision of training for women, the young and disadvantaged communities. Its voter profile was more evenly balanced between coloured and white supporters, with coloured women forming its largest constituency. In fact,

---

[32] *The Johannesburg Star*, 15 May 1999.
[33] EISA *Election Update* No. 11, 8.
[34] *Opinion 99*, IDASA, 20 June 1999.

Table 8.11 New National Party voter profile, 1999 (%)

	Black	Coloured	Indian	White
Male	8	13	4	21
Female	5	23	5	21
Household finances worse in last year		52		
Dissatisfied with SA economy		72		
Personal economic situation will improve		38		
Has full/part-time employment		49		

Source: Human Sciences Research Council, 1999.

its appeal among coloured voters increased, and 20 per cent claimed to feel 'close to the party'.[35] For coloured voters the NNP was their favoured party but, interestingly, not to the extent it was in 1994. At that time, 53 per cent of the coloured electorate identified with the party. During the 1999 elections, the NNP presented itself as a working-class, non-racial and populist party, in contrast to the allegedly elitist Democratic Party. Certainly, its voter profiles (see Table 8.11) indicate that less than half its supporters were employed, and 72 per cent were dissatisfied with the country's economy. But in contrast to the very negative number of DP supporters who expected economic improvement, 38 per cent of the NNP's voters felt that their personal situation would improve. Despite the New National Party's redefinition, the party found it difficult to move away from its historical background. For many analysts, it could never be a legitimate force in a consolidating democracy as its past was too tainted with the apartheid years.

The Inkatha Freedom Party's electoral slogan of 'make South Africa governable' was central to its manifesto, which included providing jobs, reducing crime, poverty alleviation and education. The party planned to 'get very tough on criminals, including the imposition of mandatory sentencing for certain crimes against children, women and the police'.[36] One important issue of the IFP campaign was the call for powers to be changed at provincial and local level. The party wanted authority devolved to the lowest level of government capable of administering policies adequately and properly. The party advocated that local government should run its own hospitals, schools, police stations and welfare centres: 'When communities are directly involved in the administration of the public services they consume, they are always less likely to squander money or tolerate inefficiency'.[37] The IFP's core constituency was among Zulu speakers in KwaZulu Natal. Two in every five supporters were employed. Although not positive about the national economy or their domestic financial circumstances, nearly half

---

[35] *Ibid.*
[36] *Ibid.* No. 12, 14 May 1999, 7.
[37] *Independent on Saturday*, 3 April 1999.

Table 8.12 Inkatha Freedom Party voter profile, 1999 (%)

	Black	Coloured	Indian	White
Male	42	0	0	0
Female	56	1	0	1
Household finances worse in last year		60		
Dissatisfied with SA economy		65		
Personal economic situation will improve		46		
Has full/part-time employment		41		

Source: Human Sciences Research Council, South Africa, March 1999.

believed that their personal economic situation would improve in the following year (see Table 8.12).

When former ANC and National Party members Bantu Holomisa and Roelf Meyer, respectively, united to form the United Democratic Movement (UDM), it was intended that the mould of South African politics would be broken and that the ANC would be confronted with a genuinely non-racial opposition party. The UDM presented itself as a party with cross-cutting racial and national appeal. Holomisa was popular in the former territory of Transkei, where as a soldier, he displaced the corrupt homeland government, thereby permitting the ANC to engage politically and militarily during the final years of apartheid. It was this contribution that earned him a place on the ANC national list in 1994 and an appointment as junior minister, before his dismissal for revealing instances of government corruption. Meyer's identification as a 'progressive moderate' seemed capable of attracting disaffected NNP supporters, and the party's sights were set on the Eastern Cape. The UDM's strategy was to mobilise support among those voters discontented with the ANC. Central to this effort was the overture to traditional chiefs in the area, who felt undermined by the ANC government's emphasis on democratic rights. The ANC, however, campaigned strongly in the region, emphasising how traditional leaders had helped to take South Africans forward. Relations between the UDM and the ANC were strained, and violence erupted at times. The UDM claimed that under Mbeki, South Africa would become a 'banana republic'. As a counter to these assertions, the ANC promised increased resources to the region, which resulted in a resounding ANC victory in the Eastern Cape. However, the UDM had fielded candidates across the country in its attempt to become a national party. At a national level it gained only 3.42 per cent of total votes cast, which placed it fifth in the national party hierarchy. The party had received no public funding on the grounds that it was a new organisation and needed to have representatives elected to parliament before it could qualify. Inevitably, the party complained of its shortage of money to fund campaigning. Yet one of the central elements in the party's lack of success was the allegation made against Holomisa at the Truth and Reconciliation Commission's amnesty committee. It was declared that while in the Transkei, Holomisa had been involved in the murder of a South African colonel, who had been tortured and

Table 8.13 United Democratic Movement voter profile, 1999 (%)

	Black	Coloured	Indian	White
Male	30	3	2	5
Female	51	4	0	5
Household finances worse in last year		77		
Dissatisfied with SA economy		79		
Personal economic situation will improve		41		
Has full/part-time employment		42		

Source: Human Sciences Research Council, March 1999.

then executed in front of him. Many commentators suggested that these revelations damaged the party nationally.[38] Potentially, the UDM, had it been more successful, could have challenged the ANC in a way that the IFP could not. The UDM attracted a similar constituency to the ANC, that is, isXhosa speakers, who represented 24 per cent of ANC supporters and 52 per cent of UDM voters. Also, of all the parties' voter profiles compiled by the HSRC, UDM supporters had suffered the worst level of household finances in the previous year, 77 per cent (see Table 8.13). With its campaign commitment to narrow the gap between the 'haves' and 'have nots' and ensure rural revitalisation, it might have expected greater support from poorer constituencies.

The picture that emerged from the HSRC voter profiles indicated that only one party had a majority of supporters in employment, and that was the predominantly white Democratic Party. Of the parties that attracted significant support from black South Africans – the ANC, the IFP and the UDM – three out of five supporters were unemployed. However, when party voters were asked to prioritise the policies that they wished to see introduced, UDM supporters prioritised crime prevention (see Table 8.14).

Voters' policy priorities and evaluation of government

As Table 8.14 demonstrates, the policy preferences of voters varied according to the voters' political affiliations. Job creation and fighting crime were the predominant issues of concern to the electorate. The polls outlined in Table 8.14 were conducted by the HSRC on the eve of the 2 June elections, and there were marked differences between the priorities identified by potential voters. Among supporters of the ANC and IFP almost half, 48 and 45 per cent, respectively, cited job creation as the most critical issue. For more than half of the potential supporters of the DP, UDM and FF the number one priority for the government was fighting crime. In contrast, only around one-quarter of ANC and IFP supporters saw crime as being in most urgent need of attention. The Electoral Institute of South

---

[38] EISA *Election Update* No. 11; TRC Report: website.

Table 8.14 Policy priorities of party supporters (%)

	African National Congress	New National Party	Democratic Party	Inkatha Freedom Party	United Democratic Movement	Freedom Front	African Christian Democratic Party
Job creation	48	30	14	45	36	4	13
Fighting crime	26	40	67	28	52	56	46
Better services	7	2	2	5	0	12	5
Improved education	4	6	5	9	3	23	5
More housing	6	4	2	6	0	0	4

Source: Human Sciences Research Council, March 1999.

Africa believes that ANC and IFP supporters saw unemployment as a major underlying cause of crime that had to be addressed first. The ANC's manifesto had emphasised its commitment to be 'tough on the causes of crime', which it identified as poverty and inequality.

It is interesting to see how the population's priorities had changed since 1994 and the large differences in responses to certain categories. As Table 8.15 indicates, crime and security has become a major concern to the population, but fear of indiscriminate violence has decreased dramatically from its 1994 figure, from 49 to 4 per cent. Equally, housing and education have fluctuated, while concern about poverty has remained at the same level. Job creation has become increasingly important. South Africans of all races cite the same overall package of problems, with jobs and crime being the two most often cited among respondents of all racial groups. However, national surveys conducted jointly by the South African Broadcasting Corporation, the Institute for Democracy in South Africa (IDASA) and Markinor, public opinion analysts, found that as the country approached the election there was a 'gradually widening difference of emphasis between the issues of jobs and crime'. IDASA found that white South Africans were more likely to cite crime as an important issue, while black South Africans were likely to mention jobs.[39] As we have seen, these concerns tended to be reflected in party political positions (see Table 8.14).

Signficantly, the IDASA study noted a range of issues that commanded a great deal of attention from activists, the media and politicians but were rarely cited by voters before the election. These included land, rates and taxes, wages, the environment, the death penalty, and affirmative action. As the election approached,

[39] *Opinion 99*, IDASA.

Table 8.15 The most important problems that the government should address, 1994–1999 (%)

	Sept./ Oct. 1994	Nov. 1995	July 1997	Sept. 1998	Oct./Nov. 1998	Feb./Mar. 1999	April 1999
Job creation	67	74	68	73	75	75	79
Crime and security	6	32	58	64	61	62	65
Housing	46	54	44	22	34	32	32
Education	34	20	20	24	23	28	26
Health care	2	7	10	13	11	14	12
Water	0	2	6	6	13	13	11
Corruption	0	2	6	6	7	8	10
General economy	21	10	8	18	16	12	10
Electricity	–	2	4	4	11	8	7
Poverty	9	6	3	9	12	7	9
Violence	49	32	8	8	5	4	4
Discrimination	19	4	2	2	4	4	3
Immigration	–	3	1	4	2	1	2
Political violence	7	6	1	0	1	1	1

Source: *Opinion 99*, IDASA, Cape Town, 1999.

voters were expected to consider rationally which party could best deal with the issues they had prioritised. A survey asked respondents to choose the appropriate party: 48 per cent of those interviewed chose the ANC, 5 per cent the NNP, 4 per cent the DP, and 2 per cent for both the UDM and IFP. However, over a third, 36 per cent, gave a variety of negative replies: no party could deal with the problem, or they did not know which party could solve it or, in any case, all parties were the same.[40] IDASA believed that these voters were waiting for a political party to convince them that it was able to create jobs and fight crime. In the end, IDASA concluded, the results of the election suggested that the ANC had managed to convince voters that it was the party that could best cope with the two issues of job creation and crime.

However, a further national survey revealed that the public gave negative performance ratings of the government's ability to deal with precisely these two problems. As Table 8.16 demonstrates, only about a quarter of those interviewed believed that the government was handling job creation or crime efficiently. Although the figures for April were a slight improvement on those for February/March and suggest that a small portion of the electorate were persuaded by ANC electioneering, the percentages remain very low. In a sense, the responses

[40] *Ibid.*

Table 8.16 Government performance on the 'most important problems' (%)

	% who say government is handling issue 'very well' or 'fairly well'			
	Sept. 1998	Oct./Nov. 1998	Feb./Mar. 1999	April 1999
Job creation/ unemployment	12	23	18	24
Crime/security	18	27	19	26
Housing	53	54	54	61
Education	47	55	n/a	64
Basic services: water/electricity	67	68	68	72
The economy	22	36	41	47
Health care	57	64	60	66
Corruption	26	37	n/a	44
Political violence	62	53	n/a	62

Source: *Opinion 99*, IDASA, Cape Town.

in Table 8.16 are not surprising. The government had not performed well in the areas of unemployment and crime, and these two issues continue to present challenges to Thabo Mbeki's administration. Yet a counter to these two issues, and perhaps one reason why the ANC increased its share of the total vote, is the positive ratings given to other issues that concern the population. Housing, health, education and basic services all received positive responses from interviewees in the survey and reflected a degree of satisfaction with the government. Equally, the fact that approval ratings were increasing suggests that the ANC was running an effective election campaign and was successfully convincing more people about the performance of the government. Also, we must not forget the special factor in the campaign: the stature of President Mandela, whose positive performance rating had reached 85 per cent by April 1999.

Public evaluation of the performance of Deputy President Mbeki improved towards the end of the electoral campaign, with seven in ten voters approving Mbeki's ability to do his job. The government's own responses to corruption and accountability, however, received rather mixed replies. While figures for both issues were improving, only the government's approach to transparency and accountability shifted into positive ratings, from 31 per cent in September 1998 to 55 per cent in April 1999 (see Table 8.17). On the more worrying issue of corruption in government, a majority, 52 per cent, of interviewees believed that the government was not controlling the problem (see Table 8.18).

Inevitably, public views of government performance have an impact on party support, and the ANC receives a large degree of support from those who feel the government is doing a good job. Equally, supporters of opposition parties regard the government as performing badly. Yet there are large differences when undecided voters are divided into racial groups. Undecided white, coloured and Indian voters were harsh in their criticism of the government, while undecided black voters were generally supportive. At first sight, these figures may appear unusual

Table 8.17 Maintaining transparency and accountability (%)

	September 1998	April 1999
Very/fairly well	31	55
Not very well/not well at all	44	38
Don't know	25	7

Source: *Opinion 99*, IDASA.

Table 8.18 Fighting corruption in government (%)

	September 1998	Oct.–Nov. 1998	April 1999
Very/fairly well	26	37	44
Not very well/not well at all	58	60	52
Don't know	16	3	4

Source: *Opinion 99*, IDASA.

as it is assumed that approval of government indicates concomitant approval of the party in government. However, as IDASA points out, 'the way undecided voters eventually decide how to vote depends on what messages parties aim at them and their overall images of a party and its leaders'.[41]

Like the 1994 elections, those of 1999 were still 'race-based'.[42] For some, the 'downside' of the election was its failure to break racial voting patterns: 'Beneath the veneer of civilised discourse ... exists among most South Africans a hardened

Table 8.19 Profile of different party supporters' views of government performance (%)

	ANC	NNP	DP	IFP	UDM	FF	PAC	Black undecided voters	White/ coloured/ Indian undecided voters
Very/fairly well	80	37	23	31	28	11	48	43	24
Not very well/not at all well	15	56	73	66	68	84	52	40	57
Don't know	5	7	4	3	4	5	0	17	19

Source: *Opinion 99*, IDASA.

---

[41] *Ibid*.
[42] Uys 1994; K. Nyatsumba, *The Star*, 9 December 1998.

racial crust.'[43] Although shifts in voting behaviour across racial lines took place among the coloured and Indian communities, white and black voters tended not to change their racial political identities. Conclusions were drawn that it would be 'difficult for a white-led party to make significant inroads in black areas'.[44] But given South Africa's racially defined apartheid years it would have been naive to believe that predominantly white-based political parties could attract significant levels of black support. As Tom Lodge makes clear: 'In a society in which racial distinctions coincide with massive socio-economic inequalities, African voters ... are generally poorer than members of minority communities.'[45] Inevitably, poverty eradication schemes, affirmative action programmes and employment equity legislation – policies so disliked by minority white parties – were likely to be attractive to black voters. These potential material advantages probably accounted for the racially differentiated perceptions of the economy. The white and Indian communities have negative views of economic development, whereas black voters are far more optimistic. Yet it would be wrong to believe that a state of happy idealism exists among the black electorate. When asked the question: 'Is the country going in the right direction?' all racial groups registered less positive ratings than those recorded in 1994 (see Table 8.20). This form of question was intended to elicit more generalised feelings about the country as a whole or, put another way, expose the existence of 'feel good' factors. In other words, to what extent did the wider population feel content and generally pleased about living in South Africa? If the April 1999 figures are considered in this light, the responses suggest that although over two-thirds of the black population were positive, this was lower than the earlier response of 77 per cent. Only one-third of the coloured community felt confident that the country was moving along the right lines, and the white and Indian ratings of 12 and 17 per cent, respectively, are excessively negative. These attitudes may indicate a far greater level of disaffection among these communities, not only with South Africa's politico-economic policies but also with the country as a whole.

Table 8.20 Assessment of the overall direction of the country by racial group

% saying the country is going in the right direction	November 1994	April 1999
Black	77	66
White	50	12
Coloured	54	35
Indian	55	17

Source: *Opinion 99*, IDASA.

[43] *Sunday Independent*, 6 June 1999.
[44] Themba Sono, president of the Institute of Race Relations. *The Star*, 8 June 1999.
[45] T. Lodge in EISA *Election Update* No. 15.

The verdict: free and fair elections

Elections are by definition adversarial as parties compete with each other for the electorate's vote. In the process of attempting to win votes, political parties often criticise each other's programmes and manifestos, impugn each other's intentions and sometimes question the character of party candidates. This form of election-eering is intended to be instrumental in helping voters to decide which party to support. One of the central uncertainties about the 1999 elections, and one for which the IEC had to prepare, was the possibility of violence and conflict. It was feared that electoral competition could enhance levels of political intolerance and lead to a violent situation in which free and fair elections could not be held. Various surveys conducted in 1998 measured the extent to which people would tolerate other parties. In February 1999, reports asserted that the elections were under a 'direct threat of fears engendered among voters by political intolerance in their communities'.[46] And 22 per cent of African voters claimed that it would be 'impossible or dangerous' to disagree politically with politicians.[47] Political violence and terror had been features of the pre-1994 electoral period, but those actions had declined once the election had taken place. In 1999, anxieties focused on the new party, the UDM, and the possibility that it would arouse fierce political competition and, potentially, violent outbursts. Yet in KwaZulu Natal, high levels of political intolerance were registered in opinion polls before the election, and 44 per cent of ANC supprters, 39 per cent of IFP supporters and 36 per cent of UDM supporters claimed that they would not allow an opposition party political meeting to take place in their neighbourhood. Analysts argued that a causal link existed between political intolerance and political violence, and thus fears were fuelled that the 1999 election would be disrupted.[48] The IEC took the issue of security very seriously and employed police and defence staff at registration-voting areas in order to prevent disturbances. Handbooks and instructions on conflict management were issued to officers presiding over the electoral process, and considerable resources were devoted to the task: 85,000 security personnel were deployed across the country.[49] The UN-coordinated electoral observer mission, which the IEC had invited to witness the elections, commended the 'positive' roles played by the South African police service and the defence force in ensuring security in 'a calm and discreet manner'. Even in areas of maximum deployment, the security presence was neither 'oppressive nor intrusive'.[50] In the event, the threat of violence had been overexaggerated, and minister of safety and security, Sydney Mufamadi declared the election 'free of politically motivated violence'.[51]

[46] See Johnson 1999: 29.

[47] *Ibid*. Survey conducted by Helen Suzman Foundation, MarkData, October 1998.

[48] Marius Steyn, interview; EISA *Election Update* No. 13; Johnson 1999.

[49] Marius Steyn, interview.

[50] UN Joint International Observer Group, 4 June 1999. Statement delivered by President Nicephore Soglo, former head of state of Benin, Johannesburg; ERIS Report, Johannesburg, 7 June 1999.

[51] Marius Stein, interview; *Mail and Guardian Special Election Supplement*, 4–10 June 1999.

One of the IEC's tasks was to ensure that a clear definition of the term 'free and fair' was properly understood by all agencies concerned with the election. Voters had to have information about political alternatives, be able to attend political meetings, vote in polling stations that were properly organised, and not be placed under any influence or coercion. No party was to be given any special privileges, and all were entitled to access to the media and the electorate. Fairness in the electoral context as defined by the commission meant that there would be 'no attempt to deceive voters or withhold or distort information vital to the making of good voting decisions'. All organisations involved in the election were to be transparent and accountable.[52] In accordance with the Electoral Act, party agents and candidates were not permitted to display or distribute posters or leaflets at voting stations on election day. In the event, South Africa's second democratic general election was a success. The media commended the IEC on doing 'extremely well' and felt that the election had been marked by 'patience, tolerance and goodwill'.[53] International observers from the Commonwealth observer group praised the 'tolerant atmosphere' of the electoral process: 'We have seen unhindered and vigorous political campaigning and there can be no doubt about the political freedom enjoyed by all candidates.' The European observer group pronounced the elections 'transparent, inclusive and free from censorship and tension'. Jan Scholten, president of the Association of Western European Parliamentarians, reported on a campaign period that was 'characterised by dignity, a lack of violence and vastly increased political tolerance'.[54] By consensus, the 1999 elections were viewed as significantly more peaceful than those of 1994, with far less tension between the political parties. According to an HSRC national survey of 11,140 voters at 214 polling stations, 96 per cent of respondents felt that the elections had been free and fair. The survey revealed similarities in the responses of different racial groups, with a massive 99 per cent of voters indicating that they had been neither forced nor intimidated to support a specific party. The media felt that the responses reflected a major advance towards a political culture that was tolerant of opposition. In future years, it would be the responsibility of all political parties to build on the 'positive consciousness among voters' and to deepen further the process of democratisation.[55] Certainly, the international observers viewed the elections as an 'enhancement' of the democratic process and a further step towards its consolidation.[56]

One interesting aspect of the voting patterns in the election was the variability between party support at national and provincial levels (see Table 8.21). Some parties attracted more votes regionally than nationally and demonstrated a strong provincial presence, e.g. the Inkatha Freedom Party and the New National Party. Ten parties contested all nine provincial legislatures as well as the National

---

[52] *A Handbook on Conflict Management*, EISA 1998: 5.
[53] *Mail and Guardian Special Election Supplement*, 4–10 June 1999.
[54] ERIS Report 1999.
[55] *The Sowetan*, 8 June 1999; *Business Day*, 4 June 1999.
[56] ERIS Report 1999.

Table 8.21 Total National Assembly votes compared with total provincial legislature votes

	Votes for National Assembly	Votes for provincial legislatures	Difference in votes
African Christian Democratic Party	228,975	219,471	9,504
ANC	10,601,330	10,493,175	108,155
Afrikaner Eenheids Beweging	46,292	47,645	(1,353)
Democratic Party	1,527,337	1,416,352	110,985
Federal Alliance	86,704	82,058	4,646
IFP	1,371,477	1,415,541	(44,064)
New National Party	1,098,215	1,141,362	(43,147)
Pan Africanist Congress of Azania	113,125	146,757	(33,632)
United Democratic Movement	546,790	535,930	10,860
Freedom Front	127,217	142,538	(15,321)

Note: figures in parentheses indicate more votes were cast for the provincial legislature than for the National Assembly.
Source: IEC, June 1999.

Assembly. As Table 8.21 indicates, 108,155 voters who wanted the ANC to govern nationally cast their votes in favour of other parties for provincial government. Equally, while 44,064 voters wanted the IFP to govern at provincial level, they cast their votes for another party in the National Assembly. The Independent Electoral Commission was intrigued by this pattern of voting and considered that vote splitting – voting for one party for provincial government and a different one for the National Assembly – was an indication of rational voting. When voters adopt such a strategy they exercise choice and compare party policy positions, deciding that a given party is best for the nation while another party is more suitable at provincial level. Vote splitting was apparent in the 1994 elections, as Tom Lodge points out, and clearly 'voters can differentiate between a range of dimensions of political performance'.[57] This form of voting behaviour conforms to the ideal of the informed citizen fully participating in the democratic exercise rather than one of an unthinking electorate 'blindly committed' to one party.[58]

In spite of the anxieties about identity cards, registration procedures, turnout rates, political intolerance and electoral violence, South Africa's second democratic general election elicited plenty of enthusiasm from voters and was declared 'a trouble-free poll'.[59] As in 1994, the electorate was prepared to demonstrate the depth of its political conviction by lining up at polling stations from daybreak to sunset. The ANC gained an overwhelming victory, improving on its 1994 posi-

---

[57] cf. T. Lodge in EISA *Election Update* No. 15; Mattes 1999.
[58] Marius Steyn, interview; Mattes 1999.
[59] *The Star*, 3 June 1999.

tion and thus ensuring that it had received a 'renewed and strengthened mandate'. The media recorded that a vast majority had accepted the ANC's credentials and its commitment to 'clean, transparent and accountable government'. Many tributes were paid to the party's 'masterly campaign' orchestrated by 'able and clever' people, which reflected the organisation's growing maturity. The party was praised for rejecting negative campaigning and being prepared to 'ditch old ideas and embrace new ones'.[60] Yet, beyond the hyperbole, Thabo Mbeki recognised that the people of South Africa had placed their trust in the ANC to deliver jobs, housing and a better life, a trust the ANC could not afford to betray.[61] No one had been in any doubt that the ANC would win the election, but it had also increased its share of the vote and gained fourteen seats. In 1994, the runner-up was the National Party with 20 per cent of the votes and eighty-two seats, whereas in 1999, the Democratic Party came second and secured less than 10 per cent of the vote, winning only thirty-eight seats. The Democratic Party claimed a great victory, and clearly it had improved on its previous position, but the overall result meant that parliamentary opposition to the government was more fragmented.

Concern has been expressed about the ANC's dominant political position and whether it would be tempted to abuse its power. No government should become too complacent, and adequate checks by the media, civil society, pressure groups and the public protector are essential to ensure accountability and transparency. Equally, the parliamentary portfolio committees are open to the public and potentially able to provide greater accountability to the policy-making process (see Appendix 5). The significant level of Afrikaner support for the DP may have demonstrated that 'white South Africans were no longer able to stomach the past misdeeds of the New National Party'. Yet many suffered 'racial resentment of new black authority' and were attracted to the Democratic Party because of its 'aggressive record of opposition'.[62] There are dangers in this new conservative constituency, particularly if the DP's policies were to become affected by white racist interests at the expense of wider society.[63] Ironically, the NNP attempted to attract multiracial support and resisted approaches based on racial division. Some analysts suggested that it was precisely this multiracialism that cost the party its white support.[64] However, rallying people on the basis of their racial feelings or insecurity as minorities is likely to be counter-productive and self-restrictive in the medium term. Although the DP benefited from racial division, if it is too closely identified with its right-wing, former pro-Nationalist Party supporters, its potential for development could be constrained. Ultimately, the party would be unable 'to face the daunting task of taking the debate beyond the racial divides of the past'.[65] South Africa is a country moving away from a deeply racist past, and

---

[60] *The Sowetan*, 4 June 1999; *The Saturday Star*, 5 June 1999; *The Sunday Independent*, 6 June 1999.

[61] *Mail and Guardian Special Election Supplement*, 4–10 June 1999.

[62] cf. *Citizen*, 9 June 1999; T. Lodge in EISA *Election Update* No. 15.

[63] *Mail and Guardian*, 4 June 1999; *Citizen*, 9 June 1999.

[64] Denis Venter, interview.

[65] *Mail and Guardian Special Election Supplement*, 4–10 June 1999.

the last thing it needs is for party politics to be continually mired in racial prejudice. Political parties are sustained by electoral support, but in a new democracy they also need to act responsibly.[66]

The Inkatha Freedom Party still remained a 'major political player', although its strength continued to be centred in KwaZulu Natal. The IFP retained its black support in KwaZulu and Gauteng but lost white voters, who had supported it in 1994, to the Democratic Party. Ultra-right and left-wing parties such as the Freedom Front and the Pan Africanist Congress failed to attract high levels of support, unlike the successful newcomer, the United Democratic Movement. The poor organisation, low funds and lacklustre campaigns of the marginal parties attracted their dismissal as 'political amateurs'. Yet the shift away from fringe parties suggests that the electorate wants pragmatic policies rather than populist slogans.[67] South Africa's 1999 election affirmed the country's democratic processes and gave the ANC a resounding victory. But Thabo Mbeki and his government need to deliver the right policies before the next presidential and provincial elections in 2004. As Jack Spence states:

> The 1999 election provides the ANC with a second chance to make good the failures in economic and social performance over the last five years; to strengthen its democratic credentials; to build on the work of the TRC and in the long term to provide a firmer basis for new national identity within a shared society.[68]

---

[66] The new alignment between the NNP and the DP into the 'Democratic Alliance' in preparation for the local elections due in 2000/2001 requires close monitoring.

[67] *The Sunday Times*, 6 June 1999; *The Star*, 9 June 1999.

[68] Spence 1999: 6.

Chapter 9

From Mandela to Mbeki

Goodbye to Nelson Mandela

> ### Box 9.1 Nelson Mandela
>
> Born on 18 July 1918 into the royal Xhosa clan in the village of Qunu, southern Transkei, Nelson Mandela was educated at the University of Fort Hare. His life was marked by political activism: from a student campaigning for equality for blacks, to a lawyer defending victims of apartheid, to commander of the African National Congress's underground guerrilla army. In June 1964, he was convicted of trying to overthrow the white minority government and sentenced to life imprisonment. He spent twenty-seven years in jail before being released in February 1990.

On 26 March 1999, Nelson Mandela delivered his final parliamentary speech after five years as head of state. He paid tribute to his colleagues and their achievements: a new constitution and 534 new laws. The new laws had created 'a framework for the revolutionary transformation of society and government so the legacy of the past could be undone'. However, not all the challenges facing the country had been met:

> We still have to reconcile and heal our nation, to the extent that the consequences of apartheid still permeate our society and define the lives of millions of South Africans as lives of deprivation.

Although these challenges remained unchanged, the foundations had been laid for a better life.[1] Before the 80-year-old president took the podium, political leaders lined up to deliver unstinting praise. Thabo Mbeki, at the time deputy president but shortly to assume the status of president of the country, delivered a stirring speech:

> You have walked along the road of heroes and heroines. You have faced death and said – do your worst. You have inhabited the dark dungeons of freedom denied ... You have been where nobody should be asked to be.

---

[1] *Cape Argus*, 26 March 1999.

Table 9.1 'How well do you think President Mandela is performing his job?'

	May–June 1995	November 1997	April 1999
Very well/fairly well	76%	81%	85%

Source: *Opinion 99*, SABC/IDASA.

The leader of the New National Party, Marthinus van Schalkwyk, hailed Mandela as 'everybody's president'. 'Is it not one of the great ironies of life that those who suffered greatly, so often have the capacity to forgive greatly?' he said, 'You not only possessed generosity of spirit, as president, you lived it.' Tony Leon of the Democratic Party described Mandela as one 'born with a special kind of grace, who seemed to transcend the politics of his age. He graces this house of parliament. He graces this country. He graces humanity.'[2] As Mandela left the chamber for the last time, MPs applauded him and chanted his name.

Few political leaders have aroused such widespread affection and respect, and it is impossible to separate the qualities of Nelson Mandela from South Arica's transition to democracy. On his retirement, his standing in the country was at its highest level. Mandela's performance evaluations were exceptionally strong and widespread, with 85 per cent approval ratings (see Table 9.1). The Post Office distributed special cards through newspapers so that the public could send personal messages to 'Madiba' free of charge (see Figure 9.1). Mandela was often addressed as 'Madiba', the name of his clan, as a sign of respect.

Yet Mandela was no paragon and readily admitted the arrogance of his youth.[3] He recognised that the long years in prison had matured his personality and taught him to reach out to other communities, to find common ground. He had spoken of democracy in his address to the court during the Rivonia trial in 1964. Facing a possible death sentence for treason against the apartheid state, Mandela told the court:

> During my lifetime I have dedicated myself to the struggle of the African people. I have fought against black domination. I have cherished the ideal of a democratic and free society in which all persons live together in harmony and with equal opportunities. It is an ideal that I hope to live for and to achieve. But if needs be, it is an ideal for which I am prepared to die.[4]

When revisiting Robben Island in 1994, Mandela recalled his first prison cell:

> When I lay down, I could feel the wall with my feet and my head grazed the concrete at the other side. The width was about six feet. I was 46 years old, a political prisoner

---

[2] *Ibid.*

[3] Mandela 1994; Sampson 1999.

[4] cited in President Mandela's 80th Birthday Celebration, Independent Newspapers/Mondi 17 July 1998; Mandela repeated these words when he was released from prison – see Appendix 3.

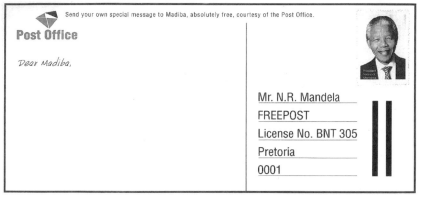

Figure 9.1 Special card distributed by post offices to enable the public to send personal messages to President Mandela

with a life sentence, and that small cramped space was to be my home for I knew not how long.

It turned out to be eighteen years.[5] Anthony Sampson's authorised biography of Mandela outlines an interesting character assessment made in 1981. The then minister of justice, Kobie Coetsee, requested of the prison service a detailed analysis of the character of Nelson Mandela (see Box 9.2). For Sampson, the assessment is a 'remarkably accurate analysis of Mandela's personality and thinking'. He also points out that Mandela was being studied as a political leader long before the country slid further into violent conflict and nine years before he was released from prison.[6]

---

[5] *Ibid.*
[6] Sampson 1999.

Box 9.2 Character assessment of Nelson Mandela made while he was on Robben Island, 1981

(1) Mandela is exceptionally motivated and maintains a strong idealistic approach.
(2) He maintains outstanding personal relations, is particularly jovial and always behaves in a friendly and respectful way towards figures of authority.
(3) He is manipulative, but nevertheless not tactless or provocative.
(4) There are no visible signs of bitterness towards whites, although this may be a fine game of bluff on his part.
(5) He acknowledges his own shortcomings, but nevertheless believes in himself.
(6) He has a capacity for integrated and creative thought.
(7) He has an unbelievable memory to reproduce things in the finest detail.
(8) He has an unflinching belief in his cause and in the eventual triumph of African nationalism.
(9) He regards himself as called to the task and this elevates him above the average white who, according to him, has apparently lost his idealism.
(10) He believes self-discipline, and continually taking the initiative, to be the prerequisites for success.

There exists no doubt that Mandela commands all the qualities to be the Number One black leader in South Africa. His period in prison has caused his psycho-political posture to increase rather than decrease and with this he now has acquired the characteristic prison-charisma of the contemporary liberation leader.

Source: Sampson 1999.

The 1994 government's performance and future challenges ____

No one could doubt the personal character of Nelson Mandela and the dignity he brought to the presidency of South Africa's first democratic government. But what are the achievements of those years and how far have they moved the country towards reducing the deep-seated imbalances of the past? Certainly, there is a general consensus, even among sceptics, that South Africa made the transition from apartheid to democracy in a context of national reconciliation. The fears expressed by many white commentators in 1994 of a country in which increased political violence and disarray would predominate have not materialised. Equally, a new constitution was crafted at the beginning of the administration, partly through a consultative exercise with the general public, and became effective in 1997. Under the new constitution, a comprehensive framework for the practice of good governance was established that repeatedly affirmed the need for accountable, open and effective government. All members of the cabinet are accountable collectively and individually to parliament. A variety of parliamentary portfolio and select committees have been introduced in the National Assembly to scrutinise policy pro-

posals. These committees, now numbering fifty as opposed to the previous thirteen, may initiate legislation and for the first time are open to the public. With
around twenty-six independent groups monitoring the progress and management
of the committees, they are widely regarded as a vibrant part of the law-making
process[7] (see Appendix 5). These innovations should be seen as major strides
towards greater transparency, and although notions of a 'people's parliament' are
extravagant, the new democratic institutions are moving in the right direction.[8]
Yet institutions alone cannot provide democracy; there must be a willingness at
government level to accept scrutiny and criticism.

The new rules of parliament, framed in the 1996 constitution, have placed considerable responsibility on members not only for policy making but also for over-
seeing the management of a broad range of issues. Yet it must be remembered that
the majority of parliamentarians elected in 1994 had no experience of governance.
Many were former freedom fighters turned conventional politicians. As Jovial
Rantao explained: 'The newly-baptised MPs had to learn the legislative process,
and how to manage and transform an institution that had previously existed to
protect the interests of a few.' In the select committees of both the National
Assembly and the National Council of Provinces, which came into being in 1997,
there were endless arguments, emotional battles, walk-outs and name calling.
However, by 1999, political representatives 'felt proud they have done their bit
for the transformation of the country'.[9]

The economy

Critics of the 1994 government argue that it made 'insufficient progress' in deliv-
ering higher living standards for the mass of the population,[10] while other analysts
believe that the ANC became increasingly compromised by its economic policy
and the adoption of 'neo-liberal macro-economic' programmes such as GEAR.[11] A
'systematic ideological conversion' took the ANC from a socialist-inclined liberation movement to an organisation that readily embraced capitalism. For those
concerned about social equity, the government was seen as a traitor to the cause of
equality.[12] The government has critics from a range of quarters: communists who
continue to desire the great socialist experiment and rail against big business; left-
of-centre pundits concerned about social democracy; and liberals worried that the
government is insufficiently *laissez-faire*. On the one hand, the GEAR programme
has been judged inappropriate, undesirable and overly involved with the business
community, while on the other hand, it is judged to have moved too slowly in the

[7] Joval Rantao, *The Star*, 26 March 1999.
[8] Frene Ginwala, Speaker of the National Assembly, cited in *The Star*, 26 March 1999.
[9] *Ibid.*
[10] Blumenfeld 1999: 47.
[11] Marais 1998: 56.
[12] *Ibid.*

area of labour-market policy.[13] Jesmond Blumenfeld believes that wages should have been lowered and privatisation pursued more aggressively. This is a contentious issue, especially as Mondli Hlatshwayo points out that 'many local workers already earn starvation wages'. According to the National Economic Development and Labour Council report of 1997–1998, the income of the poorest 20 per cent is a mere 3.32 per cent of the country's total income.[14] Any reduction in wages, he argues, would inevitably exacerbate this situation.

However, the labour problem will not disappear automatically. Employment in the regularly surveyed formal non-agricultural sectors of the economy declined by 189,000 workers, or 3.7 per cent, in 1998.[15] The South African Reserve Bank attributed this fall to the slowdown in global economic activity and the constant pressure on domestic producers to be competitive in an increasingly integrated world economic system. Yet variations were evident between different areas of the private sector. Although employment actually increased in the trade, catering and accommodation sectors as well as in laundries and dry-cleaning services, the rate of job losses in the construction industry accelerated from 9.6 to 20.5 per cent.[16] Whereas during the apartheid years the public sector would absorb job losses in the private sector, thereby reducing the level of unemployment, the policy of the 1994 government has been to resist expansion in public-sector bodies. This policy did not remedy unemployment levels, but the Reserve Bank viewed the government's action favourably. The policy was evidence of the government's resolve 'to improve efficiency in public-service delivery' and to reduce the overall size of the public sector.[17] Clearly, unemployment levels would fall if the government introduced a public-sector job creation scheme, but the focus of its policy has been to streamline that sector and reduce the size of state bureaucracy in order to stay within budgetary constraints. What has been unusual during a period of high unemployment is that wage rates have increased. For 1998 as a whole, the growth in remuneration per worker in the public sector rose from 10.9 per cent in 1997 to 11.7 per cent, while wage rises in the private sector were around 8 per cent. Although labour productivity, i.e., growth of output per worker, improved, it remained below the level of wage growth. In other words, labour costs rose, placing great pressure on producers to raise prices. However, in areas such as diamonds, gold and other metals, prices are set by international commodity markets rather than indigenous pressures. Equally, if prices of other producer goods increase, companies may risk losing their market share to their competitors. As the Reserve Bank points out, in such an economic setting, businesses would not normally increase wages faster than their current price levels.

Usually, when wages increase, domestic consumption also increases as people have more money to spend. However, in the case of South Africa, by 1999 there

---

[13] cf. Ibid.; Blumenfeld 1999.
[14] Hlatshwayo 1999.
[15] South African Reserve Bank Review 1999.
[16] Ibid.
[17] Ibid.

had been a decline in household spending, particularly on durable goods such as cars and furniture. The Reserve Bank believes that a set of circumstances contributed to this development. As employment prospects turned bleaker and job security became threatened, consumer confidence fell and there was a disinclination to spend unnecessarily. Although the income of some households had increased through higher wages, these resources were used to pay off outstanding debts that had accumulated in previous months. After 1994, consumer demand, fuelled by easy access to credit, rose dramatically. However, as interest rates and debts increased the public became more pragmatic and decided to resist spending.

Clearly, there are 'no simple formulae' that would guarantee 'sustained regeneration, let alone employment', given the 'immensity of the economic challenges' confronting the country, but issues of labour flexibility and privatisation are unlikely to disappear.[18] The South African Reserve Bank's Monetary Policy Committee expressed concern about the 'continued shedding of jobs' but regarded unemployment as 'a structural problem'.[19] However, the bank believes that certain legislation had a direct impact on the economy's capacity to create jobs, namely the Employment Equity Act, which is directed at the elimination of unfair discrimination in employment practices; the Basic Conditions of Employment Act, which provides a legal framework for regulating the minimum working conditions of South African employees; and the Skills Development Act, which was intended to strengthen education and training efforts.[20] Mbeki has accepted that in part the labour laws hinder job creation and place an 'unreasonable' burden on small businesses.[21] The pressures of globalisation will affect South Africa increasingly in the twenty-first century as international investors call for the privatisation of state assets, flexible labour legislation and the abolition of exchange control regulations.[22] However, other vital tasks, such as tax collection, have been important for the economy.[23] In March 1998 alone, the revenue service collected 22 billion rand (£2.2 billion), which was an increase of 22.5 per cent on the previous year.[24]

Governance and education

In terms of governance, institutional and parliamentary procedures have evolved in a democratic direction. The interim constitution, in effect up to 1997, did not provide clear definitions of legislative authority, so unlike Nelson Mandela in 1994, Thabo Mbeki leads a country in which the constitutional framework provides for far greater levels of openness in all branches of government. Such

---

[18] *Ibid.*: 46.

[19] South African Reserve Bank, Statement of the Monetary Policy Committee, 13 January 2000.

[20] *South African Reserve Bank Review* 1999.

[21] *The Star*, Johannesburg, 9 February 2000.

[22] cf. *South African Reserve Bank Review* 1999; Garrow 1999.

[23] President Mandela's Government's Report to the Nation 1998: 14.

[24] Ngcobo 1999.

developments pose challenges to both Mbeki's government and the opposition parties, all of which require political accountability and commitment. Before the 1999 elections, Thabo Mbeki spoke of the need for continuity between successive administrations in that the actions of former legislators defined what subsequent ones can do. Studies commissioned by the 1994 parliament on the important issues of power, privilege and delegated legislation are available to the 1999 National Assembly and may assist in taking the 'process of transformation further'.[25] Interestingly, reports indicate that the government's greatest success stories in terms of delivery – equal rights and anti-discrimination legislation – are no longer priority issues for the mass of the population. Employment and crime prevention are the top priorities of the general public (see Tables 8.14 and 8.15).

Nelson Mandela admitted in his address to parliament in 1998 that obstacles to policy implementation were often the result of restricted resources. However, he did point to the fact that 1.3 million more South Africans had access to clean water, the primary school feeding scheme reached 4.9 million children, electricity connections attained 58 per cent of the target, over half a million homes were linked to telecommunications and over 700,000 homes had been built. Although, he accepted, there was 'no magic in numbers', he felt that the country should be proud of programmes that were having an impact on the lives of the poor.[26] The Restitution of Land Rights Act restored land to people who had been forcefully removed from their territories during the apartheid years. Over 23,000 claims were made by dispossessed landowners, and many won the right to return to their land. President Mandela presided over ceremonies celebrating the transferral of title deeds.[27]

However, with regard to educational reforms, the 1994 government only 'touched the surface of the legacy of apartheid education'.[28] Many children still studied under trees, in dilapidated buildings and without appropriately trained teachers. Some schools were hollow shells without even the most basic equipment and few textbooks. Poor management, malfunctioning school governing bodies and low standards hampered attempts to improve educational levels for all children. With eleven official national languages, the government focused on cross-language communication in the classroom for both pupils and teachers. Inevitably, certain languages, e.g. English, have become dominant. While most South Africans are multilingual, very few speak English at home, preferring their indigenous African languages. As a result of the years of neglect in the past, the teaching of languages, including English, at most of the country's schools is very poor. Even children who manage to pass examinations after twelve years of schooling do not usually speak, write or read English well. Their poor knowledge of the language often makes it impossible for them to gain employment. To counter

---

[25] F. Ginwala, see footnote 21.
[26] President Mandela's Government's Report to the Nation 1998.
[27] *Khanyisa*, 1998.
[28] *Ibid.*

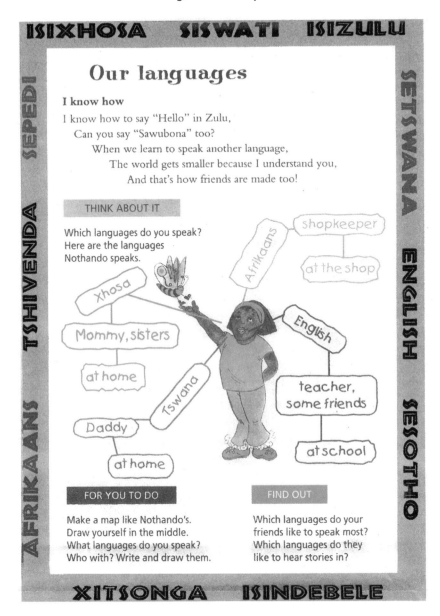

Figure 9.2 South Africa's different languages (source: Liberty Life, Actively Supporting Education Via Africa, Cape Town, 1999)

these difficulties and assist in the development of bilingualism the government introduced its Language in Education policy, which is intended to provide a better understanding of linguistic differences (see Figure 9.2). But improved educational opportunities for all demand increased government resources and improved management. In 1996, children under the age of 10 represented nearly a quarter of the

Table 9.2 Population of South Africa, 2000

Racial group	% of total population
Black	77.4
White	11.7
Coloured	8.4
Asian	2.5
Total population	44.7 million

Source: Compiled from Bureau of Market Research, University of South Africa, Pretoria, 2000.

Table 9.3 Projections of life expectancy (in years)

	Blacks	Coloureds	Asians	White
2011	57.6	61.8	66.8	72.3
2021	50.1	61.6	69	73.1

Source: Compiled from Bureau of Market Research, University of South Africa, Pretoria, 2000.

Table 9.4 Actual and projected demographic trends.

Year	Children under 10 years as a percentage of the total population	People aged 60 years and older as a percentage of the total population
1996	23.5	6.4
2021	17.2	10.8

Source: Compiled from Bureau of Market Research, University of South Africa, Pretoria, 2000.

country's total population, 23.5 per cent, and consequently required a great commitment from the government. However, educational provision may be only a medium-term problem as declining fertility levels and life expectancy have lowered projections of demographic growth. The impact of AIDS has included a decrease in the life expectancy of some sections of society, yet the number of people over 65 is predicted to increase (see Tables 9.2–9.4).

Crime

Crime has become one of South Africa's major problems. As Tables 9.5 and 9.6 indicate, reported cases of murder and attempted murder are particularly high in some provinces, yet other crimes have a high profile in the media and a particular impact on tourism and foreign investment confidence. Crimes such as car hijacking, theft of motor vehicles, hijacking of trucks with freight and robbery of cash in transit have been reported regularly and serve to create a climate of fear and

Table 9.5 Reported cases of murder

	1994	1995	1996	1997
Eastern Cape	950	1058	853	1078
Free State	336	287	334	331
Gauteng	1544	1236	1367	1206
KwaZulu Natal	2285	1794	1699	1455
Mpumalanga	287	227	291	303
North West	348	256	332	327
Northern Cape	123	138	178	144
Nothern Province	267	212	233	248
Western Cape	662	727	888	771

Source: SAPS Quarterly Report, 1998.

Table 9.6 Reported cases of attempted murder

	1994	1995	1996	1997
Eastern Cape	447	517	790	813
Free State	256	212	311	295
Gauteng	1959	1816	1650	1684
KwaZulu Natal	2139	2008	1826	1668
Mpumalanga	416	309	413	406
North West	304	272	391	450
Northern Cape	58	83	105	105
Northern Province	573	442	358	468
Western Cape	680	679	858	873

Source: SAPS Quarterly Report, 1998.

danger (see Tables 9.7 and 9.8). The high incidence of motor vehicle theft, particularly in the Johannesburg and Pretoria areas (Gauteng), raises the perception of crime among the more affluent members of society, especially among the white community. Since 1996, crimes such as car hijacking have been listed as separate criminal categories at the Crime Information Management Centre (CIMC), which was established by the South African Police Service (SAPS) on 1 January 1996. This unit, consisting of a head office and nine provincial offices, coordinates, processes and analyses crime information, which is then passed directly to the government and police service.

During 1996, the CIMC analysed a range of murder cases reported in the Eastern Cape and found that 3 per cent were related to taxi violence and 1 per cent were linked to gang-related violence, while 93 per cent of cases were linked to alcohol and drug abuse. An analysis of records in Northern Cape, Free State and Mpumalanga revealed similar links between alcohol and violence. In the

Northern Cape, most murders occurred on Saturdays, with 68 per cent of all victims stabbed with a knife or other object. In the overwhelming majority of cases, no planning or motive could be associated with the murder. Alcohol and family disputes featured in most cases. Again in the Free State, murders were committed with knives or other objects. Firearms were used in a minority of cases and were usually legally owned by either the perpetrator or the victim. In most cases, the motives for the murders committed were personal, e.g. marital problems, jealousy, self-defence, arguments, etc. Many murders occurred in or in the vicinity of drinking places, and in the majority of cases either the victim or the perpetrator, or both, were under the influence of alcohol when the attack occurred.[29] Follow-up research conducted by the CIMC in Mpumalanga confirmed the patterns observed in other provinces: 59 per cent of murders took place in drinking establishments or shebeens; a further 20 per cent were murdered in their immediate locality; and only 15 per cent of murders appeared to involve any premeditation or planning on the part of the perpetrator.[30] In the case of serious assault, 67 per cent of all incidents occurred at weekends. The majority of both male and female victims were aged between 18 and 29. Most incidents of robbery with aggravating circumstances, that is, with armed threat, occurred on the streets. Knives were used to commit 45 per cent of this type of robbery, and in 56 per cent of cases, cash of between 1 rand and 100 rand (between 10 pence and £10) was stolen. The CIMC found this type of crime particularly difficult to solve because of its prevalence in areas of high unemployment. In such circumstances, crime was resorted to 'as a means of livelihood'.[31]

A strong relationship exists between certain forms of crime and unemployment, and the qualitative research that the CIMC conducted in the Eastern Cape suggests a strong connection between the two. In fact, the research indicated that gang-related violence was 'something of a survival mechanism in a world of poverty and unemployment'. So embedded was the gang culture that the CIMC maintained it could not be eradicated by prosecution alone. Socio-economic upliftment combined with a process of resocialisation would be necessary to address the problem. In the Eastern Cape, the coloured community living in the northern areas of Port Elizabeth has known gangsterism since the 1970s and suffered its consequences. A culture of gang-related violence and the selling and smuggling of banned substances became entrenched in deprived and poverty-stricken communities. As the CIMC report stated:

> Shacks were rented out to families needing shelter and some of the gang members act as banks, lending money to members of their communities on a monthly basis. Many families having to cope with insufficient government grants were forced to borrow money. In this way the community was kept indebted, which ensured their loyalty.

---

[29] SAPS Quarterly Report 1998. A selection of research results received from provincial crime information management centre offices – http://www.saps.co.za.
[30] *Ibid.*
[31] *Ibid.*

Table 9.7 Reported cases of car hijacking

	1996	1997
Eastern Cape	138	145
Free State	47	47
Gauteng	1855	1856
KwaZulu Natal	669	710
Mpumalanga	125	168
North West	124	102
Northern Cape	6	1
Northern Province	51	53
Western Cape	77	62

Source: SAPS Quarterly Report, 1998.

These people will not testify against gangsters, because they know that they receive a service from the gangs. Gang leaders often pay people's rent, water and electricity bills in return for using their homes to hide drugs. Home-owners' legally registered firearms were often hired to commit crimes. Children tend to drop out of school at a very young age and gang members living among them serve as their role models. A strong fear factor is present within the community.[32]

In these circumstances, crime becomes an endemic part of the locality. More recently, the anti-crime organisation People Against Drugs and Violence (PADAV) has acted as a pressure group fighting against drugs and gang-related violence. However, relations between PADAV and the police have been under severe strain, especially as PADAV shows a strong tendency towards vigilantism. Its search and patrol operations have resulted in confrontations with the public and gang members. Yet if crime and vigilantism are not to spiral out of control, the processes of law and order must be strengthened.

Table 9.7 shows the very high incidence of car hijackings in Gauteng, which includes Johannesburg and Pretoria. In fact, Gauteng and KwaZulu Natal accounted for a combined total of 81.6 per cent of car hijackings. Reported cases of motor vehicle and motorcycle theft have also remained consistently high in the Gauteng area, as Table 9.8 demonstrates.

As one of its tasks, the CIMC also instigated research into the nature and incidence of rape and conducted an operational analysis in three provinces, Western Cape, Northern Cape and the Free State. Although these areas have different incidences of rape and cannot be regarded as fully representative of all regions, the preliminary findings revealed some similarities (see Table 9.9). In the Western Cape, over one-quarter of all the suspects involved had been under the influence of alcohol or drugs at the time the rape occurred. Also, 61 per cent of those suspected of carrying out the rapes were known to the complainant before the act

[32] *Ibid.*

Table 9.8 Reported cases of theft of motor vehicles and motorcycles

	1994	1995	1996	1997
Eastern Cape	1,428	1,352	1,287	1,281
Free State	928	961	951	772
Gauteng	12,875	13,854	12,027	12,948
KwaZulu Natal	4,048	4,565	4,300	3,998
Mpumalanga	887	1,002	982	998
North West	1,019	965	887	886
Northern Cape	97	130	136	105
Northern Province	392	441	453	521
Western Cape	2,185	2,154	2,014	2,145

Source: SAPS Quarterly Report, 1998.

Table 9.9 Reported cases of rape

	1994	1995	1996	1997
Eastern Cape	1258	1405	1569	1722
Free State	880	958	1038	1015
Gauteng	2382	3006	3339	3204
KwaZulu Natal	1681	1854	2131	2292
Mpumalanga	596	682	773	820
North West	841	1001	1106	1223
Northern Cape	292	324	436	428
Northern Province	588	713	833	966
Western Cape	1327	1420	1837	1744

Source: SAPS Quarterly Report, 1998.

occurred. In the Northern Cape, alcohol played a role in 36 per cent of all the rape cases analysed, and again in two-thirds of cases, the suspect was known to the victim. In the Free State, 56 per cent of the rapes took place in the victims' homes, and 43 per cent of the cases involved people previously known to one another. On these early and provisional findings, the CIMC felt that the occurrence of rape in many instances was related to 'date rape' or 'acquaintance rape' rather than to the actions of strangers.[33]

Nelson Mandela's 1998 report to the nation stated: 'Since 1994 there has been a marked decline in virtually all serious crimes such as murder, robbery, taxi violence and car-hijacking.' He attributed the alleged decline to 'better coordination'

---

[33] *Ibid.*

Table 9.10 Incidences of public violence

	1994	1995	1996	1997
Eastern Cape	73	64	86	52
Free State	41	13	13	21
Gauteng	154	54	60	79
KwaZulu Natal	61	32	26	32
Mpumalanga	21	5	3	4
North West	16	7	14	7
Northern Cape	35	10	11	11
Northern Province	19	9	10	8
Western Cape	143	63	35	28
Total	563	257	258	242

Source: SAPS Quarterly Report, 1998.

between the police, the intelligence services and the defence force.[34] Unfortunately, as desirable as those sentiments were, the actual figures were rather less positive. The police service's own assessment indicated that although the incidence of murder had fallen in some provinces, in others – the Eastern Cape, Northern Cape, Western Cape and Mpumalanga – it has increased since 1994 (see Table 9.5). Such statistics can always be intepreted in a variety of ways, and crime is still at very high levels, but some figures have provided cause for optimism. As Table 9.10 outlines, in all regions there were significant reductions on 1994 levels of public violence. Although there were some fluctuations in the reported cases of public violence between 1995 and 1996, at no time did the figures reach the high levels of 1994. Also, as was evidenced during the 1999 election, political violence and associated manifestions of public disorder were far lower than that experienced at the time of the 1994 election. Clearly, then, although crime is undoubtedly one of the greatest problems confronting South Africa, it tends not to be linked to political intolerance and community hatred. However, one aspect that does connect it with the wider political environment is the close relationship between socio-economic disadvantage and criminal activity. It is not uncommon in Johannesburg to see unemployed men hawking artifacts in the street with placards tied around their necks proclaiming 'I don't do crime. Help me to live'. It is also no coincidence that President Mbeki reminded the nation of these problems in his inaugural speech:

> Our nights cannot but be nights of nightmares while millions of our people live in conditions of degrading poverty ... No night can be restful when millions have no

[34] President Mandela's Government's Report to the Nation 1998: 10.

jobs, and some are forced to beg, rob and murder to ensure they and their own do not perish from hunger.[35]

President Thabo Mbeki

Although political pundits forecast that South Africa's second democratic elections would arouse less popular enthusiasm than those of 1994, the inauguration of President Mbeki on 16 June 1999 at the Union Buildings in Pretoria was a momentous occasion. As the crowds jostled to see Thabo Mbeki declare his covenant to the country, people were moved to tears by the euphoria of the

---

Box 9.3 President Thabo Mbeki

Born in the Transkei in June 1942 to teachers and members of the South African Communist Party, Govan and Epainette Mbeki, Thabo Mbeki, at the age of 10, was sent away to live with relatives, later becoming a boarder at Loveday College. He joined the youth wing of the Communist Party and the ANC and was expelled from school for organising a boycott. At 16, Thabo fathered a son, Kwanda, by the daughter of the school principal. He left his family behind to travel to Johannesburg to study for examinations and at the age of 20, shortly before his father was imprisoned on Robben Island with Nelson Mandela, he was smuggled out of South Africa and acquired a place at Sussex University, UK. He was the only black student of his year and allegedly acquired a taste for malt whisky, W.B. Yeats, tweed caps and Sherlock Holmes pipes. He was, however, loyal to the Communist Party and supported the widely condemned Soviet invasions of Hungary and Czechoslovakia. Mbeki worked in London for the ANC before going to Moscow for military training. He was subsequently posted to a number of African states but returned to Britain to marry in 1974. Mbeki rose swiftly through the ANC and the South African Communist Party and was head of the ANC's international department in 1989. He was avowedly anti-capitalist, but when the ANC and the SACP were unbanned he left the Communist Party and returned from exile in the early 1990s. It was after the release of Mandela that Mbeki acquired his reputation for ruthlessness. After his old rival, Chris Hani, was assassinated, he outmanoeuvred the chief contender for the deputy presidency and Mandela's choice, Cyril Ramaphosa, the then trade union leader. In 1994, he was appointed deputy president of South Africa and began to be groomed as Nelson Mandela's successor. Regarded as an 'enigma' and lacking the warmth and charisma of Nelson Mandela, he had in effect been running the country since 1996 as Nelson Mandela adopted a more ceremonial role.

---

[35] Thabo Mbeki, *Business Day*, 17 June 1999.

moment. The South African Air Force and South African Airways staged a magnificent fly-past after the president took the oath of office and people sang the national anthem. The spectacle and ceremony of the event gave rise to a sense of pride, achievement and hope that a five-year-old democracy was maturing. Journalists spoke of how 'good' it felt to be a South African as people of all races danced, sang and partied late into the night in the grounds of the executive buildings. Nelson Mandela's dignified exit from the central political stage and President Mbeki's sobering inauguration speech provided a stately framework for the occasion. Nelson Mandela reiterated his privilege to have been part of South Africa's achievements and 'inspired to serve a country that demonstrated how conflicts could be resolved peacefully', while Mbeki declared that the government had 'entered into a contract with the people', to work in partnership 'to build together a winning nation'. The country, he urged, must be 'driven by the talents of all its people, black and white', all of whom shared a 'common destiny'.[36]

At a political level, Mbeki exercises greater power than Mandela in that the ANC has increased its parliamentary majority and the Democratic Party now sitting at the head of the opposition is numerically weaker than the National Party was in 1994. Inevitably, with such a dominant party there are worries as to where real opposition to the government or political dissent may be voiced. With the Inkatha Freedom Party relegated to a regional force and the United Democractic Movement displaying an unspectacular result in the 1999 elections, there is no national political movement likely to attract significant electoral support from the black community, other than the ANC. Equally, it is unlikely that the Democratic Party, the New National Party or the newly configured Democratic Alliance will gain sizeable numbers of votes from black South Africans. There is no doubt that the racial divisions of the apartheid years continue to affect the country's political environment. However, a report by the Human Sciences Research Council (HSRC) pointed to a change in political tendencies among the wider population. As Table 9.11 indicates, the active membership of political parties by all racial groups other than the coloured community fell between 1994 and 1999. According to the HSRC, the survey indicated that the country was 'approaching normal levels of active political party membership' and was moving away from highly politicised attitudes. Although the turnout in the 1999 election was relatively high, the trend among South Africans has been to terminate their membership of political parties.[37] It seems that although the general population is prepared to vote in national elections its interest in political activism and party politics has waned.

These tendencies may reflect a general shift in the population's concerns with the minutiae of politics now that the country has moved away from the apartheid years. However, Tom Lodge cautions that there may be a more serious cause for concern if significant sections of the white, coloured and Indian electorates are 'disengaging' from the political process. If communities begin to suspect that

---

[36] cf. *Pretoria News*, 17 June 1999; *The Star*, 17 June 1999; *The Sowetan*, 17 June 1999.
[37] HSRC survey, Johannesburg, February 2000.

Table 9.11 Active membership of political parties, 1994–1999 (%)

	1994	1999
Blacks	24	10
Whites	17	9
Indians	5	2
Coloureds	5	5

Human Sciences Research Council survey, February 2000.

their 'preoccupations and interests have no effective representation within the political system', democratic consolidation will suffer. Such a situation would be especially 'damaging to the fortunes of opposition parties'.[38] Despite the ending of apartheid, those years of racial segregation and fear cast a long shadow over South Africa's new polity. The country's democracy is too young to banish racial mistrust immediately, but the real challenge for the future will be the extent to which the nation can move forward towards racial understanding.

---

[38] Tom Lodge, EISA *Election Update* No. 15, Johannesburg, 25 June 1999.

Appendices

Harare Declaration, August 1989

Declaration on the Question of South Africa by the Organisation of African Unity.

1. Preamble

The people of Africa, singly, collectively and acting through the Organisation of African Unity (OAU), are engaged in serious efforts to establish peace throughout the continent by ending all conflicts through negotiations based on the principle of justice and peace for all. We affirm our conviction that where colonial, racial and apartheid domination exist, there can be neither peace nor justice. Accordingly, we reiterate that while the apartheid system in South Africa persists, the peoples of our continent as a whole cannot achieve the fundamental objectives of justice, human dignity and peace.

With regard to the region of southern Africa, the entire continent is vitally interested that the processes in which it is involved, leading to the complete and genuine independence of Namibia, as well as peace in Angola and Mozambique, should succeed in the shortest possible time. Equally, Africa is deeply concerned that the destabilisation of all the countries in the region by South Africa, whether through direct aggression, sponsorship of surrogates, economic subversion or other means, should end immediately.

We recognise the reality that permanent peace and stability in southern Africa can only be achieved when the system of apartheid in South Africa has been liquidated and South Africa has been transformed into a united, democratic and non-racial country. We, therefore, reiterate that all the necessary measures should be adopted now, to bring a speedy end to the apartheid system. We believe that as a result of the liberation struggle and international pressure against apartheid, as well as global efforts to liquidate regional conflicts, possibilities exist for further movement towards the resolution of the problems facing the people of South Africa. For these possibilities to lead to fundamental change in South Africa, the Pretoria regime must abandon its abhorrent concepts and practices of racial domination and its record of failure to honour agreements, all of which have already resulted in the loss of so many lives and the destruction of much property in the countries of southern Africa. We reaffirm our recognition of the right of all peoples, including those of South Africa, to determine their own destiny, and to work out for themselves the institutions and the system of government under which they will, by general consent, live and work together. OAU remains committed to do everything possible and necessary to assist the people of South Africa in whichever ways as the representatives of the oppressed may determine, to achieve this objective. We are certain that, arising from its duty to help end the criminal apartheid system, the rest of the world community is ready to extend similar assistance to the people of South Africa.

We make these commitments because we believe that all people are equal and have equal rights to human dignity and respect, regardless of colour, race, sex or creed. We believe that all men and women have the right and duty to participate in their own government, as equal members of society. No individual or group of individuals has any right to govern others without their consent. The apartheid system violates all those fundamental and universal principles. Correctly characterised as a crime against humanity, it is responsible for the deaths of countless numbers of people in South Africa. It has sought to dehumanise entire peoples. It has imposed a brutal war on the whole region of southern Africa, resulting in untold loss of life, destruction of property and massive displacement of innocent men, women and children. This scourge and affront to humanity must be fought and eradicated in its totality. We have therefore supported all those in South Africa who pursue this noble objective through political, armed and other forms of struggle. We shall continue to do everything in our power to help intensify the liberation struggle and international pressure against the system of apartheid until it is ended.

2. Statement of principles

We believe that a conjuncture of circumstances exists which, if there is demonstrable readiness on the part of the Pretoria regime to engage in negotiations genuinely and seriously, could create the possibility to end apartheid through negotiations. The outcome of such a process should be a new constitutional order based on the following principles:

- South Africa shall become a united, democratic and non-racial state,
- All its people shall enjoy common and equal citizenship and nationality regardless of race, colour, sex or creed,
- All its people shall have the right to participate in the government and administration of the country on the basis of universal suffrage, exercised through the one-person, one-vote system, under a common voters' roll,
- All shall have the right to form and join any political party of their choice, provided that this is not a furtherance of racism,
- All shall enjoy universally recognised human rights, freedoms and civil liberties, protected under an entrenched Bill of Rights,
- South Africa shall have a new legal system which shall guarantee equality of all before the law,
- South Africa shall have an independent and non-racial judiciary,
- There shall be created an economic order which shall promote and advance the well-being of all South Africans,

- A democratic South Africa shall respect the rights, sovereignty and territorial integrity of all countries and pursue a policy of peace, friendship and mutually beneficial cooperation with all peoples.

We believe that agreement on the above principles shall constitute the foundation for an internationally acceptable solution which shall enable South Africa to take its rightful place as an equal partner among the African and world community of nations.

3. Climate for negotiations

Together with the rest of the world, we believe that it is essential before any negotiations can take place that the necessary climate for negotiations be created. The apartheid regime has the urgent responsibility to respond positively to this universally acclaimed demand and thus create this climate. Accordingly, the present regime should, at the very least:

- Release all political prisoners and detainees unconditionally and refrain from imposing any restrictions on them,
- Lift all bans and restrictions on all proscribed and restricted organisations and persons,
- Remove all troops from the townships,
- End the state of emergency and repeal all legislation, such as and including the Internal Security Act, designed to circumscribe political activity, and
- Cease all political trials and political executions.

These measure are necessary to produce the conditions in which free political discussion can take place – an essential condition to ensure that the people themselves participate in the process of remaking their country.

4. Guidelines to the process of negotiation

We support the view of the South African liberation movement that upon the creation of this climate, the process of negotiations should commence along the following lines:

- Discussions should take place between the liberation movement and the South African regime to achieve the suspension of hostilities on both sides by agreeeing to a mutually binding cease-fire,
- Negotiations should then proceed to establish the basis for the adoption of a new constitution by agreeing on, among others, the principles enunciated above,
- Having agreed to these principles, the parties should then negotiate the necessary mechanism for drawing up the new constitution,
- The parties shall define and agree on the role to be played by the international community in ensuring a successful transition to a democratic order,
- The parties shall agree on the formation of an interim government to supervise the process of the drawing up and adoption of a new constitution,

govern and administer the country, as well as effect the transition to a democratic order, including the holding of elections.

After the adoption of the new constitution, all armed hostilities will be deemed to have formally terminated. For its part the international community would lift the sanctions that have been imposed against apartheid South Africa. The new South Africa shall qualify for membership of the OAU.

5. Programme of action

In pursuance of the objectives stated in this document, the OAU hereby commits itself:

- To inform governments and intergovernmental organisations throughout the world, including the Movement of Non-aligned Countries, the United Nations General Assemby, the Security Council, the Commonwealth and others of these perspectives and solicit their support,
- To mandate the OAU, assisted by the front-line states, to remain apprised of the issue of a political resolution of the South African question,
- To step up all-round support for the South African liberation movement and campaign in the rest of the world in pursuance of this objective,
- To intensify the campaign for mandatory and comprehensive sanctions against apartheid South Africa: in this regard, immediately mobilise against the rescheduling of Pretoria's foreign debt; work for the imposition of a mandatory oil embargo and the full observance by all countries of the arms embargo,
- To ensure that the African continent does not relax existing measures for the total isolation of apartheid South Africa,
- To continue to monitor the situation in Namibia and extend all necessary support to the South West African People's Organisation (SWAPO) in its struggle for a genuinely independent Namibia,
- To extend such assistance as the governments of Angola and Mozambique may request in order to secure peace for their peoples,
- To render all possible assistance to the front-line states to enable them to withstand Pretoria's campaign of aggression and destabilisation and enable them to continue to give their all-round support to the people of Namibia and South Africa.

We appeal to all people of good will throughout the world to support this programme of action as a necessary measure to secure the earliest liquidation of the apartheid system and the transformation of South Africa into a united, democratic and non-racial country.

Extracts from the address by State President F.W. de Klerk to parliament, 2 February 1990

Mr Speaker, Members of Parliament,

The general election on 6 September 1989 placed our country irrevocably on the road of drastic change. Underlying this is the growing realisation by an increasing number of South Africans that only a negotiated understanding among the representative leaders of the entire population is able to ensure lasting peace. The alternative is growing violence, tension and conflict. That is unacceptable and in nobody's interest. The well-being of all in this country is linked inextricably to the ability of the leaders to come to terms with one another on a new dispensation. No one can escape this simple truth. On its part, the government will accord the process of negotiation the highest priority. The aim is a totally new and just constitutional dispensation in which every inhabitant will enjoy equal rights, treatment and opportunity in every sphere of endeavour – constitutional, social and economic.

I hope that this new Parliament will play a constructive part in both the prelude to negotiations and the negotiating process itself. I wish to ask all of you who identify yourselves with the broad aim of a new South Africa:

- Let us put petty politics aside when we discuss the future during this session,
- Help us build a broad consensus about the fundamentals of a new, realistic and democratic dispensation,
- Let us work together on a plan that will rid our country of suspicion and steer it away from domination and racialism of any kind.

Foreign relations

The government is aware of the important part the world at large has to play in the realisation of our country's national interests. Without contact and cooperation with the rest of the world we cannot promote the well-being and security of our citizens. The dynamic developments in international politics have created new opportunities for South Africa as well. Important advances have been made, among other things, in our contacts abroad, especially where these were precluded previously by ideological considerations.

For South Africa and for the whole world the past year has been one of change and major upheaval. The year 1989 will go down in history as the year in which Stalinist Communism expired and will be of decisive importance to Africa. The collapse of the economic system in Eastern Europe serves as a warning to those who insist on persisting with it in Africa. The countries of southern Africa are faced with a particular challenge that they now have a historical opportunity to set aside conflicts and ideological differences and draw up a joint programme of reconstruction. Unless the countries of southern Africa achieve stability and a common approach to economic development rapidly they will be faced by further decline and ruin. The government is prepared to enter into discussions with other southern African countries with the aim of formulating a realistic development plan. Hostile postures have to be replaced by cooperative ones, confrontation by contact, disengagement by engagement, slogans by deliberate debate. The season for violence is over. The time for reconstruction and reconciliation has arrived.

Human rights

The government accepts the principle of recognition and protection of the fundamental individual rights which form the constitutional basis of most Western democracies. We acknowledge, too, that the most practical way of protecting those rights is vested in a declaration of rights justifiable by an independent judiciary. It is neither the government's policy nor its intention that any group – in whichever way it may be defined – shall be favoured above or in relation to any other group. The government is requesting the Law Commission to undertake a task and report on it. This task is directed at the balanced protection in a future constitution of the human rights of all our citizens. This investigation will also serve the purpose of supporting negotiations towards a new constitution.

The death penalty

The death penalty has been the subject of intensive discussion in recent months. We have now reached the position in which we are able to make concrete proposals for reform and the government has decided on the following broad principles:

- The death penalty should be limited as an option of sentence to extreme cases.
- An automatic right of appeal should be granted to those under sentence of death.

Negotiation

Today I am able to announce far-reaching decisions. I wish to urge every political and community leader to approach the new opportunities constructively. The new steps that have been decided are the following:

- The prohibition of the African National Congress, the Pan Africanist Congress, the South African Communist Party and a number of subsidiary organisations is being rescinded.
- People serving prison sentences merely because they were members of one of these organisation or because they committed another offence which was merely an offence because prohibition on one of the organisations was in force will be identified and released. Prisoners who have been sentenced for other offences such as murder, terrorism or arson are not affected by this.
- The media emergency regulations as well as the education emergency regulations are being abolished in their entirety.
- The security emergency regulations will be amended to still make provision for effective control over visual material pertaining to scenes of unrest.
- The restrictions in terms of the emergency regulations on 33 organisations are being rescinded.
- The period of detention in terms of the security emergency regulations will be limited henceforth to six months. Detainees also acquire the right to legal representation and a medical practitioner of their choosing.

These decisions by the Cabinet are in accordance with the Government's declared intention to normalise the political process in South Africa without jeopardising the maintenance of good order. They were preceded by thorough and unanimous advice by a group of officials which included members of the security community. The most important facets of the advice the Government received in this connection are the following:

- The fall of the Soviet Union weakens the capability of organisations which were previously supported strongly from those quarters.
- The activities of the organisations from which the prohibitions are now being lifted no longer entail the same degree of threat to internal security which initially necessitated the imposition of the prohibitions.
- There have been important shifts of emphasis in the statements and points of view of the most important of the organisations concerned, which indicate a new approach and a preference for peaceful solutions.
- The South African Police is convinced that it is able, in the present circumstances, to combat violence and other crimes perpetrated by members of these organisations.

About one matter there should be no doubt. The lifting of the prohibition on the said organisations does not signify in the least the approval or condonation of terrorism or crimes of violence committed under their banner or which may be perpetrated in the future. Equally, it should not be interpreted as a deviation from the Government's principles, among other things, against their economic policy and aspects of their constitutional policy. At the same time I wish to emphasise that the maintenance of law and order dare not be jeopardised. The Government will not forsake its duty in this connection. Violence from whichever source will be fought with all available might. Peaceful protest may not become the springboard for lawlessness, violence and intimidation. Strong emphasis will be placed on even more effective law enforcement. Proper provision of manpower and means for the police and all who are involved with the enforcement of law will be ensured. I wish to thank members of our security forces and related services for the dedicated service they have rendered the Republic of South Africa. Their dedication makes reform in a stable climate possible.

Our country and all its people have been embroiled in conflict, tension and violent struggle for decades. It is time for us to break out of the cycle of violence and break through to peace and reconciliation. The silent majority is yearning for this. The youth deserve it. With the steps the Government has taken it has proven its good faith and the table is laid for sensible leaders to begin talking about a new dispensation, to reach an understanding by the way of dialogue and discussion. The agenda is open and the overall aims to which we are aspiring should be acceptable to all reasonable South Africans. Among other things, those aims include a new, democratic constitution; universal franchise; no domination; equality before an independent judiciary; the protection of minorities as well as of individual rights; freedom of religion; a sound economy based on proven economic principles and private enterprise; dynamic programmes directed at better education, health services, housing and social conditions for all.

In this connection Mr Nelson Mandela could play an important part. The Government has noted that he has declared himself to be willing to make a constructive contribution to the peaceful political process in South Africa. I wish to put it plainly that the Government has taken a firm decision to release Mr Mandela unconditionally. I am serious about bringing this matter to finality without delay. The Government will take a decision soon on the date of his release. In the case of Mr Mandela there are factors in the way of his immediate release, of which his personal circumstances and safety are not the least. He has not been an ordinary prisoner for quite some time. Because of that, his case requires particular circumspection. Today's announcements, in particular, go to the heart of what Black leaders, also Mr Mandela, have been advancing over the years as their reason for having resorted to violence. The allegation has been that the Government did not wish to talk to them and that they were deprived of their right to normal political activity by the prohibition of their organisations. Without conceding that violence has ever been justified, I wish to say today to those who argued in this manner:

- The Government wishes to talk to all leaders who seek peace.
- The unconditional lifting of the prohibition on the said organisations places everybody in a position to pursue politics freely.
- The justification for violence which was always advanced, no longer exists.

These facts place everybody in South Africa before a *fait accompli*. On the basis of numerous previous statements there is no longer any reasonable excuse for the continuation of violence. The time for talking has arrived and whoever still makes excuses does not really wish to talk. Therefore, I repeat my invitation with greater conviction than ever:

> Walk through the open door, take your place at the negotiating table together with the Government and other leaders who have important power bases inside and outside of Parliament.

Henceforth, everybody's political points of view will be tested against their realism, their workability and their fairness. The time for negotiation has arrived. To those political leaders who have always resisted violence I say thank you for your principled stand. These include all the leaders of the parliamentary parties, leaders of important organisations and movements, such as Chief Minister Buthelezi, all of the other chief ministers and urban community leaders. Through their participation and discussion they have made an important contribution to this moment in which the process of free political participation is able to be restored. Their places in the negotiating process are assured.

Conclusion

In my inaugural address I said the following:

> All reasonable people in this country – by far the majority – anxiously await a message of hope. It is our responsibility as leaders in all spheres to provide that message realistically with courage and conviction. If we fail in that, the ensuing chaos, the demise of stability and progress, will forever be held against us. History has thrust upon the leadership of this country the tremendous responsibility to turn our country away from its present direction of conflict and confrontation. Only we, the leaders of our peoples, can do it. The eyes of responsible governments across the world are focused on us. The hopes of millions of South Africans are centred around us. The future of South Africa depends on us. We dare not falter or fail.

This is where we stand:

- Deeply under the impression of our responsibility.
- Humble in the face of the tremendous challenges ahead.
- Determined to move forward in faith and with conviction.

I ask Parliament to assist me on the road ahead. There is much to be done. I call on the international community to re-evaluate its position and to adopt a positive attitude towards the dynamic evolution which is taking place in South Africa. I pray that the Almighty Lord will guide and sustain us on our course through uncharted waters and will bless your labours and deliberations.

Nelson Mandela's speech in Cape Town following his release from prison, 11 February 1990

A mass rally at Cape Town's City Hall greeted Nelson Mandela on the day of his release from prison. In addition to being heard by the tens of thousands in attendance, his address to the rally was televised and seen by millions throughout the world.

Amandla! [Power] I-Africa!

Friends, comrades and fellow South Africans:

I greet you all in the name of peace, democracy and freedom for all. I stand here before you not as a prophet but as a humble servant of you, the people. Your tireless and heroic sacrifices have made it possible for me to be here today. I therefore place the remaining years of my life in your hands. On this day of my release, I extend my sincere and warmest gratitude to the millions of my compatriots and those in every corner of the globe who have campaigned tirelessly for my release. I extend special greetings to the people of Cape Town, the city which been my home for three decades. Your mass marches and other forms of struggle have served as a constant source of strength to all political prisoners. I salute the African National Congess. It has fulfilled our every expectation in its role as leader of the great march of freedom. I salute our president, Comrade Oliver Tambo, for leading the ANC even under the most difficult circumstances. I salute the rank-and-file members of the ANC. You have sacrificed life and limb in the pusuit of the noble cause of our struggle. I salute combatants of Umkhonto we Sizwe, who have paid the ultimate price for the freedom of all South Africans. I salute the South African Communist Party for its sterling contribution to the struggle for democracy. You have survived forty years of unrelenting persecution. I salute General Secretary Joe Slovo, one of our finest patriots. We are heartened by the fact that the alliance between ourselves and the party remains as strong as it always was. I salute the United Democratic Front, the National Education Crisis Committee, the South African Youth Congress, the Transvaal and Natal Indian Congresses and the Congress of South African Trade Unions and the many other formations of the Mass Democratic Movement.

I also salute the Black Sash and the National Union of South African Students. We note with pride that you have acted as the conscience of white South Africans. Even during the darkest days in the history of our struggle, you held the flag of liberty high. The large-scale mass mobilisation of the past few years is one of the few factors which led to the opening of the final chapter of our struggle. I extend my greetings to the working class of our country. Your organised strength is the pride of our movement. You remain the most dependable force in the struggle to end exploitation and oppression. I pay tribute to the many religious communities who carried the campaign for justice forward when the organisations of our people were silenced. I greet the traditional leaders of our country. I pay tribute to the endless heroes of youth. You, the young lions, have energised our entire struggle. I pay tribute to the mothers and wives and sisters of our nation. You are the rock-hard foundation of our struggle. Apartheid has inflicted more pain on you than on anyone else. On this occasion we thank the world community for their great contribution to the anti-apartheid struggle. Without your support our struggle would not have reached this advanced stage. The sacifice of the front-line states will be remembered by South Africans for ever.

My salutations will be incomplete without expressing my deep appreciation for the strength given to me during my long and lonely years in prison by my beloved wife and family. I am convinced that your pain and suffering was far greater than my own. Today the majority of South Africans, black and white, recognise that apartheid has no future. It has to be ended by our own decisive mass action in order to build peace and security. The mass campaigns of defiance and other actions of our organisation and people can only culminate in the establishment of democracy. The apartheid destruction on our subcontinent is incalculable. The fabric of family life of millions of my people has been shattered. Millions are homeless and unemployed. Our economy lies in ruins and our people are embroiled in political strife.

Our resort to the armed struggle in 1961 with the formation of the military wing of the ANC, Umkhonto we Sizwe, was a purely defensive action against the violence of apartheid. The factors which necessitated the armed struggle still exist today. We have no option but to continue. We express the hope that a climate conducive to a negotiated settlement will be created soon so that there may no longer be the need for the armed struggle. I am a loyal and disciplined member of the ANC. I am therefore in agreement with all of its objectives, strategies and tactics. The need to unite the people of our country is as important a task now as it always has been. No individual leader is able to take on this enormous task on his own. It is our task as leaders to place our views before our organisation and to allow the democratic structures to decide on the way forward. On the question of democratic practice, I feel duty-bound to make the point that a leader of the movement is a person who has been democratically elected at a national conference. This is a principle which must be upheld without any exceptions.

Today I wish to report to you that my talks with the government have been aimed at normalising the political situation in the country. We have not as yet begun discussing the basic demands of the struggle. I wish to stress that I myself had at no time entered into negotiations about the future of our country, except to insist on a meeting between the ANC and the government. Mr de Klerk has gone further than any other Nationalist president in taking real steps to normalise the situation. However, there are further steps as outlined in the Harare Declaration that have to be met before negotiations on the basic demands of our people can begin. I reiterate our call for the immediate ending of the state of emergency and the freeing of all political prisoners. Only such a normalised situation which allows for free political activity can allow us to consult our people in order to obtain a mandate. The people need to be consulted on who will negotiate and on the content of such negotiations. Negotiations cannot take place above the heads or behind the backs of our people. It is our belief that the future of our country can only be determined by a body which is democratically elected on a non-racial basis.

Negotiations on the dismantling of apartheid will have to address the overwhelming demand of our people for a democratic, non-racial and unitary South Africa. There must be an end to white monopoly on political power and a fundamental restructuring of our political and economic systems to ensure that the inequalities of apartheid are addressed and our society thoroughly democratised. It must be added that Mr de Klerk himself is a man of integrity who is acutely aware of the dangers of a public figure not honouring his undertakings. But as an organisation, we base our policy and strategy on the harsh reality we are faced with, and this reality is that we are still suffering under the policy of the Nationalist government.

Our struggle has reached a decisive moment. We call on our people to seize this moment so that the process towards democracy is rapid and uninterrupted. We have waited too long for our freedom. We can no longer wait. Now is the time to intensify the struggle on all fronts. To relax our efforts now would be a mistake which generations to come will not be able to forgive. The sight of freedom looming on the horizon should encourage us to redouble our efforts. It is only through disciplined mass action that our victory can be assured. We call on our white compatriots to join us in the shaping of a new South Africa. The freedom movement is the political home for you too. We call on the international community to continue the campaign to isolate the apartheid regime. To lift sanctions now would be to run the risk of aborting the process towards the complete eradication of apartheid. Our march to freedom is irreversible. We must not allow fear to stand in our way. Universal suffrage on a common voters' roll in a united, democratic and non-racial South Africa is the only way to peace and racial harmony. In conclusion, I wish to go to my own words during the trial in 1964. They are as true today as they were then. I quote:

> I have fought against white domination, and I have fought against black domination. I have cherished the idea of a democratic and free society in which all persons live together in harmony and with equal opportunities. It is an ideal which I hope to live for and to achieve. But if needs be, it is an ideal for which I am prepared to die.

Bill of Rights, 1996

Rights

1. This Bill of Rights is a cornerstone of democracy of South Africa. It enshrines the rights of all people in our country and affirms the democratic values of human dignity, equality and freedom.
2. The state must respect, protect, promote and fulfil the rights in the Bill of Rights.
3. The rights in the Bill of Rights are subject to the limitations contained or referred to elsewhere in the Bill.

Application

The Bill of Rights applies to all law and binds the legislature, the executive, the judiciary and all organs of state.

Equality

- Everyone is equal before the law and has the right to equal protection and benefit of the law.
- Equality includes the full and equal enjoyment of all rights and freedoms. To promote the achievement of equality, legislative and other measures designed to protect or advance persons, or categories of persons, disadvantaged by unfair discrimination may be taken.
- The state may not unfairly discriminate against anyone on grounds of race, gender, sex, pregnancy, marital status, ethnic or social origin, colour, sexual orientation, age, disability, religion, conscience, belief, culture, language or birth.
- No person may unfairly discriminate directly or indirectly against anyone.

Human dignity

Everyone has inherent dignity and the right to have their dignity respected and protected.

Life

Everyone has the right to life

Freedom and security of the person

1. Everyone has the right to freedom and security of the person, which includes the right:
    - not to be deprived of freedom arbitrarily or without just cause;
    - not to be detained without trial;
    - to be free from all forms of violence from both public and private sources;
    - not to be tortured in any way; and
    - not to be treated or punished in a cruel, inhuman or degrading way.
2. Everyone has the right to bodily and psychological integrity, which includes the right:
    - to make decisions concerning reproduction;
    - to security in and control over their body;
    - not to be subjected to medical or scientific experiments without their informed consent.

Slavery, servitude and forced labour

No one may be subjected to slavery, servitude or forced labour.

Privacy

Everyone has the right to privacy, which includes the right not to have:

- their person or home searched;
- their property searched;
- their possessions seized; or
- the privacy of their communications infringed.

Freedom of religion, belief and opinion

1. Everyone has the right to freedom of conscience, religion, thought, belief and opinion;
2. Religious observances may be conducted at state or state-aided institutions provided that:
    - those observances follow rules made by the appropriate public authorities;
    - they are conducted on an equitable basis; and
    - attendance at them is free and voluntary.
3. (a) This section does not prevent legislation recognising:
    - marriages concluded under any tradition or a system or religious, personal or family law; or

- systems of personal and family law under any tradition or adhered to by persons professing a particular religion.

  (b) Recognition in terms of paragraph (a) must be consistent with this section and the other provisions of the Constitution.

Freedom of expression

1. Everyone has the right to freedom of expression, which includes:
   - freedom of the press and other media;
   - freedom to receive and impart information and ideas;
   - freedom of artistic creativity; and
   - academic freedom and freedom of scientific research.
2. The right in subsection (1) does not extend to:
   - propaganda for war;
   - incitement of imminent violence; or
   - advocacy of hatred that is based on race, ethnicity, gender or religion, and that constitutes incitement to cause harm.

Assembly, demonstration, picket and petition

Everyone has the right, peacefully and unarmed, to assemble, to demonstrate, to picket and to present petitions.

Freedom of association

Everyone has the right to freedom of association.

Political rights

1. Every citizen is free to make political choices, which includes the right:
   - to form a political party;
   - to participate in the activities of, or recruit members for, a political party; and
   - to campaign for a political party or cause.
2. Every citizen has the right to free, fair and regular elections for any legislative body established in terms of the Constitution.
3. Every adult citizen has the right:
   - to vote in elections for any legislative body established in terms of the Constitution, and to do so in secret; and
   - to stand for public office and, if elected, to hold office.

Citizenship

No citizen may be deprived of citizenship.

Freedom of movement and residence

- Everyone has the right to freedom of movement.
- Everyone has the right to leave the Republic.
- Every citizen has the right to enter, to remain in and to reside anywhere in the Republic.
- Every citizen has the right to a passport.

Freedom of trade, occupation and profession

Every citizen has the right to choose their trade, occupation or profession freely. The practice of a trade, occupation or profession may be regulated by law.

Labour relations

1. Every worker has the right to fair labour practices.
2. Every worker has the right:
   - to form and join a trade union;
   - to participate in the activities and programmes of a trade union; and
   - to strike.
3. Every employer has the right:
   - to form and join an employers' organisation; and
   - to participate in the activities and programmes of an employers' organisation.
4. Every trade union and every employers' organisation has the right:
   - to determine its own administration, programmes and activities;
   - to organise;
   - to bargain collectively; and
   - to form and join a federation.

Environment

Everyone has the right:

- to an environment that is not harmful to their health or well-being; and
- to have the environment protected, for the benefit of present and future generations, through reasonable legislative and other measures that:
  (a) prevent pollution and ecological degradation;
  (b) promote conservation; and
  (c) secure ecologically sustainable development and use of natural resources while promoting justifiable economic and social development.

Property

1. No one may be deprived of property except in terms of law and general application, and no law may permit arbitrary deprivation of property.

2. Property may be expropriated only in terms of law of general application:
    - for public purposes or in the public interest; and
    - subject to compensation, the amount, timing, and manner of payment of which must be agreed, or decided or approved by a court.
3. The amount, timing and manner of payment of compensation must be just and equitable, reflecting an equitable balance between the public interest and the interests of those affected, having regard to all relevant factors, including:
    - the current use of the property;
    - the history of the acquisition and use of the property;
    - the market value of the property;
    - the extent of direct state investment and subsidy in the acquisition and beneficial capital improvement of the property; and
    - the purpose of the expropriation.
4. For the purposes of this section:
    - the public interest includes the nation's commitment to land reform, and to reforms to bring about equitable access to all South Africa's natural resources; and
    - property is not limited to land.
5. The state must take reasonable legislative and other measures, within its available resources, to foster conditions which enable citizens to gain access to land on an equitable basis.
6. A person or community whose tenure of land is legally insecure as a result of past racially discriminatory laws or practices is entitled, to the extent provided by an Act of Parliament, either to tenure which is legally secure, or to comparable redress.
7. A person or community dispossessed of property after 19 June 1913 as a result of past racially discriminatory laws or practices is entitled, to the extent provided by an Act of Parliament, either to restitution of that property, or to equitable redress.
8. No provision of this section may impede the state from taking legislative and other measures to achieve land, water and related reform in order to redress the results of past racial discrimination.

Housing

1. Everyone has the right to have access to adequate housing.
2. The state must take reasonable legislative and other measures, within its available resources, to achieve the progressive realisation of this right.
3. No one may be evicted from their home, or have their home demolished, without an order of court made after considering all the relevant circumstances. No legislation may permit arbitrary evictions.

Health care, food, water and social security

1. Everyone has the right to have access to:
    - health care services, including reproductive health care;
    - sufficient food and water; and
    - social security, including, if they are unable to support themselves and their dependants, appropriate social assistance.
2. The state must take reasonable legislative and other measures, within its available resources, to achieve the progressive realisation of each of these rights.
3. No one may be refused emergency medical treatment.

Children

1. Every child has the right:
    - to a name and a nationality from birth;
    - to family care, parental care, or appropriate alternative care when removed from the family environment;
    - to basic nutrition, shelter, basic health care services and social services;
    - to be protected from maltreatment, neglect, abuse or degradation;
    - to be protected from exploitative labour practices;
    - not to be required or permitted to perform work or provide services that:
      (a) are inappropriate for a person of that child's age; or
      (b) place at risk the child's well-being, education, physical or mental health, or spiritual, moral or social development;
    - not to be detained except as a measure of last resort, in which case, in addition to the rights a child enjoys under other sections, the child may be detained only for the shortest appropriate period of time, and has the right to be:
      (a) kept separately from detained persons over the age of 18 years; and
      (b) treated in a manner, and kept in conditions, that take account of the child's age;
    - to have a legal practitioner assigned to the child by the state, and at state expense, in civil proceedings affecting the child, if substantial injustice would otherwise result; and
    - not to be used directly in armed conflict, and to be protected in times of armed conflict.
2. A child's best interest is of paramount importance in every matter concerning the child.
3. In this section, 'child' means a person under the age of 18 years.

Education

1. Everyone has the right:
    - to a basic education, including adult basic education; and

- to further education, which the state must take reasonable measures to make progressively available and accessible.
2. Everyone has the right to receive education in the official language or languages of their choice in public educational institutions where that education is reasonably practicable. In order to ensure the effective access to, and implementation of, this right, the state must consider all reasonable educational alternatives taking into account:
   - equity;
   - practicability; and
   - the need to redress the results of past racially discriminatory law and practice.
3. Everyone has the right to establish and maintain, at their own expense, independent educational institutions that:
   - do not discriminate on the basis of race;
   - are registered with the state; and
   - maintain standards that are not inferior to standards at comparable public educational institutions.

Language and culture

Everyone has the right to use the language and to participate in the cultural life of their choice, but no one exercising these rights may do so in a manner inconsistent with any provision of the Bill of Rights.

Cultural, religious and linguistic communities

1. Persons belonging to a cultural, religious or linguistic community may not be denied the right, with other members of their community, to:
   - enjoy their culture, practise their religion and use their language; and
   - form, join and maintain cultural, religious and linguistic associations and other organs of civil society.
2. This right may not be exercised in a manner inconsistent with any provision of the Bill of Rights.

Access to Information

1. Everyone has the right of access to:
   - any information held by the state; and
   - any information that is held by another person and that is required for the exercise or protection of any rights.
2. National legislation must be enacted to give effect to this right, and may provide for reasonable measures to alleviate the administrative and financial burden on the state.

Just administrative action

1. Everyone has the right to administrative action that is lawful, reasonable and procedurally fair.
2. Everyone whose rights have been adversely affected by administrative action has the right to be given written reasons.

Access to courts

Everyone has the right to have any dispute that can be resolved by the application of law decided in a fair public hearing in a court or, where appropriate, another independent and impartial forum.

Arrested, detained and accused persons

1. Everyone who is arrested for allegedly committing an offence has the right:
   - to remain silent;
   - to be informed promptly of the right to remain silent, and of the consequences of not remaining silent;
   - not to be compelled to make any confession or admission that could be used in evidence against that person;
   - to be brought before a court as soon as is reasonably possible, but not later than 48 hours after the arrest, but if that period expires outside ordinary court hours, to be brought before a court on the first court day after the end of that period;
   - at the first court appearance after being arrested, to be charged or to be informed of the reason for the detention to continue, or to be released; and
   - to be released from detention if the interests of justice permit, subject to reasonable conditions.
2. Everyone who is detained, including every sentenced prisoner, has the right:
   - to be informed promptly of the reason for being detained;
   - to choose, and to consult with, a legal practitioner, and to be informed of this right promptly;
   - to have a legal practitioner assigned to the detained person by the state. and at state expense, if substantial injustice would otherwise result, and to be informed of this right promptly;
   - to challenge the lawfulness of the detention in person before a court and, if the detention is unlawful, to be released;
   - to conditions of detention that are consistent with human dignity, including at least exercise and the provision, at state expense, of adequate accommodation, nutrition, reading material and medical treatment; and
   - to communicate with, and be visited by, that person's:
     (a) spouse or partner;
     (b) next of kin;

　　　　(c) chosen religious counsellor; and
　　' (d) chosen medical practitioner.
3.　　Every accused has a right to a fair trial, which includes the right:
- to be informed of the charge with sufficient details to answer it;
- to have adequate time and facilities to prepare a defence;
- to a public trial in an ordinary court;
- to have their trial begin and conclude without unreasonable delay;
- to be present when being tried;
- to choose, and be represented by, a legal practitioner, and to be informed of this right;
- to have a legal practitioner assigned to the accused by the state, and at state expense, if substantial injustice would otherwise result, and to be informed of this right;
- to be presumed innocent, to remain silent and not to testify during the proceedings;
- to adduce and challenge evidence;
- not to be compelled to give self-incriminating evidence;
- to be tried in a language that the accused person understands or, if that is not practicable, to have the proceedings interpreted in that language;
- not to be convicted for an act or omission that was not an offence under either national or international law at the time it was committed or omitted;
- not to be tried for an offence in respect of an act or omission for which that person has previously been either acquitted or convicted;
- to the benefit of the least severe of the prescribed punishments if the prescribed punishment for the offence has been changed between the time that the offence was committed and the time of sentencing; and
- of appeal to, or review by, a higher court.
4.　　Whenever this section requires information to be given to a person, that information must be given in a language that the person understands.
5.　　Evidence obtained in a manner that violates any right in the Bill of Rights must be excluded if the admission of that evidence would render the trial unfair or otherwise be detrimental to the administration of justice.

Limitation of rights

The rights in the Bill of Rights may be limited only in terms of law of general application to the extent that the limitation is reasonable and justifiable in an open and democratic society based on human dignity, equality and freedom, taking into account all relevant factors, including:

- the nature of the right;
- the importance of the purpose of the limitation;
- the nature and extent of the limitation;

- the relation between the limitation and its purpose; and
- less restrictive means to achieve the purpose.

States of emergency

1. A state of emergency may be declared only in terms of an Act of Parliament and only when:
    - the life of the nation is threatened by war, invasion, general insurrection, disorder, natural disaster or other public emergency; and
    - the declaration is necessary to restore peace and order.
2. A declaration of a state of emergency, and any legislation enacted or other action taken in consequence of that declaration, may be effective only:
    - prospectively from the date of the declaration; and
    - for no more than 21 days from the date of the declaration, unless the National Assembly resolves to extend the declaration. The National Assembly may extend a declaration of a state of emergency for no more than three months at a time. The first extension of the state of emergency must be by a resolution supported by a majority of the members of the National Assembly. Any subsequent extension must be by a resolution supported by at least 60 per cent of the members of the Assembly. A resolution in terms of this paragraph may be adopted only following a public debate in the Assembly.

Enforcement of rights

Anyone listed in this section has the right to approach a competent court, alleging that a right in the Bill of Rights has been infringed or threatened, and the court may grant appropriate relief, including a declaration of rights. The persons who may approach a court are:

- anyone acting in their own interest;
- anyone acting on behalf of another person who cannot act in their own name;
- anyone acting as a member of, or in the interest of, a group or a class of persons;
- anyone acting in the public interest; and
- an association acting in the interest of its members.

Interpretation of Bill of Rights

1. When interpreting the Bill of Rights, a court, tribunal or forum:
    - must promote the values that underlie an open and democratic society based on human dignity, equality and freedom;
    - must consider international law; and
    - may consider foreign law.

2.   When interpreting any legislation and when developing the common law or customary law, every court, tribunal or forum must promote the spirit, purport and objects of the Bill of Rights.

3.   The Bill of Rights does not deny the existence of any other rights or freedoms that are recognised or conferred by common law, customary law or legislation, to the extent that they are consistent with the Bill.

The structures of South Africa's democratic government

Proportional representation

South Africa's national and provincial legislatures are elected on the basis of PR, using the party list and proportional allocation of seats system. This is based on the idea that the number of seats that a party occupies in the national and provincial parliaments should be in proportion to the number of votes it received in the elections. A party that wins 10 per cent of the votes in the national election should therefore occupy 10 per cent of the seats in parliament. The number of seats it occupies in each of the provincial legislatures depends on the proportion of votes it received in each of the provincial elections.

Who takes up the seats as MPs (members of parliament) and MPLs (members of provincial legislatures) on behalf of the parties is decided before the elections are held. Each party has to submit a party list of its candidates for each legislature that it is contesting in a fixed order of preference. If a party is allocated twenty seats on the basis of the proportion of votes it received in the national election, the first twenty people named on its national list become MPs. The number of MPLs each party is entitled to in each provincial legislature is proportional to the number of votes it received in each provincial election. The balance of power between the parties will remain the same until the next general election. If an MP dies, resigns or is expelled from the party, he or she will lose the seat and be replaced by the next person on the party list. Parties can, however, change the order of their lists, and once a year they are allowed to change the list by adding new people. The PR system prevents MPs 'crossing the floor' to join other parties and gives the parties considerable power in enforcing party discipline. This is because seats in the legislatures are owned by the party, not by individual MPs.

National legislative authority

There are two categories of legislation, defined by a list of functions:

1. Laws which the national and provincial legislatures are jointly competent to pass; and
2. Laws which the provincial legislatures are exclusively competent to pass.

Parliament may amend the Constitution and pass legislation in category 1. It may not pass legislation in category 2 unless this is necessary to:

- Maintain national security;
- Maintain economic unity;
- Maintain essential national standards;
- Establish minimum standards for the rendering of services;
- Prevent unreasonable action taken by a province which prejudices another province or the country as a whole.

A Bill which falls into category 1 must be passed by both houses, i.e. the National Assembly and the National Council of Provinces, before it can become an Act. If the houses are unable to agree, it is referred to a Mediation Committee to try to reach agreement. If the Mediation Committee is unable to agree within 30 days of the Bill having been referred to it, the NA (National Assembly) can pass the Bill into law on its own by a two-thirds majority.

With a Bill which falls outside category 1 the NA has the power to force a Bill through Parliament even if the National Council of Provinces (NCOP) rejects it or proposes amendments which the NA does not accept. Under these circumstances, the NCOP's power is limited to delaying the passage of the Bill while its objections and amendments are considered more carefully by the NA. If the Bill is an amendment to the Constitution which affects the NCOP or the provinces, it must be passed by both houses to become an Act. Any other amendments to the Constitution are not referred to the NCOP – they may become Acts when they are passed by the NA.

National Assembly and parliamentary committees

The NA must consist of no less that 350 MPs and no more than 400. The various parties are represented in proportion to the number of votes they received in the elections. Parliament has a range of committees that serve different functions:

Constitutional committees

- Joint Committee on Human Rights;
- Joint Committee on Public Protector;
- Joint Standing Committee on Defence;
- Joint Standing Committee on Finance.

Statutory committees

- Joint Standing Committee on Appointment of Commission on Gender Equality;
- Joint Standing Committee on Intelligence;
- Joint Committee on Conditions of Service of Public Protector.

Parliamentary committees

The National Assembly and the National Council of Provinces have committees responsible for the oversight of government departments and consideration of legislation produced by and relating to those departments. In the National Assembly these committees are called Portfolio Committees and in the National Council of Provinces they are called Select Committees. There are also Joint Committees, which consist of members of both houses.

National Council of Provinces

The NCOP is intended to ensure that provincial interests are represented in national parliamentary decision making. It does this mainly by participating in the national legislative process and by providing a national forum for public consideration of issues affecting the provinces. The NCOP is made up of 90 members – one ten-member delegation for each of the nine provinces. Each delegation is made up of six permanent members and four 'special' delegates, which may include the premier of the province. Each province's delegation is generally proportionately representative of the political parties that contested the election in that province. Provision is made for municipal delegations to represent the interests of local government in the NCOP when necessary, but municipal representatives may not vote. The NCOP and any of its committees also have the power to summon anyone to give evidence or produce documents and may request any individual or institution to report to them. Each delegation has one vote, and most decisions require five delegations to vote in favour of the motion. Amendments to the Constitution which affect the NCOP or the provinces must be supported by six of the nine delegations.

Parliamentary privilege

MPs and cabinet ministers have freedom of speech in parliament and its committees. This means that they are able to say, produce or submit anything without having to worry about any legal consequences, subject to the rules and orders of Parliament and its committees. Anything that is said in parliamentary debates or questions is a matter of public record.

Terms and sessions

An election is held every five years, although the President has the power to dissolve the NA and call an early election if a majority of members support the move, or if three years have passed since the last election. Parliament is in session for most of the year, and committee meetings may continue during the recess.

Composition of committees

Parliament delegates much of its most important work to parliamentary committees. Members of the public may present submissions to a committee, which means the views of citizens, including experts, can be heard in a parliamentary committee. There is a portfolio committee for every government department. Each portfolio committee consists of about 30 MPs and is responsible for shadowing a government department, for instance, education, health or housing. The political parties are represented roughly in proportion to the number of seats they hold in the NA. The committees must monitor the government department they oversee and may investigate and make recommendations relating to any aspect of the legislative programme, budget, rationalisation, restructuring, functioning, organisation, structure, personnel, policy formulation or anything else they think is relevant. They may make inquiries and hear evidence and it is their duty to debate, amend and put forward proposals for legislation. They are potentially powerful bodies that have a crucial role to play in the legislative process. Each committee elects its own chairperson, although the majority party parliamentary caucus is effectively able to decide who will chair the committees and ensure that those candidates are elected.

The President and the National Executive

The President and Cabinet together make up the executive body. Their task includes implementing national legislation, developing and implementing national policy, coordinating state departments, and preparing and initiating legislation. The Cabinet consists of the President, Deputy President and ministers. The Deputy President and ministers are appointed by the President. All but two of the ministers must be members of the NA. The Cabinet is collectively and individually accountable to Parliament, and members of the Cabinet must report regularly to Parliament. Deputy ministers may also be appointed by the President. The Cabinet may intervene in a province when a province does not fulfil its executive functions. It may assume responsibility to the extent necessary to maintain essential services, economic unity and national security. If the Cabinet intervenes in the affairs of a province, it must give notice of the intervention in the NCOP, which must approve the intervention within 30 days of its first sitting after the intervention began, and must review the intervention regularly. If, by a majority vote, the NA passes a motion of no confidence in the Cabinet, excluding the President, the President, the entire Cabinet and any deputy ministers must all resign.

State institutions supporting constitutional democracy

Six independent institutions are established. They are to act without state interference and are to be directly accountable to the NA:

- The Public Protector (appointed for a non-renewable period of seven years) has the task of investigating improper conduct in state affairs. The only thing he/she may not investigate is court decisions.
- The Human Rights Commission is to promote respect for human rights and to monitor the observance of human rights in South Africa. Organs of state are required to report to it annually on the steps they have taken towards the realisation of the rights in the Bill of Rights concerning housing, health care, food, water, social security, education and the environment.
- The Commission for the Promotion of Protection of the Rights of Cultural, Religious and Linguistic Communities is to promote tolerance and respect for the different groups in South Africa.
- The Commission for Gender Equality is to facilitate the attainment of gender equality.
- The Auditor-General audits and reports on the accounts of all national and provincial state departments and municipalities as well as on any institution funded from a national or provincial revenue fund or by a municipality or any institution that is authorised by law to receive money for a public purpose.
- The Electoral Commission manages all national, provincial and municipal elections.

1999 elections: checklist for ensuring gender equality in the context of free and fair elections

The Convention on the Elimination of all Forms of Discrimination Against Women (CEDAW), described as the 'definitive international legal instrument requiring respect for and observance of the human rights of women', was ratified by South Africa in 1995. Article 7 requires state parties to take measures to eliminate discrimination against women in political life and to ensure their right to vote in all elections; to hold public office and to participate in the formulation and implementation of government policy. The following list is intended to serve as a mechanism for enhancing the free and fair aspects of an election, taking gender equality into account. These conditions must be met:

Citizenship

- A definition and understanding of citizenship that has inherent in it a commitment to substantive equality with regard to gender.

Conducting elections

- The structure which manages elections must be committed to this conception of gender equality.
- In accordance with this commitment the structure which manages elections must employ women at all levels of its operation.
- All policy formulated and legislation promulgated which is relevant to conducting elections must give effect to substantive equality with regard to gender.
- All policy and legislation must be implemented to give effect to substantive equality.
- The criteria for demarcation of voting districts or constituencies (where applicable) must not affect women adversely. For example, a particular voting district must not be established so that it comprises areas in which women are particularly susceptible to violence or harm. In rural areas

voting districts must be established so that access to the voting station does not constitute any (further) impediment to the right of rural women to vote.

Registration of voters

- The right of women citizens to an effective, impartial and non-discriminatory procedure for registration of voters.
- The stipulation of clear criteria for the registration of voters: *inter alia* age, identification and citizenship. Citizenship as a criterion must guarantee the right to vote in the same way to men and women.
- The right of women citizens to have easy access to registration stations.

The right to vote

- The right of women citizens to vote on a non-discriminatory basis in elections of legislative bodies.
- The right to vote for a political party which has a record of addressing issues which affect women.
- The right to vote for a political party which has women in leadership positions.
- The right of every citizen to be eligible as a voter, subject only to disqualification in accordance with criteria established by law that are objectively verifiable and not subject to artbitrary decisions based on sex or gender.
- The right of women citizens to have equal and easy access to a polling station in order to exercise their right to vote.
- Women citizens' right to vote must take place without fear of any form of violence or intimidation.

The right to stand for public office

- The right of women citizens to present themselves as candidates for election.
- An express commitment to gender equality on the part of political parties.
- The inclusion of women in the structures that formulate party lists and choose election candidates.
- The inclusion of women in decision making which relates to the composition of party lists and choice of election candidates.
- An electoral system which facilitates the electoral success of women on party lists or as candidates.
- A mechanism inherent in the electoral system which facilitates the electoral success of women, for example internal party committee quotas, voluntary party list quotas, mandated party list quotas and double-member constituencies (where appropriate).

Voter education

- The state must ensure that through national programmes of civic and voter education, the electorate becomes familiar with gender equality as central to electoral issues and procedures.
- Civic and voter education programmes must entrench gender equality as a central feature of democratic citizenship.
- Voter education programmes must develop an understanding of substantive equality with regard to gender.
- Voter education programmes must be aimed specifically at women.
- Voter education programmes must explain complex electoral processes in a manner which will be understood by illiterate voters (the majority of whom are women in South Africa).
- Voter education workshops must take place at times suitable to accommodate the domestic and economic roles performed by women.
- Voter education workshops must take place in venues accessible to women (these venues must be chosen to accommodate children, who may have to accompany their mothers to workshops).
- Voter education workshops must take place in an environment in which women feel confident that they can express themselves without fear of disruption and ridicule.

The right to express political opinions

- The right of women citizens to express political opinions without interference otherwise than as permitted by law.

The right to access to information

- The right of women citizens to seek, receive and impart information and to make an informed electoral choice.

The rights of freedom of association, assembly and movement

- The right of women to join or together with others, to establish a political party for purposes of competing in an election.
- The right of women party members and candidates to move freely within the country in order to campaign for elections.

The right to campaign

- The right of women party members, candidates and voters to campaign on an equal basis with their male counterparts.
- The right of women party members to campaign around issues that are of particular concern to women, for example domestic violence.

- The right of women party members, candidates and voters to security with respect to their lives and property during campaigns (and throughout the electoral process).
- The content of campaign messages must be directed at men and women so that stereotypes are not entrenched.
- Campaign messages must be formulated so that they express a commitment to substantive equality with regard to gender issues.
- The right of women party members and candidates to have access to the media in order to put forward political views on an equal basis with their male counterparts.
- The provision and regulation of funding to political parties and electoral campaigns in order to ensure the promotion of equality of opportunity between women and men candidates.
- Ensure parties and women and men candidates equal access to government-controlled media for purposes of campaigning.
- The media must recognise the importance of gender equality as an important aspect of democracy and report on it in relation to an election.
- The media must report on all women candidates as often as they report on their male coounterparts.

Secrecy of the ballot

- The unrestricted right of women citizens to vote in secret.
- The right to respect for the integrity of their choice must be assured to women.
- The secrecy of the ballot must be explained to men and women during voter education workshops.

Review of electoral procedures or decisions

- Where the right of women citizens to vote or to be registered, or other political right, is negatively affected by an action or omission of the state, its organs or officials, there must be access to a procedure which permits the review of such actions promptly and effectively before an independent tribunal or court.

Source: *Gender Checklist for Free and Fair Elections*, Electoral Institute of South Africa, Johannesburg, 1999.

References

ABSA Bank Quarterly (1996) *South African Economic Monitor*, Johannesburg.

Adabunu, K. (1995) *Africa World Review*, May–September.

Adam, H. and Moodley, K. (1993) *South Africa International*, Vol. 23 No. 4.

Adam, H., Slabbert, V. and Moodley, K. (1998) *Comrades in Business*, Utrecht.

Africa Today (1995) November/December.

Africa World Review (1994) November–April 1995.

African Analysis (1996) No. 249.

African National Congress (1988) Constitutional Guidelines for a Democratic South Africa, reprinted in 1994 by ANC, Johannesburg.

African National Congress (1994a) Constitution, ANC Department of Information and Publicity, Marshaltown, South Africa.

African National Congress (1994b) Strategy and tactics, 49th National Conference.

African National Congress (1996a) Annual Statement of the National Executive Committee.

African National Congress (1996b) South African Youth Day, ANC Youth League.

Alexander, J. (1995) Sculpture and photomontage exhibition, Monument Gallery, Grahamstown.

Antonie, F. (1998) Banking and apartheid, University of Sussex Conference.

Ballington, J. (1999) *Gender and Elections*, EISA, Johannesburg.

Barber, J. (1999) *South Africa in the Twentieth Century*, Blackwell, Oxford.

Barberton, C. (1995) *Prioritising Prioritisation in Government*, South Africa.

Beinart, W. (1994) *Twentieth Century South Africa*, Oxford University Press, Oxford.

Beinart, W. and Dubow, S. (eds) (1995) *Segregation and Apartheid in Twentieth Century South Africa*, Routledge, London.

Bell, P. (1998) *Africa Today*, December.

Berelson, R., Lazerfield, P. and McPhee, W. (1954) *Voting*, University of Chicago Press, Chicago.

Bernstein, A. (1994) NGOs and a democratic South Africa, *Development and Democracy*, No. 7.

Bernstein, H. (1983) *For their Triumphs and for their Tears. Women in Apartheid South Africa*, IDAF, London.

Best, A. (1976) Black federation in South Africa, in D. Smith (ed.) *Separation in South Africa*, occasional paper no. 7.

Billy, A. (1996) Ground down, *Democracy in Action*.

Blumenfeld, J. (1999) The Post-apartheid economy, in J. Spence (ed.) *After Mandela*, RIIA, London.

Blumer, H. (1967) Industrialisation and race relations, in G. Hunter (ed.) *Industrialisation and Race Relations*, Oxford University Press, Oxford.

Boraine, A., Levy, J. and Scheffer, R. (eds) (1994) *Dealing with the Past*, IDASA, Cape Town.

Bossuyt, J. and Develtere, P. (1995) Between autonomy and identity: the financing dilemma of NGOs, *The Courier*, No. 152.

Bratton, M. (1994) Civil society and political transitions, in J. Harbeson, D. Rothchild, N. Chazan (eds) *Civil Society and the State in Africa*, Lynne Rienner, Boulder, Colo.

Buijs, G. (1995) Risk and benefit as functions of savings and loan clubs: an examination of rotating credit associations for poor women in Rhini, University of Port Elizabeth, African Studies Association of South Africa.

Bush, R. (1983) The United States and South Africa in a period of world crisis, *Contemporary Marxism*, No. 6.

Business Day, various editions.

Business Report, various editions.

Cape Argus, various editions.

Cawthra, G. (1993) *Policing South Africa*, Zed Books, London.

Cawthra, G. (1997) Towards an holistic approach to security management in Southern Africa and Africa, African Studies Association of South Africa, Broederstroom.

Claude, N. (1997) KwaZulu Natal, *Briefing*, No. 7, May 1997.

Coetzee, Z., Rian, Z. and Naude, W.A. (1995) Township economic infrastructure: quantifying the imbalances, *Development Southern Africa*, Vol. 12, No. 6.

Commonwealth Observer Mission to South Africa (COMSA) (1994) *Phase III: August–December 1993*, Commonwealth Secretariat, London.

Constitution of the Republic of South Africa (1996).

Daily Despatch, 29/3/99.

Deegan, H. (1984) British party policy: Palestine 1937–1950, PhD dissertation, University of Keele, UK.

Deegan, H. (1998) *South Africa Reborn*, UCL/Taylor & Francis, London.

de Kiewiet, C.W. (1941) *A History of South Africa, Social and Economic*, Oxford University Press, London.

de Klerk, F.W. (1999) *The Last Trek*, Jonathan Ball, Johannesburg.

de Klerk, W. (1991) *F.W. de Klerk*, Jonathan Ball, Johannesburg.

de Klerk, W. (1994) The process of political negotiation 1990–1991, in B. de Villiers (ed.) *Birth of a Constitution*, Juta & Co., Kenwyn, South Africa.

Democratic Party Election Manifesto (1999) Democratic Party Provincial Office, Pretoria.

Denoon, D. and Nyeko, B. (1984) *Southern Africa Since 1800*, Longman, Harlow.

de Villiers, B. (ed.) (1994) *Birth of a Constitution*, Juta & Co., Kenwyn, South Africa.

Diamond Fields Advertiser, 28/4/99.

Dugard, J., Haysom, N. and Marcus, G. (eds) (1992) *The Last Years of Apartheid: Civil Liberties in South Africa*, Ford Foundation, Washington.

Duvenage, P. (1995) In a field of tension: historical interpretation after and through Auschwitz and apartheid, University of Port Elizabeth, South Africa.

Electoral Institute of South Africa, Updates 1998–1999.

Ellis, S. (1992) The South African Communist Party and the Soviet Union, in A. Hughes (ed.) *Marxism's Retreat from Africa*, Frank Cass & Co., London.

Eloff, T. (1994) The process of giving birth, in B. de Villiers (ed.) *Birth of a Constitution*, Juta & Co., Kenwyn, South Africa.

Erasmus G. (1994) *Politikon*, Vol. 21, No. 1, South Africa.

ERIS interim reports, 1994 and 7 June 1999, Johannesburg.

Everatt, D. (1995) *Finishing the Job? Focus Group Survey on Local Government Elections*, Project Vote 1995, Cape Town.

Faure, M. and Lane, J.E. (1996) *South Africa: Designing New Political Institutions*, Sage, London.

Flood, T., Hoosain, M. and Primo, N. (1997) *Beyond Inequalities: Women in South Africa*, Southern Africa Research and Documentation Centre, Harare.

Frankel, S.E. (1938) *Capital Investment in Africa*, Oxford University Press, Oxford.

Freedman, R. (1971) *Marx on Economics*, Penguin Books, London.

Garrow, C. (1999) *Business Times*, 20 June.

Gastrow, P. (1995) *Bargaining for Peace*, US Institute of Peace, Washington.

Gauteng Provincial Government (1995) *RDP Vision*, 1, January.

Giliomee, H. (1989) The beginnings of Afrikaner ethnic consciousness, in L.Vail (ed.) *The Creation of Tribalism in Southern Africa*, James Currey, London.

Giliomee, H. (1994) The National Party's campaign for a liberation election, in A. Reynolds (ed.) *Election 94 South Africa*, James Currey, London.

Giliomee, H., Schlemmer, I. and Hauptfleisch, S. (1994) *The Bold Experiment: South Africa's New Democracy*, Southern Book Publishers, South Africa.

Gotz, G. (1995) Cracks in the edifice, *Indicator South Africa*, Vol. 12, No. 3.

Guelke, A. (1999) *South Africa in Transition: The Misunderstood Miracle*, I.B. Tauris, London.

Gumede, W.-M. (1996) Civics at the crossroads, *Democracy in Action*, Vol. 10, No. 5.

Hamber, B. and Kibble, S. (1999) *From Truth to Transformation*, CIIR, London.

Hamilton, G. and Mare, G. (1994) The Inkatha Freedom Party, in A. Reynolds (ed.) *Election 94 South Africa*, James Currey, London.

Handbook on Conflict Management (1998) EISA, Johannesburg.

Hanekom, K. (1998) *Siyaya*, No. 2, winter.

Haysom, N. (1992) The total strategy in J. Dugard, N. Haysom and G. Marcus (eds) *The Last Years of Apartheid: Civil Liberties in South Africa*, Ford Foundation, Washington.

Hlatshwayo, M. (1999) *The Sowetan*, 16 June.

Hlope, D. (1998) *The Mercury*, Durban, 20 August.

Hooper-Box, C. (1996) New gen(d)eration, *Democracy in Action*, Vol. 10, No. 3.

Horowitz, D. (1992) *A Democratic South Africa?* University of California Press, Berkeley.

Human Rights Commission (1992) *Political Assassination in the Nineties*, Johannesburg.

Human Rights Watch Africa (1995) Vol. 17, No. 3.

Independent Board of Enquiry (1994) *Fortresses of Fear*, Johannesburg.

Independent Electoral Commission (1999) *Elections '99*, Pretoria.

Infospec (April/May 1995) South Africa.

Inkatha Freedom Party (1987) *Inkatha and the Struggle for Liberation in South Africa*, Durban.

Institute for Democracy in South Africa (IDASA) (1994–1997) *Public Opinion Survey Reports*, Cape Town.

James, W. (1996a) *Democracy in Action*, Vol. 10, No. 3.

James, W. (1996b) *Public Opinion Survey*, No. 3, IDASA.

James, W. (1998) *Parliamentary Whip*, No. 2, IDASA.

James, W., Caliguire, D. and Cullinan, K. (1996) *Now that We Are Free*, Lynne Rienner, Boulder, Colo.

Jaster, R., Mbeki, M., Nkosi, M. and Clough, M. (eds) (1992) *Changing Fortunes: War, Diplomacy and Economics in Southern Africa*, Ford Foundation, Washington.

Johnson, R.W. (1996) *Focus Letter*, No. 4, Helen Suzman Foundation, Parklands.

Johnson, R.W. (1997) *Focus*, No.7, May, Helen Suzman Foundation, Parklands.

Johnson, R.W. (1999) Voting and the fear factor, *Focus*, No. 13.

Johnson, R.W. and Schlemmer, L. (eds) (1996) *Launching Democracy in South Africa*, Yale University Press, New Haven, Connecticut.

Johnston, A. (1996) Peace and realignment, *KwaZulu Natal Briefing*, No. 3.

Johnston, A. and Spence, J.E. (1995) *South Africa's Local Government Elections*, RIIA briefing paper No. 27.

Johnstone, F.R. (1976) *Class, Race and Gold*, Routledge, London.

Khanyisa Vol. 1, No. 2, April/June 1998.

Kibble, S. (1999) *From Truth to Transformation*, CIIR report, London.

Krog, A. (1998) Truth and Reconciliation Commission, in W. James and M. Levy (eds) *Pulse*, IDASA, Cape Town.

Kuper, A. (1988) Anthropology and apartheid, in J. Lonsdale (ed.) *South Africa in Question*, CUP, in association with James Currey, London.

Legassick, M. (1995) British hegemony and the origins of segregation in South Africa 1901–1914, in W. Beinart and S. Dubow (eds) *Segregation and Apartheid in Twentieth Century South Africa*, Routledge, London.

Lemon, A. (1976) *Apartheid*, Saxon House, Farnborough.

Lewis, S. (1994) Economic realities and prospects for trade, investment and growth in Southern Africa, *Africa Insight*, Vol. 24, No. 4.

Lipton, M. (1986) *Capitalism and Apartheid*, Gower, Aldershot.

Lipton M. (1999) Democracy and stability in the new South Africa: human rights with special reference to the TRC, in J. Spence (ed.) *After Mandela*, RIIA, London.

Lipton, M., Ellis, F. and Lipton, M. (1996) *Land, Labour and Livelihoods in Rural South Africa*, Vols 1 and 2, Indicator Press, Durban.

Lodge, T. (1983) *Black Politics in South Africa since 1945*, Longman, London.

Lodge, T. (1996) South Africa: a post apartheid society, in A. Leftwich (ed.) *Democracy and Development*, Polity Press, Cambridge.

Lodge, T. (1997) *Political Corruption in South Africa*, African Studies Association of South Africa, Broederstroom.

Lodge, T. and Nasson, B. (1991a) *All Here and Now: Black Politics in South Africa in the 1980s*, Ford Foundation, Washington.

Lodge, T. and Nasson, B. (1991b) *South Africa: Time Running Out*, Ford Foundation, Washington.

Lonsdale, J. (ed.) (1988) *South Africa in Question*, CUP, in association with James Currey, London.

Maasdorp, G. (1976) The development of the homeland with special reference to Kwa Zulu, in D. Smith (ed.) *Separation in South Africa*, occasional paper no. 7.

Macmillan, W. (1930) *Complex South Africa*, Faber and Faber, London.

Macozoma, S. (1998/99) *Transit*, summer, IDASA.

Mafenya, J. (1997) *Parliamentary Whip*, IDASA, Cape Town.

Magliolo, J. (1998) Investment strategist, *The Business Report*, 21 January.

Magubane, B. (1983) Imperialism and the making of the South African working class, *Contemporary Marxism*, No. 6.

Mahomed, D.P. (1998) *Final Report*, Truth and Reconciliation Commission, Vol. 1, Chapter 2.

Mail & Guardian Special Election Supplement, 4–10 June 1999.

Make Yourself Heard (1999) educational programme on democracy and the electoral process for high schools, Johannesburg.

Mamdani, M. (1998) An analysis of 'truth' in the Truth and Reconciliation Commission, University of Sussex Conference.

Mandela, N. (1994) *Long Walk to Freedom*, Little Brown, London.

Marais, H. (1998) *South Africa Limits to Change: The Political Economy of Transition*, Zed Books, London.

Marks, S. (1970) *Reluctant Rebellion: The 1906–8 Disturbances in Natal*, Clarendon Press, Oxford.

Maseko, S. (1998) Looking Back, *Siyaya*, No. 1 autumn.

Mathiane, N. (1989) *South Africa: Diary of Troubled Time*, Freedom House, New York.

Matshitse, P. (1998) *Siyaya*, Issue 1, autumn.

Mattes, R. (1995) *The Election Book*, IDASA, Cape Town.

Mattes, R. (1999) *Election Talk Newsletter*, EISA, Johannesburg, 4 April.

Mattes, R., Giliomee, H. and James, W. (1996) The election in the Western Cape, in R.W. Johnson and L. Schlemmer (eds) *Launching Democracy in South Africa*, Yale University Press, New Haven, Connecticut.

Mayibuye (1996) South Africa.

Mbeki, T. (1999) *Business Day*, 17 June.

Mboweni, T. (1998) *Transformation and Equity Programme*, IDASA, Cape Town.

Meintjes, J. (1973) *The Voortrekkers*, Cassell, London.

Mokaba, P. (1997) *Parliamentary Whip*, IDASA, Cape Town.

Molise, P. (1996) *Business Report*, Institute of Personnel Management, Johannesburg, 10 June.

Moller, V. and Hanf, T. (1995) *Learning to Vote*, Indicator Press, Durban.

Motsei, M. (1995) *RDP News*, South Africa.

Mtintso, T. (1996) *The Star*, Johannesburg.

Mzabalazo (1994) African National Congress publication.

Nazo Elections '99 (1999) Independent Electoral Commission, Pretoria.

Ngcobo, S. (1999) *Business Report*, 19 June.

Ngwema, S. (1996) No consultation no cash flow, *Democracy in Action*, Vol. 10, No. 1.

Ngwema, S. (1997) *Parliamentary Whip*, IDASA, Cape Town.

Ntsebeza, D. The impact of the Truth and Reconciliation Commission on South Africa, University of Sussex Conference.

Nyatsumba, K. (1996a) *Cape Argus* 24 September.

Nyatsumba, K. (1996) Challenges facing South Africa, *The Star*, 11 September.

Opinion 99 (1999) IDASA, Cape Town.

Ottoway, M. (1993) *South Africa, The Struggle for a New Order*, Brookings Institute, Washington.

Overseas Development Institute (1994) *Economic Policies in the New South Africa*, London, ODI.

Peires, J.B. (1995) Ethnicity and pseudo-ethnicity in the Ciskei, in W. Beinart and S. Dubow (eds) *Segregation and Apartheid in Twentieth Century South Africa*, Routledge, London.

Poulantzas, N. (1970) *Fascism and Dictatorship*, François Maspero, London.

President Mandela's 80th Birthday Celebration, Independent Newspapers/Mondi, 17 July 1998.

President Mandela's Government's Report to the Nation (1998) *The Building Has Begun*, Government Communication and Information System, Durban.

Pretoria News, various editions.

Race Relations Survey (1978/1979) South African Institute of Race Relations, Johannesburg.

Race Relations Survey (1994/1995) South African Institute of Race Relations, Johannesburg.

Ramphele, M. (1995) *Affirmative Action*, IDASA, South Africa.

Rantao, J. (1999) *The Star*, 26 March.

Reynolds, A. (ed.) (1994) *Election 94 South Africa*, James Currey, London.

Robertson, M. (1991) *Human Rights for South Africans*, Oxford University Press.

RSA Review (1995) Vol. 8.

Sampson, A. (1999) *Mandela: The Authorised Biography*, HarperCollins.

Sandifer, D. and Scheman, L.R. (1966) *The Foundations of Freedom*, Praeger, New York.

Sanibona (1998) No. 12, October.

Saunders, C. (1988) Historians and apartheid, in J. Lonsdale (ed.) *South Africa in Question*, CUP, in association with James Curry, London.

Saxena, S.C. (1992) *South Africa: Walking the Last Mile*, Kalinga Publications, Delhi.

Schrire, R. (1991) *Adapt or Die*, Ford Foundation, Washington.

Scott, T. (1995) An overview of South Africa's future international economic relations, in G. Mills, A. Begg and A. van Nieuwkerk (eds) *South Africa in the Global Economy*, South African Institute of International Affairs.

Seekings, J. (1995) *Media Images of 'Youth' During the South African Transition 1989–1994*, South African Sociological Association, Rhodes University, Grahamstown.

Shaw, M. (1994) The bloody backdrop, in S. Friedman and D. Atkinson (eds) *The Small Miracle*, Ravan Press, Johannesburg.

Shillington, K. (1987) *History of Southern Africa*, Longman, London.

Sibisi, J. (1996) *Democracy in Action*, South Africa.

Simons, H. and Simons, R. (1969) *Class and Colour in South Africa 1850–1950*, Penguin, London.

Slovo, J. (1976) South Africa: no middle road, in B. Davidson, J. Slovo and A. Wilkinson (eds) *Southern Africa, the New Politics of Revolution*, Penguin, London.

Smith, D. (ed.) (1976a) *Separation in South Africa: People and Politics*, occasional paper no. 6. Queen Mary College, University of London.

Smith, D. (1976b) *Separation in South Africa: Homelands and Cities*, occasional paper no. 7. Queen Mary College, University of London.

Smith, D. (1982) *Living under Apartheid*, George Allen & Unwin, London.

Smith, D. (1985) *Apartheid in South Africa*, Cambridge University Press, Cambridge.

Sondelani Sizovota (1999) EISA, Johannesburg.

Sono, T. (1999) *The Star*, Johannesburg, 8 June.

South African Institute of Race Relations (1962) *Survey of Race Relations in South Africa 1961*, Johannesburg.

South African Institute of Race Relations (1996) *Fast-Facts*.

South African Police Service (1998) Crime Information Management Centre, South Africa.

South African Research and Documentation Centre (SARDC) (1997) *Beyond Inequalities*, Belville and Harare.

South African Reserve Bank Review (1999) Pretoria.

South Africa Yearbook (1995) South African Communication Service.

Sowetan, various editions.

Spence, J. (ed.) (1994) *Change in South Africa*, Pinter Publishing, London.

Spence, J. (ed.) (1999) *After Mandela*, Royal Institute of International Affairs, London.

Star (Johannesburg), various editions.

Thabethe, E. (1997) *Parliamentary Whip*, IDASA, Cape Town.

Todes, A. (1998) Gender, place, migration and regional policy in South Africa, in M. Mapetia (ed.) *Changing Gender Relations in Southern Africa*, Institute of Southern African Studies, Lesotho.

Transformation and Equity Programme (1998) *Transit*, IDASA, Cape Town.

Truth and Reconciliation Commission Reports.

Turok, B. (1997) Development in South Africa, in A. Adedeji (ed.) *South Africa and Africa: Within or Apart*, Zed Books, London.

Tutu, D. (1998) TRC Report Extract 1, Independent Newspapers and IDASA, 2 November.

Tutu, D. (1999) *No Future without Forgiveness*, Rider, London.

Unterhalter, E. (1989) Class, Race and Gender, in J. Lonsdale (ed.) *South Africa in Question*, CUP in association with James Currey, London.

Uys, S. (1994) *South Africa's Elections*, RIIA, London.

van den Berghe (1967) *South Africa: A Study in Conflict*, University of California Press, Berkeley.

Van der Horst, S. (1941) *Native Labour in South Africa*, Oxford University Press, Cape Town.

Van Vuuren, D.J. (ed.) (1988) *South Africa: The Challenge of Reform*, Human Sciences Research Council, Owen Burgess Publishers, Durban.

Walker, E. (1930) *The Frontier Tradition in South Africa*, Oxford University Press, London.

Weiss, A. (1998) *Siyaya*, No. 2, Winter.

Welsh, D. (1971) *The Roots of Segregation: Native Policy in Colonial Natal 1845–1910*, Oxford University Press, Cape Town.

Welsh, D. (1994a) *The South African Elections*, RIIA, London.

Welsh, D. (1994b) Negotiating a democratic constitution, in J.S. Spence (ed.) *Change in South Africa*, Pinter Publishing, London.

White, C. (1995a) *Democratic Societies? Voluntary Association and Democratic Culture in a South African Township*, Centre for Policy Studies.

White, C. (1995b) *Gender on the Agenda*, Centre for Policy Studies, Current Trends Series Vol. 8, No. 7.

Wolpe, H. (1988) *Race, Class and the Apartheid State*, James Currey, London.

Wolpe, H. (1995) Capitalism and cheap labour power in South Africa, in W. Beinart and S. Dubow (eds) *Segregation and Apartheid in Twentieth Century South Africa*, Routledge, London.

Worden, N. (1995) *The Making of Modern South Africa*, Blackwell, Oxford.

World Bank (1995) *South Africa: Reducing Financial Constraints to Emerging Enterprises*, Washington.

Zuma, J. (1997) *KwaZulu Briefing*, No. 6.

Interviews/meetings

Adams, Mpho, Kutlwanong Democracy Centre, Pretoria, 18 June 1999.

Carolus, Cheryl, high commissioner, London, formerly deputy secretary-general, African National Congress, Johannesburg, 3 June 1996.

Cronin, Jeremy, former deputy secretary-general, South African Communist Party, Johannesburg, 3 June 1996.

Dlamini, Bonginkosi, provincial youth secretary, Inkatha Freedom Party, Gauteng leadership, 6 June 1996.

du Plessis, Norman, deputy electoral officer, Independent Electoral Commission, Pretoria, 21 June 1999.

Jones, Robert, Electoral Institute of South Africa, Johannesburg, 21 June 1999.

King, Loretta, councillor, Soweto, Southern Metropolitan substructure, 3 June 1996.

Leon, Peter, leader of Democratic Party, Gauteng Legislature, Johannesburg, 4 June 1996.

Lodge, Professor Thomas, Department of Political Studies, University of Witwatersrand, August 1998.

Majodina, Pemmy, treasurer-general, ANC Youth League, Johannesburg, 6 June 1996.

Masite, Sophie, Mayor of Soweto, Southern Metropolitan substructure, Johannesburg, 3 June 1996.

Msimang, Mendi, former South African high commissioner, RIIA London, 13 December 1995.

Myeni, Musa, MP, Inkatha Freedom Party, Johannesburg, 6 June 1996.

Mzizi, Gertrude, member, Gauteng Legislature, Inkatha Freedom Party, 6 June 1996.

Naidoo, Kumi, South African National NGO Coalition, Royal Commonwealth Society, London, 23 September 1998.

Nhlapo, Pat, personal assistant to Mayor of Soweto, Johannesburg, 3 June 1996.

Ndlovu, Humphrey, member, Gauteng Legislature, Inkatha Freedom Party, 6 June 1996.

Polgeiter, Febe, secretary-general of the ANC Youth League, Johannesburg, 6 June 1996.

Rabaji, Chris, ward councillor, Soweto, Southern Metropolitan substructure, 3 June 1996.

Radue, Ray, National Party senator, RSA, Cape Town, 13 June 1996.

Razak, Sam, deputy provincial secretary, Inkatha Freedom Party, Gauteng leadership, Johannesburg, 6 June 1996.

Rubin, Helene, principal, Anchor College, 7 February 1996.

Steyn, Marius, manager, Independent Electoral Commission, Pretoria, 21 June 1999.

Tutu, Archbishop Desmond, St Paul's, London, 1 November 1999.

Villa-Vicencio, C., South African Embassy, Dublin, March 1999.

Venter, Denis, former executive director, Africa Institute of South Africa, Pretoria, 22 June 1999.

Internet

South African Police Service website: http://www/saps.co.za

South African Reserve Bank: http://www.resbank.co.za

Truth and Reconciliation Commission: http://www.truth.org.za

TRC Report Vol. 1, Chapter 2: http://www.polity.org.zan

TRC Human Rights Violations Committee: http://www.truth.org.za

Index